Divine Diversity

An Orthodox Rabbi Engages with Muslims

Al Sadiqin Press

Reprint Department
Al Sadiqin Press
abrahamson@alsadiqin.org
www.alsadiqin.org

ISBN-13: 978-1503286399
ISBN-10: 1503286398

Editor: Rebecca Abrahamson
Cover: Husada Tsalitsa Mardiansya
Interior Designer: The Publishing Pro, LLC, Colorado Springs, Colorado

Facebook® is a registered trademark of Facebook, Inc.
Pictures and some reference material derived from Wikipedia® under the Creative Common—Attributions-ShareAlike License.

The text of this book is ultimately derived from conversations shared on the social-media website Facebook®. Per Facebook® guidelines, the contributors were contacted and permission was granted to collect and publish their correspondence or a paraphrase thereof, either under their name or a pen name. Contributors who were no longer reachable and/or did not respond to requests to be included in the book were given pen names and their discussions paraphrased. The contributors were informed that this publication has no relationship whatsoever with Facebook® or any of its subsidiary operations. The conversations are informal and should be related to as such. Although an attempt has been made to give attribution to original authors, it may be possible for someone to quote in full or in part an uncredited work. Scientific and historical facts are presented informally and should be confirmed in primary sources before quoting the material presented here. This work is neither a history book, a science book nor a book on theology. It is an informal encounter between an orthodox, Chassidic Jew and devout Muslims, which achieved a surprising degree of depth and synergy. It should be enjoyed in that light.

Many of the quotations from the Torah, Qur'an and other source documents were translated by the individual participants from the Hebrew and Arabic.

Approbations

"I know his Eminent Rabbi Ben Abrahamson to be an individual of the highest calibre, greatest sincerity and a wealth of knowledge, and it gives me great joy to see a portion of his wisdom and experience now in written form.

"The extent of Rabbi Abrahamson's work in promoting and nurturing interfaith understanding and harmony shines through in this book. His combination of many years of effort and enquiry make this publication unique both in its content and style. His incorporation of real-life conversations ground the book in everyday life while the historical and liturgical information it expounds make it a valuable academic resource in the field of interfaith studies.

"I hope that this book will stimulate further dialogue between people of the Muslim and Jewish faiths, as well as others, across the globe. Just as our religions derive from common roots, it is my wish, as I am sure it is Rabbi Abrahamson's, that we once again unite, this time in the common cause of the peace and harmony we so desperately need in today's world."

—Dr Sheikh Hojja Ramzy

Sheikh Ramzy is the director of the Iqra Institue, Oxford University, chairs the Muslim Council of Great Britain and is Ambassador for the Universal Peace Federation.

***

"Rapprochement between Muslims and Jews is founded upon an understanding of our common scriptural and historical traditions.

Ben Abrahamson's work herein provides important sources that will enable the reader to appreciate our rich common heritage and thus foster good relations between our peoples."

—Rabbi Yoel Schwartz

Rabbi Yoel Schwartz is a senior lecturer at Yeshivat Dvar Yerushalayim, Jerusalem. He studied in Yeshivot Ponevitz and Mir and has authored books on the Noachide covenant including, The Source and Corpus of the Noachide Code *and* Light Unto the Nations.

***

"It is a great pleasure to recommend the book by Rabbi Benyamin Abrahamson. It is now ten years since we first met, and I first wish to commend the author. Rabbi Abrahamson has all the qualities necessary to assure us that his works are worthy of our reading and learning. He is highly intelligent, very thorough, very diligent, very serious, very logical, very imaginative and open minded, being equally a highly learned Talmid Chacham, a devoted Hareidi Jew. Rabbi Abrahamson's concepts are based upon, among others, many hardly known Midrashim, and upon historical sources usually ignored in the Jewish syllabus. Thus his work is in harmony with Jewish authentic tradition, and is of great value to introduce Jews to certain aspects of Islam which, certainly at this point in time, Jews should know. We live in a world in which Islam is becoming more important.

"It is inspiring to read about the process in which Muslims rediscover the roots of their religion and learn the affinity of Islam with Judaism. With the help of the Almighty, and with the efforts of Rabbi Abrahamson, Jews and Muslims will live together in peace."

—Rabbi Yeshayahu Hakohen Hollander

Rabbi Hollander received his rabbinical ordination from Rabbi Levanoni and Rabbi Babad and his M.Sc in physics from The Hebrew University in Jerusalem. Active in Cultural Diplomacy, he and his wife, a Holocaust survivor and social worker, live in Israel.

***

"I came across Rabbi Ben Abrahamson few years ago on Facebook® and could not believe it was possible for a Jewish scholar to be this fair and open minded to Islamic teachings; his knowledge of Qur'an and *hadith* left me speechless. For the first time in my life I started to believe that there was hope for a world where we could all live together in peace.

"Over the years I have learned so much from reading his posts and comments and have a much better understanding of Islam and Judaism. I am so glad that now through this book others will get a chance to benefit from the wealth of knowledge and wisdom that Rabbi Ben Abrahamson has and I pray that this book becomes a catalyst for peace through better understanding, mutual respect and dialogue between all the children of Ibrahim (as)."

—Maksoom Hussain

Maksoom Hussain is a Muslim woman living in England, born in Pakistan. She is a property investor, business owner, inspirational speaker and organizes networking events. She has spoken all over the country including at the Indonesian Embassy in London. She is married with three boys and believes that we can overcome any challenge when we operate from faith rather then fear.

"For the past several years the relentless work of Rabbi Ben Abrahamson has been a light in the dark, an intellectual guide, a source of inspiration, and a living example of how to transform dream into reality. His endeavors, while in the general realm of so-called 'interfaith dialogue' are actually much, much more: Rabbi Abrahamson is a pioneer fighting on the front lines for mutual recognition and respect between those Jews and Muslims who would be truly faithful to their own authentic traditions. Rather than water down our differences, Rabbi Abrahamson suggests we strengthen our unique cultural attributes and religious tenets, while revealing the revolutionary paradigm of multi-covenantism that is itself rooted deeply in both Torah and Quranic teachings. If you are seeking a new path forward — a path of unity but not of uniformity, a path wherein our differences become the key to completing and complimenting one another — then it is essential you familiarize yourself with Rabbi Abrahamson's work."

—Gabriel Reiss

Gabriel Reiss is the Director of Israel Activities for LAVI Olami and founder of its ATID student think tank. Born and raised in Los Angeles, he completed officers training in the Israeli Air Force and served operationally in the IDF's elite EGOZ anti-guerrilla unit in Lebanon. Gabriel is currently involved in several grassroots social-justice movements and peace initiatives between Jews and Palestinians in Israel's disputed Judea region where he lives with his wife and four children. He is a frequent lecturer on history, Jewish identity and Zionist ideology, having completed a triple major in philosophy, economics and political science at Hebrew University.

*** *

"Rabbi Ben Abrahamson is what I believe is "A People's Rabbi". His ability to converse with scholars and lay people in a manner that is not condescending makes communication with him most enjoyable. His field of expertise is history, his ability to read both Hebrew and Arabic and his willingness to examine sources from both Islam and Judaism without an attempt to be in conflict has led to some interesting discoveries of similarities — similarities that go deep beneath the surface that show a real connection between Islam and Judaism beyond 'there is only One God.'

"His willingness to engage with both scholar and housewife and take their comments as potential insights makes him a most sincere conversation partner that leaves no one feeling uninvited or unwelcome. It leaves all conversation as a potential gem of discovery. All feel they can contribute. It has led to real affection towards him from many Muslims.

"It is my belief that the problems in the world are not because of people of faith, but because of those who let secularism infect their faith with a disease—a disease that erodes their faith to allow immoral behavior and oppression towards others. The Rabbi is an example of someone who everyday puts his faith first, and makes his actions consistent with his faith's ideals. *Salam/Shalom.*"

—Carol Esfahanizadeh

Carol Esfahanizadeh converted to Islam in 1981. Most of that time was spent as a follower of the School of Ahlul Bayt commonly known as Ithna Ashari (Usuli), the largest school of thought in Shia Islam. She has been a serious student of Judaism under the tutelage of Keith Daus and has attended many Shabbats at a conservative synagogue. She is active on an interfaith council, a member of the Dawoodiyya and is a housewife with two adult children.

Carol has made the Hajj, visited on Ziyarat to all the Twelve Imam's tombs (Iraq, Iran, Saudi Arabia) and hopes to one day visit the tomb of Sayyedah Zaynab in Damascus Syria. She also hopes to visit Jerusalem. She is most grateful for the lovely discussion group the Rabbi has on Facebook®. She prays for the Israeli / Palestine conflict to end peacefully with the least loss of life.

Qatada ibn al-Nu'man[1] said *"al-din wahid wa al-shari'ah mukhtalifah"* (religion is one, *shari'a* is diverse).

"Oh Allah, put light in my heart, light in my tongue, light in my sight, light in my hearing, ... Put light in my soul, and give me great light" —a prayer of the Prophet Muhammed (pbuh) (*sahih* Bukhari and *sahih* Muslim).[2] In Judaism the metaphor of "light" is also used: "*Ki ner mitzvah v'Torah ohr,* the Commandments are a lamp and Torah is the light." (Proverbs 6:23).

"There is no unity [of God] like the unity found in Islam; therefore, one who forbids wine which they have handled, turns holy into profane by regarding worshippers of God as worshippers of idols, God forbid."[3]

Rabbi Yisrael MeShklov, one of the leading disciples of the Vilna Gaon,[4] in his commentary to the *Code of Jewish Law* ruled that it was permitted for a Jewish *shohet* to acknowledge Allah by proclaiming *"Allahu akbar"* (God is great) when he slaughtered meat. R. Abraham Isaac Kook,[5] finding no explicit prohibition in this matter, also ruled that it is permissible to repeat the formula when preparing kosher meat.

---

1. One of the *sahaba*, contemporary Companions of the Prophet Muhammed. The *sahaba* included scholars, disciples, family members of the Prophet and military leaders.

2. *Sahih* Bukhari and *sahih* Muslim are two of the six major collections of *ahadith. Sahih* means authentic.

3. Rabbi Joseph Messas, *Mayim Hayyim,* Yoreh Deah, no. 66, p. 159

4. Seventeenth-century rabbi, Lithuania.

5. Twentieth-century rabbi, Holy Land.

Table of Contents

Introduction

Rabbi Ben Abrahamson serves as the consultant on Islamic history and religion to Jewish religious courts in Jerusalem and elsewhere, and acts as advocate for issues pertaining to Islam. He has been active in cultural diplomacy since 2006, speaking at a UNESCO Conference in Paris, the Houses of Parliament in London, venues in Istanbul, Ankara, Jordan, India, Jerusalem, and Hebron, and at conferences at Yale University, Oxford University, and the United Nations.

His work in building understanding between Muslims and Jews was sparked by firsthand exposure to Middle East violence. Faced with the contradiction between violence and faith, he sought answers by reading every scholarly book he could find, yet books are a poor replacement for people. He then began simple discussion among people of faith who desire peace and are convinced that the way of God is indeed the way of peace. He explains, "modern rabbinic Judaism teaches that proper Muslims are perfect believers, complete in every way, guaranteed a portion in the World to Come. I believe this view reflects a fundamental teaching originally shared as part of all the Abrahamic religions."

His approach is historical, with a focus on the identities of the Jews, Christians and proto-Muslims in Arabia at the time of the Qur'an's revelation, and how they related to each other.

"Records of that period show that early Muslims and Jews originally recognized each other as believers, encouraged and supported each other, even fought and died for each other. I believe that appreciating our shared common history and heritage can help us today by making any problem between communities easier to solve, as a problem 'within the family' and not a feud between foreigners and aliens."

His Facebook® postings have given Ben the opportunity to share his research and gain feedback; his friends therein have insisted that he put his discussions into a book. Here you will be introduced to Arabic and Hebrew terms, written in italics, translated the first time the term is mentioned in each chapter, then used freely. It is essential that we become familiar, fluent even, with key terms in order to promote better understanding.

Remember that these essays are an encounter. Statements herein should not be taken as authoritative but as an effort in mutual understanding.

That this is in book form should not detract from the dynamic nature of the discussions. This is a snapshot of an ongoing movement to build a peaceful world, based on the assumption that the way of God is indeed the way of peace. Here is a small sample.

The Character of a God-Fearer

Ben Abrahamson: We have a teaching, **"He who is slow to anger is better than the strong man, and a master of his passions is better than a conqueror of a city"** (*Pirkei Avot* 4:1[1], Proverbs 16:32), I am reminded of this when I read the following *hadith*:

> Allah's Apostle said, "The strong is not the one who overcomes the people by his strength, but the strong is the one who controls himself while in anger." (*sahih* Bukhari, *sahih* Muslim).[2]

---

1. "Sayings of the Fathers", part of the *Mishnah.*

2. Collections of *ahadith* (legends) —*sahih* Bukhari 8, 73,135, *sahih* Muslim 32,6311.

Abu Hurayra[1] reported that a man said to the Prophet
Muhammed, may Allah bless him and grant him peace,
"Advise me." He said, "Do not get angry." He repeated
his request several times and the Prophet said, "Do not get
angry."[2]

'A'isha[3] reported that the Prophet, may Allah bless him and
grant him peace, said, "Whenever kindness is in a thing
it adorns it, and whenever it is removed from anything, it
disfigures it."[4]

Anas reported that the Prophet, may Allah bless him and
grant him peace, said, "Make things easy for people and do
not make them difficult. Give good news to people and do
not frighten them away."[5]

A friend: *Jazak'Allah,* brother! Can you please provide the source for this
text?

Ben: It is based on the *ayah*[6] in the Qur'an, "**Those who spend** [benevo-
lently] **in ease as well as in adversity, and those who restrain** [their]
anger and pardon men; and Allah loves the doers of good [to oth-
ers]" (Qur'an, *Al 'Imran* 3:134). It is these that will find peace.

Someone asks: Abrahamson, are you a Muslim?

---

1. One of the *sahaba,* companions of Muhammed, and a compiler of *ahadith.*

2. *sahih* Bukhari

3. One of Muhammed's wives.

4. *sahih* Muslim

5. *sahih* Bukhari 3, 69

6. Verse in the Qur'an

Ben: I am an orthodox, chassidic Jew.

Ahir: *Mash'Allah.*

Maksoom Hussain: May Allah increase your *iman*[1] as you have increased ours. Thank you, sir.

Ben: Amin

Another friend: Thank you, brother Ben.

1. Faith, similar to the Hebrew *emunah*

PART I

Our Shared Spirituality

1. Calendar

The sanctity of time is of vital importance in Islam and Judaism.
Correspondences between our calendars indicate shared historical
and theological roots.

Two key words you will need in this chapter:

- Intercalation—inserting a leap month
- Commutation—exchanging a sacred month for a regular month

Ben Abrahamson: The Islamic or *Hijra* calendar is made up of twelve lunar months. Traces of Jewish holidays like *Rosh Hashana* (new year), *Yom Kippur* (day of atonement), *Pesach* (Passover) *Shavuot* (Pentecost) and *Sukkot* (Tabernacles) are still evident in this calendar. However, because of structural differences between the Islamic and Jewish calendars, the celebration of their parallel holidays coincides only once in about thirty-three years.

The Jews of Arabia felt that they were the "true mourners of Zion" and carried customs of mourning for the destruction of the Temple to extremes not matched by Jews elsewhere. We can assume that the mourning for the Temple influenced pre-Islamic Arabian culture to some extent. But even so, it is surprising to find one of the holiest days of the Islamic calendar—the ninth of *Dhu al Hijja*, the Day of Arafat, the height of the *Hajj* pilgrimage to Mecca—corresponding to the Jewish fast day of the ninth of Av, which commemorates the destruction of the Temple in 70 CE. Another remarkable parallel is the fast of *Ramadan*, similar to the Jewish *Sefirat haOmer* (counting the days of the *Omer* temple offering between the holidays *Pesach* and *Shavuot*), which among other things is a time of mourning for those killed after Bar Kochba's failed revolt against Rome in 135 CE. In the years after the destruction of the Temple, it was a time of partial fasting as no grains were permitted until the barley had been offered, which was not possible after the Temple was destroyed.

The Gregorian calendar, the most common one in use today, measures the time it takes for the Earth to rotate completely around the Sun, 365.2422 days. It is usually abbreviated CE (or AD) and BCE (or BC). Since 1582 CE, most countries have used the Gregorian calendar.

The Julian calendar, made official by Julius Caesar in 46 BCE, measures the time it takes for the Earth to be under exactly the same constellations, 365.256 days. In 1582 CE it was ten days short and abandoned by edict of Pope Gregory XIII, and replaced by the Gregorian calendar above.

Lunar Calendars, including Islamic and Jewish calendars, measure the time it takes for the moon to orbit the Earth twelve times, 354.3667 days. The lunar calendar starts about eleven days earlier each Gregorian/solar year. This means that any given month will migrate throughout the solar year. The Islamic year is considered to have started at sunset of Thursday, July 15, 622, in the Julian calendar.

The Islamic (*Hijri*) calendar is usually abbreviated AH in Western languages from the Latinized *Anno Hejirae* "year of the *Hijra* (journey)". The Jewish calendar is abbreviated AM from the Latinized *Anno Mundi* "year of (the creation of) the world".

The month of *Muharram* is the first month of the *Hijra* calendar, and is one of the four sacred months.

The number of the months according to Allah swt is twelve, mentioned in the Book of Allah, on the day He

created heavens and the earth. Among these there are four sanctified. (Qur'an, *At-Taubah* 9:36)

These months correspond to four months of pilgrimage to Jerusalem: *Sukkot, Pesach, Shavuot,* and *Tisha b'Av.* (Below, the Hebrew month is in parentheses):

- *Muharram al-Haraam — Rosh Hashana, Yom Kippur,* and *Sukkot* pilgrimage (Tishrei)
- *Rajab al Murajjab — Pesach* pilgrimage (Nisan)
- *Dhu al Qa'dah — Shavuot* pilgrimage (Sivan)
- *Dhu al Hijjah — Tisha b'Av* pilgrimage (Av)

In both Islam and Judaism, hostilities were not permitted during these months. In Judaism it was to allow the free, unhindered passage of pilgrims to Jerusalem. The Children of Israel had three biblical pilgrimages, and a fourth (the Ninth of Av) added after the Temple was destroyed.

Irshad: The Jewish calendar has a few extra days and so it is also solar. But the *Hijri* calendar is purely lunar. When did Jews add those extra days?

Ben: The Torah relates:

This day *[Pesach]* **you are going out in the month of** *Aviv.* (Exodus 13:4)[1]

And the flax and the barley were smitten, because the barley was [in the month of] *Aviv* **and the flax was** *Giv'ol.* **And the wheat and the spelt were not smitten because they were dark.** (Exodus 9:31-32)

---

1. The second of the five books of Moses, or Pentateuch. The five books are Genesis, Exodus, Leviticus, Numbers, and Deuteronomy.

In the first month, on the fourteenth day of the month at even, ye shall eat unleavened bread, until the one and twentieth day of the month at even. (Exodus 12:18; also Deuteronomy16:1, Exodus 23:15, Exodus 34:18)

This means that *Pesach* must be in the spring (*aviv*). The sign that spring had arrived was the ripening of barley. Both the Muslim and Jewish month is purely lunar, beginning with the new moon. Since a twelve month lunar calendar is about eleven days short of a solar year, after about three years, the lunar calendar falls a month short.

If the barley was not going to ripen by the time of *aviv*, then an extra month would be inserted. This is called "intercalation" and was instituted when the Torah was first given on Mount Sinai.

Originally the calendar used in Arabia was the same, or almost the same, as the calendar used by the Children of Israel. The names of the months recall the season in which they used to fall:

- *Muharram* means sacred.
- *Safar al-Muzaffar* means whistling of the wind.
- *Rabi al-Awal* means first rains
- *Rabi al-Thaani* means second rains
- *Jumaada al-Awal* means dry, 1st month of summer
- *Jumaada al-Thaani* means dry, 2nd month of summer
- *Rajab* means majestic, great, honored, valuable .
- *Shabaan* means branch, harvest
- *Ramadhaan* means heat
- *Shawwaal* means harvest
- *Dhu al Qa'dah* means to sit
- *Dhu al Hijjah* means pilgrimage

Intercalation was forbidden by the Prophet Muhammed (pbuh) in the year 631. The classical Islamic commentaries say this is because the governors would declare intercalation and commutation for their own self-interests, to make war convenient for example.

Today the holidays float around the year in the *Hijri* Calendar; many people have forgotten their biblical origins.

Yassiah Yasser: Thanks Ben. I learned something I had not paid attention to before. There is a parallel *Hijri-Shamsi* calendar as well which is an "Islamization" of the Gregorian calendar. It was devised about a hundred years ago.

Just to mention another similarity, Muslim and Jewish days start with sunset.

Thank you for sharing. May Allah bless you.

Ben: The days of the week have the same names in Islam and Judaism:

- *yawm al-a'had = yom ehad (yom rishon)* = Sunday
- *yawm al-athnayn = yom shnayim (yom sheni)* = Monday
- *yawm al-thalatha = yom shalosh (yom shaleshi)* = Tuesday
- *yawm al-arba'a = yom arba'a (yom rivi'i)* = Wednesday
- *yawm al-khamis = yom khamesh (yom khameshi)* = Thursday
- *yawm al-jum'a = yom shishi* = Friday
- *yawm al-sabt = yom shabat* = Shabbat

Micah David Naziri: Originally *Muharram* was the month of *Tishrei,* until the Caliphate adopted a purely lunar calendar. The Qur'an indicates that the sun and moon should both be used in calculating the months.

Ben: In the Qur'an, *Al-Taubah,* 9:36-37 refers to twelve months, and is generally understood to prohibit the manipulation of the calendar.

> **Surely the number of months with Allah is twelve months in Allah's ordinance since the day when He created the heavens and the earth, of these four being sacred; that is the right reckoning;** (Qur'an, *Al-Taubah* 9:36)

Postponing [of the sacred month] **is only an addition in unbelief, wherewith those who disbelieve are led astray, violating it one year and keeping it sacred another, that they may agree in the number** [of months] **that Allah has made sacred, and thus violate what Allah has made sacred; the evil of their doings is made fair-seeming to them; and Allah does not guide the unbelieving people.** (Qur'an, *Al-Taubah* 9:37).

This last verse could refer to commutation (exchanging a sacred month for a regular month) and not intercalation (inserting a month).

When you say "the sun and moon should both be used in calculating the months", I assume you are referring to this verse:

He it is who appointed the sun a splendor and the moon a light and measured for her stages, that ye might know the number of the years, and the reckoning. (10:5)

I have not seen any of the classical commentators understand it this way. Regards.

Micah David Naziri: Correct, none of them do, but we do not see their *tafsir* (commentary) emerge until centuries after Muhammed.

Ben: I agree that originally the Arabians kept the same lunar-solar calendar that most Jews did. It seems to me that it was changed by the Prophet Muhammed, not a later Caliph.

According to the account of Creation in Genesis, it was decreed that the **"lesser light"** (the Moon) should **"rule the night"** and serve **"for signs and for festivals"** (Genesis 1:14). Psalms also says, **"He appointed the moon for festivals"** (Psalms 104:19).

A friend: Is it true that the practice to follow a lunar calendar is to distinguish Jews and Muslims from idolaters who worship the sun? What about the claim that the lunar calendar is based on worshipping a moon god? I understand that there is a claim that according to Dead Sea Scrolls the calendar should be solar.

Ben: You are referring to the Essene sect, an ascetic Jewish group which existed at the turn of the Common Era in the Holy Land. After the Dead Sea Scrolls were discovered in 1947, further excavations in the area near the Dead Sea known as Qumran revealed the Qumran Geniza (storage area of sacred texts). Some of those texts indicate that the Essene sect lived there, and that the Essenes had every book of the Torah. The Essenes did not claim to have another Torah. Also, most scholars understand that the Essenes held that the solar and lunar calendars had been in alignment. They believed that because of sin, the calendars deviated, and they followed the solar.

Concerning making distinctions, pagans worshipped both the sun and the moon, so there wouldn't be a clear distinction on that account. In the Torah and the Qur'an, when it is discussed that the moon should be used for calculating times, it is not said that the reason is to be a distinction from pagan custom.

She responds: I like your explanation, my teacher. Thank you so much.

A friend contributes: On 10 September, 2018 the first of *Muharra*m 1440 and first of *Tishrei* 5779 will correspond. The Jewish calendar is intercalated that year, and thus matches the fixed Islamic calendar. That year the holidays will correspond, as they did in the year of the *Hijra*, 622 CE.

Ben: Here, the Hebrew name of the Jewish holiday follows the Arabic name of the Islamic holiday:

- *Ras as Sana*—*Rosh Hashana*—The New Year. In Islam, commemorates the *Hijra*, the journey of Prophet Muhammed from Mecca to Medinah in 622 CE. In Judaism, Adam was created; beginning of ten days of repentance.
- *Yaum Ashura* (tenth day)—*Yom Kippur*—The Day of Atonement. In Islam, commemoration of two events: Jews were freed from Egyptian slavery; martyrdom of Husayn Ibn Ali, grandson of Muhammed, at the battle of *Karbala*. In Judaism, fast day, culmination of ten days of repentance.
- *Lailat al Baraat*—*Pesach*—Passover. In Islam, on the "night of salvation", prayer vigils are held. In Judaism, commemorates the Exodus from Egypt.
- *Ramadan*—*Sefirat HaOmer*. In Islam, fast from dawn to dusk. In Judaism, counting of the *Omer* offering between *Pesach* and *Shavuot*, a time of partial mourning.
- *Eid Al Fitr*—*Shavuot*—Pentecost. Culmination of *Ramadan* and of *Sefirat HaOmer*.
- *Yaum Arafat*—*Tisha b'Av* (ninth of the month of *Av)*. Fast day. In Islam, pilgrims gather on mount Arafat near Mecca to commemorate Muhammed's final sermon. In Judaism, mourning for destruction of Temple. *El Hajj / Eid Al Adha* is the day after *Yaum Arafat*; Muslims share meat meals. On the tenth of *Av* Jews are allowed to eat meat after having been prohibited for the nine days previous to *Tisha b'Av*.

The Islamic New Year (*Ras as Sana*) commemorates the *Hijra*, as noted above. According to the Islamic calendar used today, Muhammed's journey did not take place in the month of *Muharram*, but in the month of *Rabu'ul Awwal*. In that year *Rabu'ul Awwal* coincided with the Jewish month *Tishrei*.

There was a time when Jewish and Islamic holidays and months occurred at the same time, and celebrated the same events.

A Commentator offers: The Prophet Muhammed came to Medina and saw the Jews fasting on the day of *Ashura* (*Yom Kippur*) (*sahih* Bukhari 3.31.222).[1] He asked them why. They replied, "This is a good day, the day on which Allah rescued *Bani Israel* from their enemy. So, Moses fasted this day." The Prophet said, "**We have more claim over Moses** [more claim to Jewishness] **than you.**" So, the Prophet fasted on that day and ordered the Muslims to fast.

Ben: Apparently, there were two calendars in use in Arabia at the time. The lunar-solar calendar of the Jews was used by the farmers and Bedouins because it was useful for agriculture and farming. The other was a strictly lunar calendar used for religious reasons at the *Ka'aba*,[2] which seems to have its roots among those who did not accept the mathematical intercalation of the calendar of Hillel II.

According to Tabari[3] and the *ahadith*, the Prophet did not know that it was *Ashura/Yom Kippur* when he arrived, but immediately began fasting:

> **The Prophet** [pbuh] **ordered a man from the** [tribe of]
> **Aslam: "Announce to the people that whoever has eaten**
> **should fast the rest of the day, and whoever has not eaten**
> **should fast** [the whole day]**, because today is the** *'Ashura*
> [10th day of Muharram]**."** (*sahih* Bukhari)

---

1. One of the collections of *ahadith* (legends), it contains over 7,000 *ahadith*, compiled in the ninth century.

2. Center of worship at Mecca, holiest place on earth in Islam, said to have been built by Abraham and his son Ishmael. Muhammed removed idolatrous practices that had taken hold in the *Ka'aba* and rededicated it to the worship of One God. A Muslim is required to make a pilgrimage to the *Ka'aba* once in his lifetime.

3. Ninth-century Islamic scholar, Persia. A child prodigy, Tabari studied under a wide variety of Islamic scholars in Persia and present day Iraq, studying the various Islamic legal schools of jurisprudence. He wrote *History of the Prophet and Kings (Tarikh al Tabari)* and *The Commentary on the Qur'an (Tafsir al Tabari).*

The Prophet appears to have been unaware of the fast, yet quite willing to accept it. One possibility is that Muhammed was unaware of Jewish customs; this seems improbable. Another possibility is that the Jews and the Prophet were keeping different yet related calendars (one lunar and the other lunar-solar).

The commentator of *Mishkat al-Masabih*[1] claims that Muhammed must have arrived in the year 623 CE, "because in the first year the Prophet had arrived in Medina after *Ashura*, in the month of *Rabi al-Awal*." This is an important observation, because it assumes the Prophet kept the same strictly lunar calendar that is in use today. If Muhammed arrived in *Rabi al-Awal*, he arrived two months after the month of *Muharram*, the month containing *Ashura*, and so the above event would have taken place ten months later.

However, in that year the tenth of *Tishrei* fell on the tenth of *Rabi al-Awal*, so an interpretation that agrees more readily with the *hadith* would be that the first day of the Prophet's arrival in Medina was *Yom Kippur*. This implies that from this point in time, until intercalation was forbidden in 631 CE (Qur'an, *Al-Taubah* 9:36-37), the calendars coincided.

It is important to note that even though the calendars today do not coincide, the holidays that remained in Islam were not of pagan origin but had biblical roots.

Muhammed Ilyas[2] quotes Nadvi who wrote: "... the Islamic Era did not start with the victories of Islamic wars, nor with the birth or death of the Prophet (pbuh), nor with the Revelation itself. It starts with *Hijra* [Muhammed's journey from Mecca to Medina].... [This] reminds Muslims not of the pomp and glory of Islam but of its sacrifice and prepares them to do the same."

---

1. Collection of almost 6,000 *ahadith,* compiled in the fourteenth century by Khatib al Tabrizi.

2. Twentieth century Islamic scholar and revivalist, India. He founded *Tablighi Jamaat*, the Society for Spreading Faith, a revival movement with ten million followers worldwide.

Insha'Allah, (God willing), we are beginning to understand that the Islamic calendar is full of meaning—meaning not just to Muslims, but to Jews. And by the same logic, the Jewish calendar is full of meaning not just to Jews but to Muslims.

A Commentator interjects: As you quote above, **"Postponing the sacred month is only an addition in unbelief. Those who do not believe are led astray, violating it one year and keeping it sacred another"** (Qur'an, *Al-Taubah* 9:37), the Qur'an rejects the lunar-solar calendar and confirms lunar calendars.

Ben responds: The *ayah* that you quote refers to exchanging a sacred month for a regular month. But we must differentiate this from intercalation, which is the insertion of a leap month.

According to the historian Tabari, at around 412 CE, Qussai, the leader of the Quraish family, gained influence and married Hobbah (Chavah), daughter of Holeil (Hillel) the king of an Arabian tribe known as the Khozaites. Qussai received from King Holeil several privileges, including the right of intercalation—*al Nasa.*[1] The *Nasi* in the ancient *Sanhedrin* (highest Jewish court of law) had the same right. One of the first efforts of Qussai was to build a Council House or Town Hall called *Dar-al-Nadwa,* near the *Ka'aba* in Mecca, and with its porch opening towards it. This mimicked the ancient Sanhedrin.

Later members of the Quraish abused this privilege, adding months and exchanging them when it was convenient for them to go to war. The classical commentaries on the Qur'an explain that this is the reason intercalation and commutation were prohibited—because of abuse.

In Judaism commutation is forbidden. Even intercalation is restricted: The "leap month" may not be decided by the High Priest or anyone with a vested interest because of the potential for abuse.

---

1. The term *al-Nasa* may be related to the Hebrew *nasi*–prince, religious leader.

Instead it was based on the appearance of barley grain.

In the Torah it is commanded that Passover must always occur in the month of *aviv* and it must occur in the spring. This is not possible with a strictly lunar calendar, which is eleven days short of a full year.

It was a descendant of King David that was given the honor to announce the leap month during the Second Temple period. Prior to that, it might have been announced by the High Priest as well.

In the year 541 CE, Roman Byzantine general Belisarius summoned a council of war against Persia. Two Roman officers in command of Syrian garrisons declined to follow the army to Nisibis, Turkey, giving the excuse that their absence would leave Syria and Phoenicia exposed to attack.

Belisarius argued that because the summer solstice was at hand, when the Arabs devoted two months to the customs of their religion and forbid war, there was no cause for apprehension; and he promised to let them go when that period was expired. These were the months of *Hajj*.

The summer solstice, June 21, 541 CE, would have fallen on the tenth of *Jumaada al-Thaani* according to the strictly lunar calendar now in Islamic use, six months too early for the *Hajj* pilgrimage. Yet according to the Jewish lunar-solar calendar it falls in the correct month.

This means that intercalation must have been in use at least a hundred years before the Prophet (pbuh).

A commentator states: Ben, your comments produce more questions: What was the original Jewish calendar in the time of Moses and David? If a descendant of David was given the authority to add leap years, how did they do so beforehand?

Ben: The Torah does not specify exactly how the calendar was calculated, but it could not have been without intercalation. Before the time of David, it is possible that the High Priest announced intercalation.

Passover must be on the fifteenth of the month of *aviv* (spring), and it must be in the spring. It cannot float through the year.

This is also mentioned in both the Septuagint[1] and the Samaritan Torah.

The story of the Exodus relates, **"This day you are going out in the the month of the *aviv*"** (Exodus 13:4).

To commemorate that we left Egypt in the *aviv*, we are instructed to bring the Passover sacrifice and celebrate the Feast of Unleavened Bread (*Hag HaMatzot*) at this time of year. Deuteronomy 16:1 states:

> **Keep the month of *aviv* and make the Passover (sacrifice) to the Lord your God at night, because in the month of the *aviv* the Lord your God took you out of Egypt.**

Similarly, Exodus 23:15 states:

> **You will keep the Feast of Unleavened Bread; seven days you will eat unleavened bread, as I have commanded you, at the time of the month of *aviv*, because in it you went out of Egypt.**

The Torah commands that after Passover, the barley offering should be brought for seven weeks, which culminates in the festival of *Shavuot*. So Passover must be fixed not only in the lunar, but also the solar (agricultural) calendar.

A friend contributes: In the fourth century CE, Hillel II established a fixed calendar based on mathematical and astronomical calculations. What was the Jewish calendar before the fourth century?

Ben: Intercalation was always done by the Sanhedrin based on the testimony of witnesses. In the year 358 CE, the Byzantines disbanded the

---

1. Translation of the Torah into Greek in the second-century BCE.

Sanhedrin and ordered that anyone declaring a new month would be killed as well as the entire city in which he lived.

Thus, at the last clandestine meeting of the Sanhedrin in Tiberias, Hillel II proposed that the Sanhedrin "declare" all the intercalated months based on a mathematical calendar, until the Sanhedrin would be reassembled. This is the calendar that rabbinic Jews use today.

Some Jews, particularly those with literalist/Sadducean tendencies, did not accept the mathematical calendar. It has been suggested that they abandoned intercalation and allowed the calendar to float through the year. It has been further suggested that they used the crescent moon as the symbol of their group and continued to require witnesses for the beginning of each new month. In fact, the Samaritans and the Karaites rejected Hillel's mathematical calendar and still look for the appearance of barley to declare spring.

If you calculate going back in the *Hijri* calendar and the Jewish calendar, you will find that they coincide in the year 358 CE, the year when the mathematical calendar was proposed.

The splitting of the moon is an event during the mission of the Prophet described in Islamic tradition. Virtually all commentators accept the historicity of this event, and describe it as a miracle. This incident is explained as the context of revelation in the Qur'an in *sura Al-Qamar* 54:1-2. The commentators agree that this incident occured at Mina in Mecca about five years before the Prophet's *Hijra* to Medinah, approximately 617 CE.

The Jewish and Islamic calendars coincide twice every thirty-three years approximately. It should be noted that the two calendars were "joined" in 617 CE and 618 CE and "split" in 619 CE, the "year of sorrow".

The "splitting of the Moon" may also refer to the splitting of calendars. There is an ancient Jewish tradition[1] that the splitting of the moon refers also to the deviation and eventual reconciliation of Jew-

---

1. Noted in *Midrash Geulah*, Jewish legends.

ish and *Hijri* calendars in the end of days.

At one time the lunar-solar calendar of Judaism corresponded to the now strictly lunar calendar of Islam. The month of *Muharram* corresponded to *Tishrei,* with *Ras as Sana* as *Rosh Hashana,* and *Ashura* as *Yom Kippur.* If you continue this correspondence then *Shabaan* was equivalent *to Nisan,* with the fifteenth of that month as *Lailat al Baraat* (night of salvation, an auspicious time for prayer) and Passover.

A friend: Many thanks brother Ben!

2. Festivals

In this thread, we see that politics and semantics often derail our efforts at dialogue. Once we get our basic assumptions and semantics articulated, we can enjoy fruitful discussion of our commonalities.

Ben Abrahamson: The *'umra* pilgrimage occurs in the *Hijri* (Islamic) month of *Shawwal* and completes the *Hajj* or *'umra* pilgrimage in the service of Allah.

> **But if ye are prevented** [from completing it], **send an offering for sacrifice, such as ye may find, and do not shave your heads until the offering reaches the place of sacrifice. And if any of you is ill, or has an ailment in his scalp,** [necessitating shaving], [he should] **in compensation either fast, or feed the poor, or offer nuskin** [sacrifice] ... (Qur'an, *Al-Baqarah* 2:196).

In the Torah a similar custom is described. The Torah descibes the *'omer* offering which is an offering of grains:

> **And in the day when ye bring the *'omer*, ye shall offer a lamb without blemish of the first year for a burnt-offering unto the Lord. And the meal-offering thereof shall be two tenth parts of an *ephah* of fine flour mingled with oil, an offering made by fire unto the Lord for a sweet savour ...** (Leviticus 23:13)

It was concluded by a *nesekh* (drink offering) and included semi-fasting:

> **And ye shall eat not bread, nor parched corn, nor fresh ears, until this selfsame day, until ye have brought the offering of your God; it is a statute for ever throughout your generations in all your dwellings.** (Leviticus 23:14)

After the Temple was destroyed, mourning customs were adopted, including forbidding shaving or cutting hair or beard during this period.

A friend asks: You are a Jew?

Ben responds: I am an orthodox, chassidic Jew.

He continues, trying to return to the thread: *Shavuot* corresponds to *Eid ul-Fitr*. *Sivan* and *Shawwal* used to be the same month. Even their names are linguistically related.

Here we have a digression, seeking semantic clarification: The word "Muslim" is found in the Qur'an. But is the word "Jew" found in the Torah?

Ben: "Jew" is the name that has been given to us by others. It comes from the word Judeans. We call ourselves Israel.

Judea is related to the area given to the tribe of Judah. Samaria is related to the area given to the tribe of Shimon (according to one account), or placed under the control of Sanballat, related to the rise of the Samaritans. Today, the majority of Samaritans live in Holon, near Tel Aviv, and some near Nablus, in Samaria. According to their census, there are about 1,000 Samaritans in Israel.

In Ben's defense: Anybody here have a problem with what Ben Abrahamson is? How about getting interested in seeing his message.
With all due respect guys, if someone is coming up with a message of the Qur'an why don't you appreciate it instead of asking
what he is?

A question: Since you mention the *Hajj,* where did Jews have to perform
their equivalent of it?

Ben: The Children of Israel were commanded by Allah swt to make a pilgrimage to Jerusalem three times a year, for *Pesach* (Passover), *Shavuot* (Pentecost) and *Sukkot* (Tabernacles). After the Temple was destroyed, a fourth pilgrimage was instituted, on the ninth of *Av.* All
these traditions have their correspondence in Islam.

A political digression, we get derailed at times: Do Jews have rights in the
land of Palestine according to the Torah? If they already have rights
in this land, did the Torah order them to occupy the people of Palestine? I know that you live in Israel!

Ben responds: How do you want me to answer your question? The Torah
speaks dozens of times about the Children of Israel being assigned to
the Land of Israel. The Qur'an mentions this as well:

> **Remember Moses said to his people: "O my people! Call**
> **in remembrance the favour of Allah unto you, when He**
> **produced prophets among you, made you kings, and**
> **gave you what He had not given to any other among the**
> **peoples. O my people! Enter the holy land which Allah**
> **hath assigned unto you, and turn not back ignominiously,**
> **for then will ye be overthrown, to your own ruin." (Qur'an,**
> *Al-Maedah* 5:20-21)

However, it has nothing to do with "occupation". From our point of view, the Land of Israel is the place where the *shari'a* (covenant) of Torah should be kept. This would include any God-fearer, including Muslims. It should be a place where religious people work together to support each other.

The Palestinians today have nothing to do with the Philistines of Moses' (pbuh) time. Most Palestinians are probably descendants of Jews, and even if they weren't, the Torah prohibits any mistreatment of God-fearers in the Holy Land. Exactly the opposite, one must care for their widows and orphans, provide them employment, guarantee their safety, etc.

As far as the mess that we are in, first of all, the non-religious media is no source for information. They wish to increase the conflict between believers. We need religious courts that fear Allah—more than they fear the media or politics—to clarify what is happening, and righteous leaders who will judge according to recognized moral standards.

A friend contributes: In my opinion all of the people in the world should live in coexistence and peace, so that we can serve Allah. By the way sir, I am impressed by your knowledge about Islam, and am ashamed that I don't have that knowledge of my religion even though I am a Muslim.

Ben: That should be a good thing. The Qur'an says in a most perfect way **"so strive as in a race in all virtues. The goal of you all is to Allah; it is He that will show you the truth about the matters in which you are different"** (*Al-Maedah* 5:48). If I have encouraged you to learn more about your faith, then that is the way it is supposed to work.

A friend: If anyone kills a human being whether he is a Jew, Muslim, Christian or anyone, he is a sinful man; he killed all of humanity, according to the Holy Qur'an.

And another: There is no religion on earth which promotes terrorism.

Back to the Holy Land, a friend insists: The land of Palestine belongs to Arab Muslims who defended it many times. If the land of Palestine is where the *shari'a* of Torah is kept, Jews can live there.

Isma'eel AbdulKhaliq Alemao: "Holy Land" is the term we should use. The word "Palestine" does not exist in the Qur'an: "**O my people! Enter the Holy Land** [Palestine] **which Allah has assigned to you and turn not back** [in flight] …" (*Al-Maedah* 5:21).

> "*Al-ArD al-Muqaddasah*" (*Eretz haKodesh* in Hebrew, Holy Land) is the term used in this *ayah*.

> The nomenclature is of vital importance. It is only the righteous servants of Allah that will inherit that land. According to the Qur'an, inheritance of the Holy Land is based on personal piety.

> Allah himself said that near the end times the Jews would be brought back to the Holy Land in a mixed crowd:

> **And We said to the Children of Israel after him: "Dwell in the land, then, when the final and the last promise comes near. We shall bring you altogether as mixed crowd** [gathered out of various nations]." (Tafsir Al-Qurtubi, *Al-Isra*, 17:104)

> Yes the Jews have been brought back, but the warning has been given that piety must be the code of conduct and devotion to Allah the way of life.

Rachel: The term "Holy Land" unites us all.

Back to festivals, Ben: The faithful Muslim who can recite the Qur'an is like a citron (*'itraj*) whose fragrance (*rayh*) is good (*tayyib*) and whose taste (*ta'm*) is good (*tayyib*). The faithful Muslim who cannot recite the Qur'an is like the date [palm] (*tamr*) which has no fragrance but whose taste is good. The unbeliever *(munafiq)* who can recite the Qur'an is like an aromatic plant *(rayhan)* whose fragrance is good but whose taste is bitter *(mar)*. And the unbeliever who cannot recite the Qur'an is like the colocynth plant *(hanzal)*, which has no fragrance and tastes bitter *(sahih Bukhari,* 65:338, also 61,538; 61,579; 93,649).[1]

This reminds me of liturgy at the Jewish holiday of *Sukkot*: "Just as the citron *('etrog)* has good taste *(ta'am tob)* and good fragrance *(reyah tob)*, so Israel has among its men of learning who also perform good works. Just as the palm tree *(tamar)* has taste *(ta'am)* but no fragrance *(reyah)*, so Israel has among them men of learning who do not perform good works. Just as myrtle has good fragrance but no taste, so Israel has among them men who perform good works but lack learning. And just as the willow has neither taste nor fragrance, so Israel has among it people who neither have learning nor perform good works." (Leviticus Rabbah 30:12).[2]

Commentators interject amazement that more people do not know of a peaceful Islam.

Ben states: There are many who spread the true message of Islam, but they are not the ones you see in the media. The media benefits by encouraging conflict between believers.

Ben returns to the previous topic: In the *hadith* and the *midrash*,[3] the same words are used: *'itraj / 'etrog* (citron), *tamr / tamar* (date palm), *rayh / reyah* (fragrance), *ta'm / ta'am* (taste) and *tayyib / tob* (good). What is fascinating is the reversal of the correspondence of fragrance for learning and taste for good deeds in the *hadith*, and fragrance for good deeds and taste for learning in the *midrash*.

---

1. Collection of more than 7,000 *ahadith*.

2. Collection of Jewish legends, sixth or eighth century CE.

3. Jewish legends.

Another difference is that in the *hadith*, the person who is faithful is called a "Muslim", the person who is not is called a hypocrite (*munafiq*), whereas in the *midrash* both the one with good deeds and the one without is still called "Israel". From a Jewish point of view this is because a member of the nation of "Israel" is someone who is obligated to keep the *shari'a* of Torah, whether he or she keeps it or not. From a Muslim point of view, being a "hypocrite" is a hidden trait and that person is still treated as a Muslim.

But a commentator interjects: The Qur'an mentions Jews who are not righteous.

Ben responds: In the Qur'an, the *ayah* states:

> [However] **They are not all alike. Among the People of the Book there is an upright community who recites the revelation of Allah swt during the night and fall prostrate before Him. They believe in Allah and the Last Day, enjoin what is right and forbid what is evil, and vie with one another in good works. They are of the righteous. And whatever good they do, its reward will not be denied them. Allah knows those who fear** [Him]. (*Al-Imran* 3:113-115)

Seeing that discussions of our commonalities continue to get derailed, Ben outlines his basic assumptions, as drawn from the teachings of Rabbi Benamozegh:[1] I am always looking for commonalities between Islam and Judaism. In this thread of the citron, I also see a parallel.

---

1. Rabbi Elijah Benamozegh was a nineteenth century Italian Kabbalist and Rabbi. He studied the major religions as well as Greek philosophy in an effort to encourage universal brotherhood via finding affinities among various systems of thought, all of which, he declared, fundamentally arise from divine precepts. His book *Israel and Humanity* was published posthumously by his disciple Aime Palliere, whom he guided in following the Noahide covenant.

In Judaism, we teach that there is a universal covenant which is obligated upon all mankind. Jews have called this *Bnei Noah* (children of Noah, righteous gentiles), *Yireh Shamayim* (God-fearers), and *Ger Toshav* (non-Jewish residents in the Jewish commonwealth). In modern parlance I would call it universal human rights and obligations. Rabbi Benamozegh declared this universal *deen* is also called Islam.

The universal covenant empowers and obligates all mankind. It is one *deen* that all humanity shares. It is the foundation of every proper belief system. The Torah clearly teaches the universal message of the prophets, and goes to great lengths to show that there was no division among them from the first to the last. All proper believers form a kind of brotherhood, where one can respect and in some cases even admire the faith and traditions of other peoples.

Rabbi Benamozegh compares it to groups of craftsmen who gather to build a great palace for a king. Each group thinks that it is the best and most correct, and it is indeed so, because each group is the best and most perfect in its trade. The carpenters are best at what they do. The bricklayers are the best at what they do. The electricians are the best at what they do. What one group teaches as the best way for it to contribute to building the palace would not be correct for another group. Mixing of talents and techniques between the groups would reduce the specialty and diversity needed to create the most perfect palace. The diet, clothing and training of each group must necessarily be different. The goal of all of them is the same, and they should compete as if in a race.

There is no room for feelings of superiority or arrogance, and each of us must recognize and appreciate with gratitude the work of other believers with whom God has made different covenants.

And among His signs is the creation of the heavens and the earth, and the variations in your languages and your colours: verily in that are signs for those who know.
(Qur'an, *Al-Rum* 30:22)

From amongst all those *ummas* you are among the *umma* that
has been allotted to me and from amongst all the prophets
I am the prophet who hath been assigned to you. (Musnad
Ahmad)[1]

**To each among you have we prescribed a *shari'a* [law] and
minhaj [custom]. If Allah had so willed, He could have
made you a single *umma* [faith community], but [His plan
is] to test you in what He hath given you: so strive as in a
race in all virtues. The goal of you all is to Allah; it is He
that will show you the truth about the matters in which
you are different**; (Qur'an, *Al-Maedah* 5:48)

It's a race in which everyone wins.

In this way, I can understand the desire of those who wish to
make Islam pure of *bidah* (corruption) and outside influences. I can
understand a sense of pride which encourages fervent devotion in
the performance of the Torah's commandments. This is all what I
would expect of a team in a race. But on the other hand, I can see
that condemnation of different practices, intolerance, and generaliza-
tions work against the lofty goals of the covenants which Allah has
entrusted us.

Abrahamic religions have both universalist and particularist aspects. Rabbi Benamozegh writes that in the Torah, the universal concepts of religion were expounded by the prophets. There is a thread
running through the message of all the prophets uniting all mankind
in the universal recognition of the One God and submission to His will.

The particularistic concepts of religion were embodied by the
kings. A proper king was not a ruler of his people, above the whole
nation, but rather he is the representative and servant of every citizen
of that nation. He represented the needs and desires of the people,

---

1. Collection of *ahadith,* ninth century CE

their unique character, and was the main upholder of the covenant.

This is why, he explains, the end of times requires two significant leaders: one representing the universalist need of proper faith, one representing the particularist need of proper faith. In Judaism they are known as Elijah and Messiah. In Islam they are known as *Hazrat Mahdi* and *Hazrat Maseeh`*.

Rabbi Joseph B. Soloveitchik[1] discusses the balance between particularistic and universal aspects of religion in his essay, "Confrontation." He emphasizes the necessity of diversity and the impossibility of intimately understanding the religious expression of another faith community. He states that full cross-cultural understanding cannot be achieved, and thus rejects interfaith dialogue which involves the particulars of religious doctrine and ritual. Our goal is not to merge into one worldwide faith community, but to embrace our inherent variety.

This gives important protection to the religious minority.

This would lead me to believe that we must be cautious about learning the scriptures of another faith community. Indeed I would discourage it as it could lead to serious misunderstandings.

James David Audlin: I do think the People of the Book (Jews, Christians, and Muslims) should study each other's scriptures—this would not only help them to overcome the mistaken things some people in each group say about the others, but it would help them understand their own, since these three wonderful faiths are extremely closely related in their histories.

He points out however that it is essential to do so with the guidance of an expert from that faith community and not relying on one's own reading of the text.

---

1. Rabbi Joseph Ber Soloveitchik (1903-1993) was born in Russia, educated in Russia and Germany and emigrated to American in 1932, one of the founders of modern orthodox Judaism in America.

Ben: The reason given in Talmudic tractate *Baba Kama* 38a why many civil laws in rabbinic Judaism ceased to apply to non-Jews during Roman times was because they had become outlaws and rogue states which did not keep the most basic fundamental *deen* of Noah. The Torah did not require us to give pagan nations the legal protection that they themselves denied to the children of Israel. However, it follows that if these nations begin to keep the Covenant of Noah, then all rights and protections that Jewish law affords a proper non-Jewish citizen come into effect. We must return their lost objects, protect them from war, feed their widows and orphans, and accept their testimony in court.

It is based on this opinion that when people ask me why I write "the Prophet" when referring to Muhammed or speak about the Qur'an as a divine book, I reply, "the Torah teaches me that Muslims who follow their religion properly are perfect believers, complete in every way, and thus proper Noahides. Proper Muslims tell me that the Qur'an is a divine book, so I accept their testimony.

Keeping in mind the words of Rabbi Soloveitchik, what another faith community means by the terms "prophet", "messiah", or even "holy book" is not directly comparable to Jewish teachings. As a Jew, I can never have complete understanding of how they are using these terms. I have no right to import or export these terms across faith boundaries, to diminish boundaries or differences, to mix customs or judge traditions, only to offer support and encouragement to proper believers from a distance.

Rabbi Soloveitchik states that diverse nations, though they cannot merge, do indeed need each other as they share common political, economic and social needs; dialogue in these areas takes place within the framework of the seven basic tenets of the Noahide Covenant. They are:

1. Justice: Commandments to set up courts of law and pursue social justice

2. Blasphemy: Prohibitions against cursing God.
3. Idolatry: Prohibitions against worshipping any being except God.
4. Sexual morality.
5. Prohibitions against murder.
6. Prohibitions against theft.
7. Prohibitions against eating the limb of a living animal.

Allah knows best. May our redemption, of all of us together, come speedily and in our lifetime. Amin.

I ask Allah to accept my work and make it purely for His sake. May He benefit others through it, make it a source of reward for me in this life and the next, and make it a help for me on the Day of Reckoning. May He guide me through it to what is right, and protect me from errors of thinking, bad intentions, mistaken or misunderstood quotations, and improper honor shown to scholars and sages.

Ali paraphrases the message of Imam Iskender Ali Mihr of Turkey, who calls for unity among Abrahamic faiths: There are seventy-two different groups of faith in the world, each group pretty much considers the other to be an enemy. To imagine that God treats human beings, his most beloved creatures, with unjust favoritism by giving them different religions, only one of them leading to heaven, is pure naiveté.

The order of Allah is very clear:

You must hold fast, all of you together, to the bond of God and be not divided into sects. (Qur'an, *Al-Imran* 3:103)

This idea does not contradict variety; the Qur'an recognizes a multiplicity of righteous paths:

Through this Book, God guides to paths of Islam, those who seek His Approval. He brings them out of darkness

into the light of His grace, and guides them to the straight path. (Qur'an, *Al Maedah* 5:16

As for those who sincerely strive for Us, We surely guide them onto paths that lead to Us. God is with those who do Good. (Quran, *Al Inkabut,* 29:69)

The Imam declares that Judaism, Chrisitianity, and Islam are correct versions of the same religion. Unity comes not from all people conforming to one expression of an Abrahamic faith, but by upholding basic principals.

The Imam refers to these basics as the seven stages—*reminiscent of the seven Noahide laws!*

Now we can return to our commonalities.

Ramadan

Ben: May Allah shower His very special blessings during the blessed month of *Ramadan* to the entire Muslim *umma* by forgiving our sins. *Amin, ya Rabbal 'Alameen.*

O you who believe! Observing *As-Saum* [the fasting] is prescribed for you as it was prescribed for those before you, that you may become *Al-Muttaqun* [the pious]. [Observing *saum* (fasts)] **for a fixed number of days, but if any of you is ill or on a journey, the same number** [should be made up] **from other days. And as for those who can fast with difficulty** [e.g. an old man], **they have** [a choice either to fast or] **to feed a *miskin*** [poor person] [for every day]. **But whoever does good of his own accord, it is better for him. And that you fast, is better for you if only you know. The month of Ramadan in which was revealed the Qur'an, a guidance for mankind and clear proofs for the guidance and the criterion** [between right and wrong].

So whoever of you sights [the crescent on the first night of] **the month** [of Ramadan, ie, is present at his home], **he must observe** *saum* [fasts] **that month, and whoever is ill or on a journey, the same number** [of days which one did not observe *saum* (fasts) must be made up] **from other days. Allah intends for you ease, and He does not want to make things difficult for you.** [He wants that you] **must complete the same number** [of days], **and that you must magnify Allah** [ie, to say *Takbir* (*Allahu Akbar*— Allah is the Most Great)] **for having guided you so that you may be grateful to Him**. (Qur'an, Al-Baqarah 2:183-185)

Ben emphasies one ayah:

O you who believe! Observing *As-Saum* [the fasting] **is prescribed for you** *as it was prescribed for those before you,* **that you may become** *Al-Muttaqun* [the pious].

Judaism has seven major fast days in the rabbinical calendar, and additional minor fast days. Two of these days, Yom Kippur and the ninth of *Av* are twenty-four hour fasts. There is also an optional custom, which is also in Islam (al-Tirmidhi, 747), to fast on Mondays and Thursdays from morning until nightfall.

The month of *Ramadan* corresponds to *Iyyar* in the Jewish calendar. After *Pesach*, the barley offering would be brought during the seven weeks from *Pesach* to *Shavuot*, this spans the month of *Iyyar*. Until the barley offering was offered, it was forbidden to eat wheat, barley, oat, spelt, and rye.

And ye shall eat neither bread, nor parched corn, nor green ears, until the selfsame day that ye have brought an offering unto your God: It shall be a statute for ever throughout your generations in all your dwellings.
(Leviticus 23:14)

After the Temple was destroyed, the barley offering could no longer be offered. In a grain-based culture like Arabia, the Sadducean Jews observed this period as almost a total fast. They took the verse "until the selfsame day" to mean that the fast occurs during the day, instituting a seven-week fast from *Pesach* to *Shavuot*. This is why it is considered meritorious to fast for six more days for the first six days of *Shawwaal*. These six days complete the number of forty-nine days (seven weeks), which is equivalent to the time span from *Pesach* to *Shavuot.*

Perhaps it is timely to note that there is a custom in Judaism called *Sefirat HaOmer*. This is the time during which the barley offering (*'omer* in Hebrew, *'umar* in Arabic) would be brought to the Temple. It is a period of seven weeks between the holidays of *Pesach* and *Shavuot*. Until the barley offering was made it was forbidden to eat any grains. These seven weeks span:

- 14 days in Nisan
- 29 days in Iyyar
- 6 days in Sivan

Rabbinic Jews living in Babylon prohibited new grains but allowed other foods. For them this period became a time of mourning. Among other mourning customs that are observed, weddings and music are forbidden. Some Jews fasted during these days.

However, full mourning does not span the entire seven weeks, but for a total of thirty-three days. Different Jewish communities observe slightly different days within this seven-week period. Sephardic Jewish families begin the period of mourning during the month of Iyyar and continue for thirty-three days until the third of Sivan.[1]

---

1. "Sephardic" literally means "Spanish"; Sephardic Jews are descended from those exiled from Spain in 1492 and settled in Holland, Northern Africa through the Middle East as far as India.

The fasting was widespread, as documented by the numerous decrees by the Byzantine Empire to forbid fasting during the seven weeks after Passover. The punishment was death. Christianized Jews who feared Byzantine punishment began to fast or mourn in the seven weeks before Passover. In the Eastern Orthodox Church, these weeks became known as Lent.

In Arabia, where the Jews were mainly of the Sadducean variety, the prohibition of **"ye shall eat neither bread, nor parched corn, nor green ears"** amounted to a complete daytime fast.

Allah commanded the Prophet to observe one month as a complete fast from dawn to dusk.

> In the month of *Ramadan* the Qur'an was revealed, a guidance for mankind, plus clear proofs of the guidance, and the criterion of right and wrong. **And whosoever of you is present, let him fast the month, and whosoever of you is sick or on a journey, a number of other days. Allah desires for you ease; He desires not hardship for you; and that you should complete the period, and that you should magnify Allah for having guided you, and that perhaps you may be thankful.** (Qur'an, *Al-Baqarah* 2:185)

A friend asks: Will you be observing the fast of *Ramadan*, Ben Abrahamson?

Ben answers: I follow the *shari'a* of the Torah; however I recognize, encourage and support those who follow the *shari'a* of the Prophet (pbuh).

Our friend continues: Should not the *shari'a* of the last and final messenger be followed? It abrogates the previous *shari'a*.

And another: *Shari'a* of Torah has no value in this age, because it is the age of Muhammed. **"And We have sent you** [Muhammed] **not but as a**

mercy for the 'Alamin [mankind, *jinns* and all that exists]. (Qur'an, *Al-Anbiyā'* 21:107).

And another: When I read your words I think you must be a true Muslim, right?

Ben responds that he is a Muslim in the sense that he follows the *shar'ia* given to his *umma*:

> **When it is recited to them they say, "We believe in it; it is the truth from our Lord. We were already Muslims before it came."** (Qur'an, *Al-Qasas* 28:53)

Another commentator supports Ben:

> **... And do not argue with the People of the Scripture except in a way that is best, except for those who commit injustice among them, and say, "We believe in that which has been revealed to us and revealed to you. And our God and your God is One; and we are Muslims** [in submission] **to Him."** (Qur'an, Al-Ankabut 29:46)

Eid-ul-Fitr
Festival of the Purification after Completing the Fasting Month of Ramadan

Ben: Fasting during the six days of *Shawal* after the obligatory fast of *Ramadan* is *Sunnah Mustahabbah* (commendable tradition), not *waajib* (obligatory). It is recommended for the Muslim to fast six days of *Shawal*, and in this there is great virtue and an immense reward. Whoever fasts these six days will have recorded for him a reward as if he had fasted a whole year, as was reported in *ahadith* (traditions) from the Prophet (pbuh).

Abu Ayoub[1] reported that the Messenger of Allah (Muhammed pbuh) said: "Whoever fasts *Ramadan* and follows it with six days of *Shawal*, it will be as if he fasted for a lifetime."[2]

The Prophet (pbuh) explained this when he said: "Whoever fasts for six days after *Eid al-Fitr* has completed the year: whoever does a good deed (*hasanah*) will have ten *hasanah* like it." According to another report: "Allah has made for each *hasanah* ten like it, so a month is like fasting ten months, and fasting six days completes the year."[3] It was also narrated by Ibn Khuzaymah[4] with the wording: "Fasting for the month of *Ramadan* brings the reward of ten like it, and fasting for six days brings the reward of two months, and that is the fasting of the whole year." [5]

Ben ties this in with Jewish traditions: Six days into the month of *Sivan* the holiday of *Shavuot*[6] is celebrated. Three days before the holiday (Hebrew: *sheloshet yemei hagbalah*), the mourning customs end. This is the time when the first fruits of the field would be offered in the Temple. Today it is celebrated by decorating the home and synagogue with leafy branches, fruits and nuts and preparing a milk meal.

Based on Exodus 23:19:

The first of the firstfruits of thy land thou shalt bring into the house of the LORD thy God. Thou shalt not seethe [cook] a kid in his mother's milk.

---

1. Abu Ayoub was one of the *Sahaba*, or companions of Muhammed; those who were in close association with the Prophet.

2. Narrated by the Islamic scholars who compiled the *ahadith* collections in the ninth and tenth centuries CE: Muslim, Abu Dawood, al-Tirmidhi, al-Nisaa'i and Ibn Maajah.

3, Al-Nisaa'i and Ibn Maajah. See also *Sahih al-Targheeb wa'l-Tarheeb*, 1/421.

4. Tenth-century Muslim scholar, Persia. Compiled a collection of *ahadith* called *Sahih ibn Khuzaymah*.

5. Quoted from islamhouse.com website

6. Shavuot means "weeks" and is the festival of first fruits.

Due to the proximity of the verses, a milk meal is served.

There are also seven weeks between *Lailat al Baraat* and the "six days of fasting" in *Shawwal*.

- 13 days in *Shabaan*
- 30 days in *Ramadan*
- 6 days in *Shawal*

Ramadan is an entire month of fasting during daylight hours. Most Islamic jurists think that the intention "I will fast for this approaching month of *Ramadan*" is not legally binding enough, since the intention to fast must be formulated each night for the following day, ie, "I will fast for *Ramadan* during this day." This daily declaration is also required in Judaism during the counting of *Omer* period.

In the first days of *Shawwal*, the festival of *Eid ul-Fitr* occurs. Linguistically, *Shawwal* is related to *Sivan*. This festival is marked in many countries with a festival meal of fruits, nuts, and milk.

Thus even today, in a roundabout way, some Muslims continue to celebrate *Shavuot*, according to Exodus 23:19.

Someone sent me this: "These are the final days of Ramadan with Eid Al Fitr approaching. If the month of Ramadan is a special time in the Islamic calendar, the last ten days are a particularly special time within Ramadan. Traditionally, the last ten days are especially connected with seeking forgiveness." *This reminds us of the ten days of repentance between Rosh Hashana and Yom Kippur in the Jewish calendar.*

Eid Saeed, Kul Aam Wa Antum Bi Khair

Ben: The Muslim festival *Eid Al-Fitr* is the most important festival in the Islamic calendar. The day does not mark any historical event or episode, but it provides the Muslim an occasion to offer thanks to Allah for having given him the strength and the will to observe fast during the holy month of Ramadan.

It is also an occasion for prayers when Muslims gather in large congregations, standing shoulder to shoulder, to demonstrate the equality and equity which is the inherent feature of Islamic society all over the world.

But the greatest significance of this day of rejoicing lies in the fact that on this day every Muslim is enjoined to give the needy food at the rate of the prescribed weight per every member of his household, including servants and guests who were sheltered under his roof the preceding evening.

Eid Al-Fitr then serves a three-fold purpose: It places upon every Muslim the obligation to remember Allah and offer Him thanks; it affords him an opportunity of spiritual stock-taking in that he can now ponder over the strength of his will or the weakness of his character, as the case may be, which manifested itself during the preceding month (*Ramadan*); it also is the day for the haves to share a portion of what they have with the have-nots.

A flow of appreciative comments follow: *Salaam,* very kind Rabbi, pray for us.

Muhammed: *Salaam,* thank you very much, Rabbi.

Maksoom Hussain: *Jazak'Allah hu khair,* brother, thank you.

Amani: *Kol sana wenta taayeb,* Rabbi Abrahamson!

Sadika Ali: Thank You. May Allah swt bless you abundantly, amin. Blessed *Eid al Fitr* to you too.

Susan: *Jazak'Allahu Khiron wa Shabbat Shalom.*

Etta: Yes praise be, and good things to you.

Eka: Rabbi Ben, *toda* (thank you), may Allah bless you.

Naushad: Thank you, Rabbi. May the Lord bless you in His infinite ways!

Micah David Naziri: I'm going to read your work. It looks very interesting. Basically, I just overlay the Jewish calendar with the Muslim holidays, with *Yom Kippur/ Yaum Ashura* as the focal point. There are numerous *ahadith*, particularly Shiah ones, that talk about the revelation starting before *Ramadan*, which argues that the fast referenced in the Qur'an ("wherein revelation occurred") was one that spanned the month of *Ramadan* but started before it, went through it and ended afterwards, ending three days before *Shavuot*, which is likely where the three days of `*Eid* came from.

Ben responds: The overlay that I propose maps *Ras as Sana* to *Rosh Hashana*, *Yaum Ashura* to *Yom Kippur*, *Lailat al Baraat* to Passover, *Ramadan* to *Sefirot HaOmer*, *Eid al Fitr* to *Shavuot*, *Roz e Arafat* to the *ninth of Av* and the three holy months of *Muharram*, *Rajab* and *Dhu al Qa'dah* to the (commutated) months of *aliyat regel* (Jewish pilgrammage) for *Sukkot*, *Pesach*, and *Shavuot*. The three days of `*Eid* are referred in Talmudic literature as the *Shloshet Yemei HaHagbala* (the three juxtaposed days), where the six days of fasting in *Shawwal* have been dispersed, and the end of the fast moved up.

He responds: Yes, this seems like we have drawn very similar conclusions.

A friend offers his holiday blessings: Shalom Ben, and blessed *Eid* to all Caliphist Muslims! I think it is not wise to dismiss the traditional opinion of Islam as expressed in so many *hadith, sirah* and clarified by so many Islamic scholars on the calendar issue. Only Al-Biruni[1] makes a mistake. *Ramadan* used to always be in December during the Prophet's lifetime

.

Ben disagrees: It is noted by the commentator of *Mishkatul-Masabih* that Muhammed noticed the Sadducean Jews fasting on the tenth of *Muharram* (which parallels the Hebrew month of *Iyyar* and is not a Jewish fast) "in the second year, because in the first year the Prophet had arrived at Medina after *'Ashura,* in *Rabi'ul-awwal.*"[2]

The mistake that the commentator makes is by assuming that in the *ahadith* he quotes:

1) The Prophet (pbuh) arrived on the 10th of *Rabi al-awal.*
2) The Prophet (pbuh) fasted on the 10th of Muharram, referring to the strictly lunar calendar that was mandated in the Qur'an in 631 CE.

He concludes that traditions that Muhammed's arrival took place on the tenth of *Muharram* are not correct and refer to the Prophet's fast almost a year later in 623 CE.

However, by understanding that the first *hadith* refers to the strictly lunar calendar and the second *hadith* refers to the lunar-solar calendar, then the two days match up. This can be confirmed mathematically by reverse calculation, noting that the tenth of *Rabi al-awal,* according to the strictly lunar calendar, fell on Yom Kippur in 622 CE in the Hebrew month of *Tishrei,* and not in *Iyyar.*

Our friend: Interesting ideas, but what about the writings of scholars Ibn

---

1. Al Biruni was a tenth-century Muslim scholar in Persia; scientist, linguist and historian, known as *al-Ustdadh,* "the Master" for his knowledge of Indian cultures.

2. *Mishkat al-Masabih;* Delhi ed.; 1307 A.H.; p.l72; Collection of *ahadith*—published in fourteenth century by Khatib al Tabrizi.

Sa'd[1], Abu Ja'far[2] and Ibn Hisham?[3] All accounts agree that the strictly lunar calendar of the Sadducean Jews was not imposed upon the Muslims until they made Umar[4] their "Messiah" more than six years after the passing of the Prophet Muhammed.

Ben: Intercalation was prohibited in the Qur'an, *sura* 9:36–37, long before Umar. Most scholars date that to 631 CE. But it seems it was not universally observed until Umar's decree in 638 CE. So concerning years before 638 CE there is significant confusion as to which calendar is being referred to in the *ahadith*. All of these scholars are writing two centuries after the events.

Our friend. We can disagree but still be on the "same side": I think I will go with the majority Islamic view on this one, brother. Of course I am biased because the *Sabi* calendar from who the *Karaimi* laymen descend (not to be confused with Karaite Jews) was fixed with twelve stellar months of the zodiac for centuries.

Hanuka in Malaysia

---

1. Ninth-century Islamic biographer, Iraq

2. Tenth-century astronomer and mathematician, Persia

3. Ninth century Islamic scholar, Egypt, edited the biography of Muhammed.

4. Umar was a member of the *sahaba* and Caliph of the growing Islamic empire from 634-644 CE. Allowed Jews to reenter Jerusalem following the Byzantine ban.

Asher Adiv took the above picture and shares: Amazing, a festival like Hanuka celebrated by Malaysian Muslims during the last ten days of *Ramadan* to remind the coming of Holy Night, *Lailat al Qadr*. They call it *"Malam 7 Likur"* (Seventh Night). This occurs in Malaysia, I do not know about Muslims in other countries

Someone proposes: It's like the Jewish *Lag Ba Omer* (the thirty-third day of the *Omer* counting after Passover, bonfires are lit, music is permissible).

Ben: This reminds me of the Egyptian custom of *Fawanees* (*Ramadan* lanterns). *Fanous* is a Greek word, and means "light" or "lantern", and was historically used in reference to "light of the world" and as a symbol of hope as "light in darkness".

One story has it that the sixth Fatimid Caliph Al Hakim Bi-Amr Illah wanted to light the streets of Cairo during *Ramadan* nights, so he ordered all the sheikhs of mosques to hang *fawanees* that could be illuminated by candles. As a result, the *fanous* became a custom that has never been abandoned.

Another story states that, during the time of this Caliph, women were not allowed to leave their houses except during *Ramadan*, but even then they had to be preceded by a little boy carrying a copper *fanous*. The *fanous* was then used as a tool to announce the arrival of a woman to caution men in the street to move away. As these practices softened, women were allowed to go out as they wished but people liked the idea of the fanous, and so it became a tradition that little children carry them in the streets every day to play.

A third story even relates that the lanterns came from a different source. Some believe that the use of lanterns was originally a Coptic Christian tradition celebrated during Christmas time (Coptic version), when people used to celebrate with colorful candles. This story explains that, since many Christians converted to Islam, they took this tradition with them in the form of lanterns made of tin and lit with candles.

It is perhaps noteworthy that *Ramadan* corresponds to *Sefirat Ha Omer*. So *Lailat al Qadr* corresponds to *Lag Ba Omer*.

A commentator: Interesting!

Ben: Just to explore another possible connection, Caliph Al-Hakim bi-Amr Allah was a major proponent of Ismailism (a form of Shia Islam). Many Ismailis emigrated from India in 1920 under the guidance of Imam Sultan Muhammed Shah and were settled in the country now known as Malaysia, perhaps bringing the tradition of Ramadan Lanterns with them.

Other sources suggest the present *Ramadan fanous* tradition began during the rule of Saladin (1174-1193 CE), though the most widespread account of the lantern's origins places it a little earlier, when Fatimid leader Al-Muizz li-Din Allah entered Egypt on 15 *Ramadan* of 358 AH (969 CE), and Egyptians greeted him with lamps and torches.

There is yet another version of the origins of the lantern, attributing its development to the Fatimid caliphate. The story goes that the caliph would check for the moon marking the beginning of the holy month accompanied by children who lit his way with lanterns while singing songs.

Asher Adiv: There was a Jew who converted to Islam called Abdul Malik Israel who came to Indonesia most probably from Spain fleeing the Spanish Inquisition. I'm not sure if he was the only Jew or he came with a few others, who intermarried with some Hashemites who were also Javanese royals. There was even a sultanate known as Sultan Bani Israel in Batavia named after him I think. Some of the Javanese royals migrated to Malay land fleeing from the Dutch colonizers due to a rebellion against them. Then, there was a wave of Jews coming from Europe in late nineteenth and early twentieth century. The famous *meshulach* (fundraiser), Jacob Saphir, also came to visit Jews in this region.

A discussion branches off as to the impact of holidays
which commemorate tragedies.

A friend offers: The Muslim community has mixed feelings towards the New Year, due to the tragedy of *Karbala*; the Arab tribes of Mecca had grown fearful of the political ambitions of Muhammed's family and massacred them. An army of 30,000 clashed with the members of a caravan of less than one hundred men from the Prophet's family.

The Shia Muslims, who form about a quarter of the Middle Eastern Muslim population, go into a forty-day mourning period with the beginning of the New Year. Some Sunni Muslims also reflect with sadness on the events for the first ten days of the year, although many fault the Prophet's family for creating disunity by refusing to accept the authority of the Caliph.

Dan: From a purely mental-health standpoint, is it good to constantly be reminded of a historical tragedy? In the same vein, some Jews focus solely on the tragedy of the Holocaust and forget about the freedom struggle in Exodus, for example. So, though historical tragedies should be remembered, holding onto this sense of victimization can lead to an authoritarian mentality that leads one to victimize others as one was victimized oneself ... kind of the opposite of the "Golden Rule".

A friend offers that remembering the Karbala tragedy can inspire
Muslims to have compassion for powerless minorities, as even the
Prophet's own family met this tragic end. It can also help Muslims
see the shortcomings of their own leaders.

Dan: In general, I don't feel that maintaining a psychology of victimization is wise. If I abuse others the way that I have been abused in the past, this is a type of spiritual blindness. So, I think it would be better for all the People of the Book to come together to break the chains of violence than to repeat the tragedies of the past by dwelling on them.

The Hajj

A friend contributes: Another rite which has helped so many to eradicate racism from their lives is the *Hajj* pilgrimage to Mecca, which is obligatory upon every Muslim at least once in a lifetime. This annual pilgrimage, or *Hajj* as it is called in Arabic, is one of the five pillars, one of the five fundamental religious duties to be performed by Muslims.

The *Hajj* is the prime example of the multi-racial aspect of Islam: Muslims of all races gather with one common purpose—to worship Allah. This is a compulsory act which should be done by all those Muslims with the strength and ability to do it.

In the *Hajj* pilgrimage, you will see a multitude of men, women and children, close to two million, from every corner of the world, black and brown of complexion, yellow and white, Arabs and Iranians, Turks and Malays, Chinese and Africans, black and white Americans, blond and blue-eyed Europeans. Whether black or brown, yellow or white, rich or poor, young or old, every male that our eye beholds is dressed alike, wearing two white seamless sheets of simple material, thus eliminating completely all marks and signs of distinction of dress between the African and American, the Asian, Australian and

European, the mighty and wealthy and the poor and lowly. Here they have come, brother unto brother, sister unto sister, bearing witness to the brotherhood of mankind, to the equality of all human beings before their Creator, for it is to worship Him and to extol His glory that has brought them here.

The Hajj and the Ninth of Av

Ben: There were three holy months in the Jewish calendar when war was prohibited and uninhibited travel to Jerusalem was guaranteed. This was during the months of *Hag* (Hebrew) or *Hajj* (Arabic) or the pilgrimages for *Pesach*, *Shavuot* and *Sukkot*. After the temple was destroyed, a fourth pilgrimage was instituted, the ninth of *Av*, when the Jews would travel to Jerusalem to mourn on the Mount of Olives.

If the Jewish New Year, *Rosh Hashana*, on the first of Tishrei corresponds to *Ras as Sana* on the first of *Muharram*, then the ninth of *Av* corresponds to the ninth of *Dhu al Hijjah* (the Day of Arafat). In this way the *Hajj* and the ninth of *Av* share a common source.

This is supported by epigraphic[1] findings, such as the inscription published by Altheim and Stiehl, found in Mada'in Saleh, also called *Al-Hijr*, in the Al-Ula sector of the Al Madinah Region of Saudi Arabia. The inscription was engraved on a tomb erected by Adnun (Anan or Onias) bar Honi bar Shemuel *Rosh Higra* (Head of the Pilgrimage) for his wife Mina who died in the month of *Av* in 356 CE.

Tosefos[2] records that there was a pilgrimage on the ninth of *Av* from many places, and specifically mentions pilgrims coming from Arabia.

In the year 541 CE, Flavius Belisarius, commander of the Roman Byzantine armies, summoned a council of war against Persia. Two Roman officers in command of Syrian garrisons refused to join Belisarius' army to Nisibis. They said that their absence would leave Syria and Phoenicia exposed to the attacks of the Arabs. Belisarius argued that this would not be a problem because the summer solstice was at hand, when the Arabs went on pilgrimage and would not resort to arms, so there was no cause for apprehension. The summer solstice June 21, 541 CE would have fallen on the day after the ninth of *Jumaada al-Thaani* according to the strictly lunar calendar now in Islamic use, six months too early for the *Hajj* pilgrimage. This means that intercalation (inserting a leap month) must have been in use in the years before the Prophet. If we assume the intercalation currently used by the Jewish calendar, the solstice would have fallen on the ninth of *Dhu al-Hijja*—the correct date—which also happened to be the ninth of *Av*.

There is another indication that both holidays share the same source; the ninth of *Dhu al-Hijjah*, just like the ninth of *Av*, is a fast day.

On the ninth day, the pilgrims leave Mina for Mt. Arafat where they sit in contemplative vigil and pray and recite the Qur'an, near a hill overlooking Mecca. This hill is called *Jabal Al Rahmah* (The Hill of Forgiveness, Mount Arafat). This practice is known as *Wuquf* and is

---

1. Epigraphy is the study of inscriptions and writings

2. Commentaries on the Talmud, compiled in thirteenth and fourteenth centuries.

considered the highlight of the *Hajj*.

Roman soldiers from the tenth legion encamped on the Temple Mount after its destruction.

Jews made pilgrimages to the Mount of Olives because it was eighty meters higher than the Temple Mount and offered a panoramic view of the Temple site. It became a traditional place for lamenting the Temple's destruction on the ninth of *Av*.

Eka: It's wonderful, *sub'Anallah* (glory be to Allah), the same tradition of Abraham.

The calendar is intricately tied to festivals. Some friends ask about the calendar.

Ben: The lunar-solar calendar is commanded by the Torah, because Passover, the first month, must always be in the spring. This means approximately every three years a month must be added. However, scholars Al-Tabari and Ibn Waqidi[1] say that this privilege was abused by the leadership in Arabia. They would add or exchange

1.Eighth-century Muslim scholar, Arabia. Biographer of the prophet Muhammed.

months whenever convenient for them, to make holidays and holy months fall when best for their warfare. The Prophet (pbuh) declared that manipulating holidays is wrong and it was thus abolished.

People like intellectually honest unity.

A friend: *Mash'Allah.* Again thanks to Mr. Abrahamson we found another very interesting fact. May Allah bless you sir.

A friend asks: Does Judaism have a special kind of worship to commemorate Abraham's test to sacrifice his son?

Ben: According to the *shari'a* of Torah, the sacrifice of Abraham (pbuh) is commemorated mostly on *Rosh Hashana (Ras as-Sana),* because of the connection between the ram offered in place of Abraham's son Isaac and the ram's horn blown to announce the beginning of the New Year (also symbolizing Gabriel's trumpet blown before the Day of Judgment).

Our friend responds in an affectionate vein: Judaism is from Bani Israel, Islam from Bani Ishmael.

Eid Al Adha

Ben: *Eid Al Adha* is on the tenth of *Dhu al-Hijjah* and is a three-day holiday. It commemorates Abraham's test to sacrifice his son Ishmael. It is an *eid* (solemn festival) of sacrifice and commitment to Allah's commandments. My *dua* to Allah swt is that He bless all of us in all circles of life, and help all amongst us who are helpless, worried, especially the believers—my co-religionists—who are in great need in Syria and Egypt, waiting for His *rahmat* (mercy). Amin. *Eid Mubarak* (blessed *eid*) to all.

A friend: Amin—wish you the same!

Ben deftly mentions Abraham's test, with no qualms about the seeming contradiction of whether the son so tested was Isaac or Ishmael: I do not have a problem with the different versions of the story of Abraham's relationship with Isaac and Ishmael because rabbinic Judaism strongly disagrees with the view that there is only one exclusive covenant. It is clear from the Torah that both Isaac and Ishmael were given covenants from Avraham. According to the Torah, the commemoration of Allah's covenant with Isaac at Mount Moriah in Jerusalem is on *Rosh Hashana*. Allah's covenant with Ishmael occurred at the covenant of circumcision (Genesis 17:20-27). If you look at the correspondence on the calendar, you will see that *Shavuot* corresponds to *Eid Al Adha*. There is a tradition that whenever two things seem to contradict, you wait for a third piece of information which reconciles the two.

"Two passages that contradict each other are resolved by a third passage that reconciles between them." (*Baraisa* of Rabbi Ishmael: The Thirteen Rules by which the Torah is expounded, listed in the Jewish prayer book)

> **So strive as in a race in all virtues. The goal of you all is to Allah; it is He that will show you the truth about the matters in which you are different.** (Qur'an, Al-Maedah 5:48).

A friend contributes: Imam al-Riza[1] said, "At the twenty-fifth night of the month *Dhu'l-Qa`dah*, Prophet Abraham was born, Prophet Jesus the son of Mary was born, and the earth was spread on the water where the Holy *Ka'aba* is now situated. Hence, if one observes fasting on this day, he will be given the reward of observing fasting sixty months."

---

1. Ninth century Imam, descendant of Muhammed and one of the Twelve Imams; successors of Muhammed, the Twelve Imams are descended from Muhammed through his daughter Fatima, from whom the *Mahdi* is said to descend.

According to another narration, Imam al-Riza added, "Verily, on this day, *al-Qa'im* (*Imam al-Mahdi*, Messiah) will appear." May it be soon!

3. Prayer in Islam and Judaism

Islamic salah *(prayer) parallels Jewish prayer with its similar* qiyaam *(rising),* ruku'*(bowing) and* sujud *(prostration). In clarifying terminology used in prayer, other terms are discussed — what do the terms Jew and Israelite mean, and, which came first, Judaism or Islam?*

Ben Abrahamson: You will see below how Muslim *Salah* (prayer) is somewhat like Jewish prayer in similar *Qiyaam, Ruku'* and *Sujud*.

When I read the following *ayah* (verse) in the Qur'an: **"And remember it was said to them: 'Dwell in this town and eat therein as ye wish, but say the word of humility and enter the gate in a posture of humility: We shall forgive you your faults; We shall increase** [the portion of] **those who do good.' "** (7.161) I am reminded of this Torah verse: **"Stand in the gate of the Lord's house, and proclaim there this word, and say: Hear the word of the Lord, all Judah, that enter in at these gates to prostrate before the Lord. Thus saith the Lord of hosts, the God of Israel: Amend your ways and your doings, and I will cause you to dwell in this place."** (Jeremiah 7:2-3)

Machmud: The Rabbi has posted five, and I've heard that Jews pray three times a day. Could you please give me a reference?

Another responds: You can find the Hebrew terms in any Jewish prayerbook (*siddur*).

Machmud: Any Jewish prayerbook doesn't sound like a good reference. I need some reference from the *Tanakh* (Bible), the *Talmud* or any other authentic references.

Response: The content of the *siddur* is based on the *Tanakh* and *Talmud*. All references are in the Artscroll Siddur for example. Before you ask me to go and get mine to spend the next ten minutes typing them up here for you *habibi* (my friend), it is a greater act of love for me to tell you to go and get a *siddur* for yourself and read it.

Islamic and Rabbinic Prayer Times

Fajr (فجر)	Dawn when "white thread can be distinguished by you from a black one" to sunrise	*Brochos* (ברכות)	Dawn when "one can distinguish between blue and white." to the first quarter of the day
Zhur (ظهر)	After true noon until *Asr*	*Shacharit* (שחרית)	From sunrise to the first third of the day.
Asr (عصر)	Afternoon. According to Imam Abu Hanifa, "*Asr* starts when the shadow of an object becomes twice its height (plus the length of its shadow at the start time of *Zhur*)." For the rest of Imams, "*Asr* starts when the shadow of an object becomes equal to its length (plus the length of its shadow at the start time of *Zhur*)." *Asr* ends as the sun begins to set. According to Shia Muslims, "*Asr* prayer has no set times but is performed from mid-day. *Zhur* and 'Asr prayers must be performed before sunset, and the time for 'Asr prayer starts after *Zhur* has been performed.	*Ashrei* (אשרי) *Mincha*	Afternoon. 1/2 hour after true noon to last quarter of the day. Ideally, one should complete the prayers before sunset, although many authorities permit reciting *Mincha* until nightfall.
Maghrib (مغرب)	After sunset, until dusk According to Shia Muslims, *Maghrib* prayers must be performed before midnight.	*Ma'ariv* (מעריב)	After nightfall, until midnight
Isha'a (عشاء)	Dusk until dawn For Shia Muslims, the time for *Zhur* (dhur) and Asr is between the time the sun begins to decline from its zenith until sunset. *Maghrib* should be delayed from the setting of the sun until the redness of the sky has passed overhead, ie, no red in the eastern sky. *Isha* prayer maybe prayed directly after *Maghrib*. Both *Magrib* and *Isha* should be prayed before midnight.	*Shema* (קריאת שמע)	Dusk until dawn.

Ben: These five prayers are in every orthodox prayer book. The concept of "three prayers" is that rabbinic Jews are required to say the three middle prayers in the synagogue with a quorum of ten. The other two are usually said at home.

Yunus: Do you mean that not only Islam and Judaism are one and the same religion but they have the same practices and rituals too?

Ben says yes: When I came across this *hadith*: "**Maalik Ibn Abi Aamir An-saari narrates: 'Uthmaan Bin Affaan would recite in his *Khutbah* [sermon]: 'When the *salaat* [prayer] is ready, arrange the *sufoof* properly and line up with the shoulders'** ". *Sufoof* is similar to the Hebrew *tsafoof*, or crowded together. I thought of Zephaniah 3:9: "**I will clarify the languages of the nations, that they may all call upon the name of the Lord, to serve him shoulder-to-shoulder.**"

A friend: *Mash'Allah!* Very nice example!
      Another point about "to serve him shoulder-to-shoulder": when the biblical text says, "**I will clarify the languages of the nations**", Muslims all over the world from India to the USA pray only in one language, in Arabic. We are not allowed to pray the five daily prayers in English or any another language! *Mash'Allah ...*

A response to the above enthusiast for uniform prayer: I don't think there is any compulsion or obligation to offer your prayer in Arabic, which most Muslims don't even understand to begin with. People should know what they are uttering. It only makes sense.

Our friend above responds: All Muslims learn how to pray in Arabic, at least they memorize the first chapter in Qur'an, *Al-Fatihah* ("The Opening"), which is compulsory, and must be recited in Arabic! But I didn't say that each Muslim should pray or call to Allah in Arabic all the time, I mean only the five daily prayers! Peace!

Ben: Rabbinic Jews pray five times a day: two private and three public prayers. We do the following *raka'at*: early morning—2, mid morning—4, afternoon—4, evening—3, nightfall—1. A *raka'at* is a unit of prayer consisting of three movements. This is similar to Islamic *raka'at* 2,4,4,3,4, see chart on p. 57.

One Islamic *raka'at* consists of three movements: one *ruku*, which is bowing with hands on the knees, and two *sujuds*, which is prostration with face, hands, knees, and toes on floor

Rabbinic Jews do partial *sujud* except on major holidays because of mourning for the destruction of the Temple. Once the Mosaic system of sacrifices is reinstituted, then full *sujud* will be practiced again.

The Talmud (*Pesachim* 88a) says that we are required to pray the morning prayer because of the verse, "As it is said this day, on the mountain God is seen" (Genesis 22:14); afternoon prayer because of this verse, "And Isaac went out to pray in the field" (Genesis 24:63); and evening prayer because of this verse, "And he called the name of that place the House of God" (Genesis 28:19).

The Torah teaches that we should perform *sujud* at the gates of the Temple, "Stand at the gate of the LORD's house, and proclaim there, this word; and say: 'Hear the word of the LORD, all Judah, that enter in at these gates to prostrate *(khol yehudah habaim basha'arim lheshtachavot)* before the LORD. Thus saith the LORD of hosts, the God of Israel: Amend your ways and your doings, and I will cause you to dwell in this place" (Jeremiah 7:2-3). The Talmud teaches that there were twelve prostrations, one for each gate (Talmud, *Sheqalim Mishnah* 6:1); this was reduced to four: one at the beginning and ending of the Avot Blessing *(Brachah)* and one at the beginning and ending of the Modim Blessing *(Brachah)* (Talmud Berakhot 34a).

So at this point we have three prayers a day, each with two blessings (Hebrew *bracha*, Arabic *raka'at*) that have prostration. The number of *raka'at* were 2,2,2.

In addition, the Torah commands us to declare the oneness of God (Arabic, *tawhid*) when one rises up and when one lies down. "Hear,

O Israel: The Lord our God, the Lord is one. Love the Lord your God with all your heart and with all your soul and with all your strength. These commandments that I give you today are to be on your hearts. Impress them on your children. Talk about them when you sit at home and when you walk along the road, when you lie down and when you get up" (Deuteronomy 6:4-7). When people became more city-oriented, the prayers were said later in the day. This caused a disagreement whether the oneness of God *(tawhid)* should be said upon rising or at the first public prayers (which were later) and upon going to sleep or at the last public prayers. The Talmud declared that it should be said at both times (Talmud, *Berakhot* 4b). This increased the number of prayers from three to five. The number of *raka'at* were now 2,2,2,2,2

Also there were some communities where the prayers were known by heart, so the community prayed together silently, and other communities where the prayers were not known by heart. In those communities a prayer leader would say the prayers out loud. The Talmud declared that both customs should be followed (*Rosh Hashanah* 35a). This increased the number of prostrations from two to four in the morning and afternoon prayers. The number of *raka'at* were now 2,4,4,2,2

The *fourth* through sixth centuries were very turbulent and dangerous times for the Jewish community, so the Talmudic scholars ruled that one should lengthen the evening prayer so that it will be slightly longer and people can walk home together (*Berakhot* 29, 57b, *Pessachim* 104a). One blessing was added to the evening prayer from the nightime prayer. The number of *raka'at* were now 2,4,4,3,1

Other changes:

Shortly after the Temple was destroyed full prostration was changed to half prostration, but this will be returned to full prostration when the Temple is rebuilt (Talmud, *Megilah* 22b and commentaries)

The two prostrations of the dawn prayer *(Baruch She'amar & Yishtabah)* were moved to the morning prayer. (Tosefos on Talmud, *Berakhot* 46)

All the prayers were preceded by learning a section from the Torah. This was in turn preceded by a blessing for the reading of the Torah (*Yoma* 72a). These blessings, which start as a call to prayer "*Barkhu...*" are called *ruku* in Arabic. The *barkhu* (bowing) for the afternoon prayer was added to the end of the morning prayer. The *barkhu* (bowing) for the nightime prayer was added to the end of the evening prayer.

Also, shortly after the Temple was destroyed, the *barkhu* (bowing) that was done between two sets of blessings (prostrations) was prohibited because of the wording, "It is our duty to praise the Master of all, who has not made us like the nations of the lands. For they worship vanity and emptiness (Isaiah 30:7), who pray to gods that cannot save (Isaiah 45:20). But we bow in worship and thank the Supreme King of kings, the Holy One, Blessed be He." At first it was an offense to the Romans, and later to the Christians, who thought it must refer to them. As a result this prayer was moved to the end of the prayers and said silently. Now it is read out loud, but has not yet been returned to its place in between the two sets of blessings (prostrations). So the custom is to bow (do *ruku*) at the beginning of the Modim prayer and prostrate *(sujud)* at the end, and the second prostration *(sujud)* just before Oseh Shalom prayer *(tsalaam)*.

Considering the tension that was produced by declaring three prayers a day, having different communities implement it differently, which in turn caused the rabbis to have to rule on diverse practices, one could consider a rule of five short prayers without need for ten people together to be an easier obligation for the community of the Prophet (pbuh).

I am reminded of following *hadith*, specifically the phrase "I descended till I met Moses who asked me, 'What have you done?' I said, 'Fifty prayers have been enjoined on me.' He said, 'I know the people better than you, because I had the hardest experience to bring Bani Israel to obedience. Your followers cannot put up with such obligation. So, return to your Lord and request Him [to reduce the number of prayers].'... Ultimately Allah reduced it to five." (Sahih Bukhari Volume 4, Book 54, Number 429).

Islamic and Rabbinic Raka'at (Unit of Prayer)

Rabbinic Name	Jewish Prayer Position	Islamic Prayer Name	Islamic Prayer Position
	2,4,4,3,1 (# of raka'at)		2,4,4,3,4 (# of raka'at)
Brochos		**Fajr**	
Brochos on rising			
Birchas HaTorah Shema' Korbanos	Stand (and sit)	Ruku (bowing)	1st Raka'ah
Shakharis			
Baruch She'amar Pesukei de'zimrei	Stand Stand (and sit)	Sujud Sujud (full prostration)	
Ve Yevarech David Shema' Pesukei de'zimrei	Stand	Ruku	2nd Raka'ah
Yishtabach	Stand Stand	Sujud Sujud	
		Zhur	
Barkhu Shema'	Ruku	Ruku	1st Raka'ah
Avos	half-Sujud half-Sujud	Sujud Sujud	
Modim	Ruku	Ruku	2nd Raka'ah
Hoda'ah	half-Sujud half-Sujud	Sujud Sujud	
Kedusha	(Ruku)	Ruku	3rd Raka'ah
Avos	half-Sujud half-Sujud	Sujud Sujud	
Retzeh	(Ruku)	Ruku	4th Raka'ah
Modim	half-Sujud half-Sujud	Sujud Sujud	
		Asr	
Barkhu	Ruku	Ruku	1st Raka'ah
Mincha			
Ashrei			
Avos	half-Sujud half-Sujud	Sujud Sujud	
Modim	Ruku	Ruku	2nd Raka'ah
Hoda'ah	half-Sujud half-Sujud	Sujud Sujud	
Kedusha	(Ruku)	Ruku	3rd Raka'ah
Avos	half-Sujud half-Sujud	Sujud Sujud	
Retzeh	(Ruku)	Ruku	4th Raka'ah
Modim	half-Sujud half-Sujud	Sujud Sujud	

Islamic and Rabbinic Raka'at

Rabbinic Prayer Name	Jewish Prayer Position	Islamic Prayer Name	Islamic Prayer Posiiton
Ma'ariv		Maghrib	
Barkhu Shema'	Ruku	Ruku	1st Raka'ah
Avos	half-Sujud half-Sujud	Sujud Sujud	
Retzeh	(Ruku)	Ruku	2nd Raka'ah
Modim	half-Sujud half-Sujud	Sujud Sujud	
Barkhu	Ruku	Ruku	3rd Raka'ah
Ma'yin Sheva'	half-Sujud half-Sujud	Sujud Sujud	
Shema' al Mitah		Isha'a	
Shema'	(Ruku)	Ruku	1st Raka'ah
HaMapil	Stand	Sujud Sujud	
		Ruku	2nd Raka'ah
		Sujud Sujud	
		Ruku	3rd Raka'ah
		Sujud Sujud	
		Ruku	4th Raka'ah
		Sujud Sujud	

It is still work in progress because there are multiple customs and rabbinic prayer was never defined in terms of number of *raka'at*. Instead, rabbinic prayer was derived, in stages, from the Temple prayer service. Two differences that are documented in Jewish prayer:

1) *sujud*–full prostration (Hebrew–*qida*) was changed to half-*sujud* in mourning for the destruction of the Temple (although Jews do *sujud* on certain holidays, and *sujud* will again be practiced in the future).

2) The Morning Prayer was expanded to include parts of the dawn prayer as well as parts of the afternoon prayer.

Islamic prayer is made up of repeating, essentially identical *raka'at*s. These *raka'at*s do not have individual names but are called by number. Jewish prayer on the other hand often has different wording for the

Movement During Prayer

	Torah	3rd CE Aramaic	Rabbinic	Arabic
Rising to pray	qam	qam		qiyam
Standing prayer (as slave before master)	`amad	tzaluta	`amidah tefilah	tzalat (salat)
Raising hands	nisiyat kapayim prisat kapayim	nisiyat kapayim	nisiyat kapayim*	niyyat
Bowing down with hands resting on knees (expressing recognition)	bereikha	bereikha	barkhu torah blessing	ruku
Feet, Hands and Face to ground (expressing submission)	qida	qida	four times during `amidah **	sujud four times each raka'at
Full Prostration arms, legs spread face to ground (after sacrifice)	hishtakhawah	sajda	***	
Kneeling, supplicating prayer	Kri`ah hands outstretched, not sitting on feet	Kri`ah****	`alenu	qu'ud sitting on feet
Taking leave	shalom	shalom	oseh shalom	salaamu 'alaikum
Face to the ground (petition for forgiveness)	nifilat apayim	nifilat apayim	face rests on arm during tachnun	salatul tasbih

* Originally arms were raised during pesukei dizimrei. This was discontinued when the Temple was destroyed. This custom still survives in Jewish custom when raising hands for shema and ashrei prayer.

** When the Temple was destroyed, in the Land of Israel qida became slight movements of knees and head. It continued in Babylon as partial prostration (the way Muslims do it today).

*** When the Temple sacrifices ceased, full prostration sajda no longer occurred This caused a shift in terminology, qida took on the name sajda and kri`ah took on the name qu'ud (qida).

**** When the Temple was destroyed, Jews ceased to outstretch hands, although Christians retained this custom.

unit of prayer. A Jewish raka'at consists of bending at the waist, then twice bending at the knees and bowing the head. In the above table this is referred to as half-sujud.

Omar: I've seen it many times, full prostration, face on the floor; common among the old-time practitioners, but less so these days among the younger generation.

Full prostration (sujud) is connected with offering a sacrifice; in the Ramban's[1] opinion, Nefilat Apayim requires completely lying on the

1. Also known as Nachmanides, thirteenth-century rabbi, kabbalist and physician, Spain. Espoused reverence for tradition, perhaps in response to Greek influences that were on

floor with arms outstretched. Today this is only done by Christians (as far as I know), but is not retained as a part of prayer, rather as a part of showing submission to a higher authority during ordination or similar procedure.

Ben: What is interesting is that one can trace the actual words used to describe these positions.

It also explains Jewish customs such as not putting tefillin between the eyes because it would interfere with *sujud* prostration, which requires the forehead to touch the ground.

> **If the people knew the reward for the *Zuhr* prayer in its early time, they would race for it. If they knew the reward for the "*Isha*" and the *Fajr* prayers in congregation, they would join them even if they had to crawl. If they knew the reward for the first row, they would draw lots for it.** (*Sahih* Al-Bukhari Volume 1, Book 11, Hadith 688)[1]

Judaism has the same custom to be early for prayers, the special merit of the dawn and midnight prayers, and being in the front rows of the synagogue.

A reader: Dear Mr. Abrahamson, if I may ask, do you have in Judaism daily prayers like Muslims have and how do you perform these daily prayers in practice?

---

the rise in Spain at the time. He was forced to participate in the Disputation of Barcelona in 1263, against his will, in which he defended Judaism against Christian claims. Though he won the respect of King James I of Aragon, who granted him full freedom of expression during the debate, the humiliation of the Dominican side catalyzed his banishment from Spain for two years. This led to his immigration to the Holy Land in 1267 under the protection of its Muslim rulers.

1. Collection of *ahadith* – legends.

A commentator asserts: No they don't have, unfortunately. Allah explains it clearly in the Qur'an:

> **Those were the ones upon whom Allah bestowed favor**
> **from among the prophets of the descendants of Adam and**
> **of those We carried** [in the ship] **with Noah, and of the**
> **descendants of Abraham and Israel, and of those whom We**
> **guided and chose. When the verses of the Most Merciful**
> **were recited to them, they fell in prostration and weeping.**
> **But there came after them successors who neglected prayer**
> **and pursued desires; so they are going to meet evil—**
> **Except those who repent, believe and do righteousness; for**
> **those will enter Paradise and will not be wronged at all.**
> (Qu'ran, *Maryam* 19:58-60)

The above verse is clearly talking about the believers of the old, the people of the book, who have forgotten to pray the way they were commanded to.

Ben: The Jews continue to pray as the Muslims do, the same five daily prayers and the same number of *raka'at*. The only difference is that since the destruction of the Temple we bend halfway down to the ground, instead of all the way. It is the custom to do full prostration, just like the Muslims, on the High Holidays. We are aware of the prior custom and *insha'Allah* when the sacrificial system is restored in Jerusalem, we will return to the full prostration.

Jewish and Islamic *Raka'at*

Ben: The Jews of Arabia were Sadducean. According to Al Jahiz and Ibn Hazm[1] they differed from Jews of today in many customs. The rabbinic Jews of today are descended from the Pharisees, a group at

---

1. As illustrated in Ibn Hazm's book, *Kitab al-Fasl fi al-Milal wa al-Ahwa wa al-Nihal.*

odds with the Sadducees.

Observant rabbinic Jews pray five times a day, with a similar number of *raka'ats*: 2,4,4,3,1. They all do *ruku* and differ only in the extent of bowing during *Sujud*.

The Prophet Muhammed (pbuh) says:

When one wakes in the morning he should say: "We have come into this morning when all dominion belongs to Allah swt, the Lord of all worlds ..." and **"praise be to Allah who has returned** [my soul] **safe and sound."**

It is also Jewish custom, immediately upon arising, to say: "I offer thanks before you, living and eternal King, for You have mercifully returned my soul within me; Your faithfulness is great ..." It is interesting to note that the Jewish custom of saying this prayer (called *"Modeh Ani"*) dates to the time of Islam. Before that time, during Talmudic times, upon waking, Jews would say the prayer *Elohai Neshamah* "My God, the soul that You have placed in me is pure ..." (Talmudic tractate Berakhot 60b.) This prayer has been moved to the morning prayers.

According to Jewish custom, after saying the *Modeh Ani* prayer, one should wash the hands (three times, starting with the right hand), wash one's face and rinse one's mouth. This is not unlike the Islamic custom of *wudu*. *Wudu* consists basically of: washing the right hand up to the wrist three times, then left hand, rinsing the mouth three times, then nostrils, washing the face three times, washing entire right arm three times; then left arm. Wet hands should be passed all over the head, to ears and neck once. Wash right foot three times, then left. It is interesting that the *Shia* custom is to shape the one hand like a cup and take water into it to wash the other hand. In Judaism an actual cup is used.

Harry: *Modeh ani lefanekha melekh chay ve khayam ...* That brings back memories. Thank you, Rabbi.

Ali: But the Jews do ablution ... ?

Ben: Jews do *wudu*.

Ali: I did not know.

A friend: We have a lot in common; this is only one of the many. Thanks for
very lovely information.

Tawaf (circumabulation) and *Sujud* (prostration) in the Jerusalem Temple, Synagogue, and Mosque

Ben: The bowing in the Jerusalem Temple, synagogue and mosque finds its
roots in the Temple custom to bow at each gate in Temple. The relationship between gates and prayer is a common theme. City gates
were the places where courts were set up to regulate commerce and
taxes. Similarly, the Temple gates had courts that regulated entrance
to the Temple grounds. Each gate served a practical function in the
Temple operation. So it is probable that the prayers associated with
each gate took on a specific character. Each gate began to symbolize
a specific need: water, livelihood, justice, etc.

Even to this day, the custom in the synagogue of bowing when one
passes in front of the Torah Ark is done in remembrance of the Temple
gates. The synagogue, which coexisted with the second Temple, has
only one "gate": the Torah Ark where the Torah scrolls are stored,
symbolizing the Gate of Nicanor.

As public prayer began to take on more of a formal nature, the
congregants recited the same prayers they said by the gates of the
Temple. They would prostrate for each one. They would take three
steps backwards and forwards before the start of prayers, and also
after the end of the prayers as a symbolic gesture of approaching
and leaving the Temple gates. However, thirteen prostrations were

Correspondence between the Actual Words said in Prayer and the Gates of the Temple

Prayer	Gate*	Location	Purpose
Commemoration of the patriarchs	No name	Southern gate on western wall	Entering the temple grounds from the city.
Mightiness of God	Shaar HaEliyon (Upper Gate)	Western gate on southern wall	It was the highest gate in elevation, hence it's name.
Sanctification of God	Shaar HaDelek (Fuel Gate)	Second gate from west on southern wall	The Gate of Kindling through which wood was brought for the *Mizbe'ach* (altar)
Understanding	Shaar HaBekhorot (Firstling Gate)	Third gate from west on southern wall	The Gate of the Firstborn through which were brought the offering of first born animals (Shmos 13).
Penitence	Shaar HaMayim (Water Gate)	Fourth gate from west on southern wall	The Water Gate, opposite the *Mizbe'ach*, was opened only on Sukkot to bring water for the *Nisuch ha'Mayim*. A stream passed through the *Azarah* and flowed through this gate. When necessary, its flow was blocked, causing it to overflow and cleanse the Azarah floor
Forgiveness	Southern Nikanor gate	Southern gate on eastern wall	To the south was the Chamber of the Pancake-Makers, where twelve cakes were prepared daily, six for the morning and six for the afternoon sacrifice
Redemption			Added after destruction of the Temple
Healing	Shaar Nikanor	Middle gate on eastern wall	On these steps the Levites sang the "hymns of degrees," (Ps. 120-135), corresponding with the number of steps (Yoma 38a); these were recited at the festival of the rejoicing of the water. The reading of the Torah was heard as well.
Blessing of the harvest	Northern Nikanor Gate	Northern gate on eastern wall	On the northern side was the Chamber of Pinchas, the vestment-keeper, who had charge of the priests' lockers built in the wall and who arranged for the 24 patrols
Ingathering of the exiles			Added later
Restoration of the judges			Added later
Destruction of the sectarians			Added later
Rewarding of the righteous	Shaar HaShir (Song Gate)	Eastern gate on northern wall	The gate where the Levites entered with their musical instruments. Also where Israel's Great Sanhedrin sat, and judged the kohanim.

* The thirteen gates are described "There were in the Temple thirteen chests, thirteen tables and thirteen prostrations. [Members] of the household of Rabban Gamaliel and of R. Hananiah the Chief of Priests, used to prostrate themselves fourteen [times]. And where was the additional [prostration] In front of the store of wood, for thus they had a tradition from their forefathers that the Ark was hidden there." (Talmud Sheqalim Mishnah 6:1)

Prayer	Gate	Location	Purpose
Rebuilding of Jerusalem			Added later
Restoring the Kingdom of David			Added later
Acceptance of prayer	Shaar HaNashim (Women's Gate)	Second gate from east on northern wall	The Women's Gate, an entrance for women bringing offerings.
Restoration of the Temple Service	Shaar HaQorban (Offering Gate)	Third gate from east on northern wall	The Gate of the Offering through which Kodshei Kodshim offerings were brought.
Thanksgiving	Shaar HaNitzutz (Yeconiah Gate)	Fourth gate from east on northern wall	The Gate of the Spark, a roofed entrance under which burning coals were kept for rekindling purposes. It was formerly called the Gate of Yechanyah for it was through this gate that the kings of the Davidic line enter and king Yeconiah passed when he went into exile to Babylon. On its roof was a watchtower.
Blessing of priests, prayer for peace	No name	Northern gate on western wall	Leaving the temple grounds to the city.

thought to be a burden to the common people, and most worshipers came in by one gate and left by another, so the sages decreed that for common people they would prostrate four times: 1) at the beginning of the "patriarch's prayer" (gate), 2) at its completion, 3) at the beginning of the "thanksgiving prayer" (gate), and 4) at its completion. However, priests and kings were required to do more.

In the halachic sense, Jerusalem takes the place of the camp of Israel in the desert, as the outer circle surrounding the Temple. Har ha-bayit, the Temple Mount, corresponds to the camp of the Leviyim, and Jerusalem corresponds to the camp of Israel, with regard to laws such as the consumption of kodashim kalim and ma'aser sheni. Jerusalem is referred to as Tel Talpiyot—Tel she-kol piyot ponot elav, "The mount to which all mouths turn [in prayer]". (The original phrase appears in the hosha'not prayers of the Sukkot holiday, and the homily is based on Midrash Shir HaShirim Rabba 4:6.) Throughout the exile, Jews scattered all over the globe have centered their hopes and prayers on returning to Jerusalem and the Temple, though they may not have had a common language or common government.

It was customary to make one procession around the altar on each day of Sukkot, and seven processions around the altar on the seventh day (Talmud, *Sukkah* 4:5)

Aqeel Yousuf: I laud you for your efforts to reconcile the Abrahamic faiths through your tireless endeavours. Well done.

Ben: The interesting part is that the Talmud seems to indicate that because of the number of people who came to the Temple, it was necessary for all of them to go in the same direction, counterclockwise, so as not to create confusion. This means that it would be a regular act of worship, no matter what gate one was going to, to circumambulate (to go around) the Temple at least once and pass all the gates.

Aqeel Yousuf: *Tawaf* equivalent?

Ben: Yes, this means that the prayer we say today while standing and bowing is a direct descendant of *tawaf*.

Aqeel Yousuf: And it was anti-clockwise, correct? *Tawaf* is anti-clockwise in the *Haram* in Mecca.

Ben: Yes, the same.

Ekhwan Rusli: Anti-clockwise as the way the Earth spins on its axis. Anti-clockwise just like the Earth orbits the Sun, the Moon orbits the Earth, and the direction of spin of most heavenly objects.

James David Audlin: Fascinating, helpful, *shokran, todah!*

Gibran Malik: Thank Allah for your help in showing this truth. They didn't believe me two years ago, but now people are starting to grasp it. May Allah bless you.

Ben: Amin, *wa iyyak.*

Another friend challenges: Are you saying that every single Jew that exists today prays five times a day? So according to you, all the Jews addressed in the Qur'an, who killed the messiah, did not observe the law, did not pray five five times a day, called *Uzair* the son of God,[1] have been completely erased from this planet?

Ben: Surely there are Jews who have abandoned their religion, just as there a Muslims who are not observant and do not pray five times a day, but these people are not representative of their faith.

This commentator remains unconvinced: Then I highly doubt this Judaism, considering their devotion towards Zionism and Israeli apartheid.

Ben: Then you do not know it very well. I invite you to ask questions.

Passionate statements can easily branch off into a heated argument. But look at the response? A mere: Insh' Allah ...

And then a turnaround: May the Lord of the worlds guide us all into the right path, Amin. Peace, Rabbi Ben.

Ben responds: *Wa aleikum wa aleina salaam wa rahmatullah wa barakatahu.*

---

1. The Qur'an (9:30) has a verse that states that the Jews called a certain Uzair the son of God, a claim denied by Maimonides as being contrary to Judaism's strict monotheism. Muslim scholars have clarified that this verse refers to a small group of Jews.

And the thread ends on a note of peace. This passionate commentator did not need a list of proofs and arguments, just the sense that God-fearing Jews are interested in honest dialogue. Love is natural.

Prayer Shawls

Ben: And the LORD spoke unto Moses, saying:

> **Speak unto the children of Israel, and bid them that they make them throughout their generations fringes in the corners of their garments ... that ye may remember and do all My commandments, and be holy unto your God.** (Numbers 15:37-40)

A friend: "…the fringes in the corners of their garments ..." Is that why the prayer shawl has the fringes on the four corners as representation of this? I think it's called a *tallit* or *tallis*?

Ben: Yes, the *tallit* or *tallis* fulfills the biblical requirement in Numbers 15:38 and Deuteronomy 22:12. It is also mentioned in Josephus and in the New Testament: Matthew 9:20, 14:36, 23:5, Mark 5:27, Luke 8:44.

It is perhaps not surprising that some Palestinian *ghutra's* (head scarves) have fringes, if what Prof. Tsvi Misinai says is true: "A series of genetic and historical studies reinforce earlier works ... , in their finding: A solid majority of the Palestinians (80%-90%) are descendants of Jews who remained in the country following the destruction of the Second Jewish Temple."

Omar: Not just Palestinian—Arabian *ghutra's* have them too, keeping in mind a significant portion of the Palestinian population was Jewish.

Micah David Naziri: Yes, this is just one of the many customs retained from the Jewish roots of Islam. In Iran people still touch and kiss the doorposts of shrines when entering and exiting. This is reminiscent of touching and kissing the *mezuzah*, a small scroll that has a passage from the Torah and is posted on the doorpost.

Ben: Technically I would say "retained from the Jewish influences on Islam", because Islam came first. We should be talking about the Islamic (Noahide) roots of Judaism.

Omar: It's a common refrain in Israeli scholarship today to attribute the origins of Islam to Arabian Judaism, even if it's flawed and lacks proper chronology.

But I don't think I've heard about Islamic origins of Judaism outside of Islam. Obviously there was *Bnei Noah* before Moses, with the Noahide covenant preceding the Torah, but can you really take the argument that far?

Ben: Absolutely. This is the whole point of Rabbi Benamozegh's work *Israel and Humanity*. The main reason why God made a covenant with the Jewish people, and gave them additional laws, was so that they could play a special role in preserving the original faith of mankind, that of Abraham (pbuh) and before that Noah (pbuh) and even Adam (pbuh) himself.

In Jewish Law, once you make the equation between *"Bnei Noah"* and *"Islamic deen"*, then the religious narratives of both Islam and Judaism become surprisingly similar, if not identical.

This is supported by the Talmud, *Mishneh Torah* and Jewish Law. It is clear that the prophet Abraham and the religion that he taught to the multitudes was that of *Bnei Noah* (Islam). We as Jews can say that Abraham kept Islamic *deen*, he submitted to Allah, and as such he was a Muslim, not a Jew. Judaism came much later, as a covenant (*shari'a*) with a special purpose and many laws to guard and protect the Torah so that it could preserve the pure faith of Abraham for all the nations. The Jewish people were meant to serve, facilitate, and act as ministers or a nation of priests, to see this pure faith spread to all mankind.

Zara: Muslims believe that Adam was the first man and prophet and was a Muslim. He practiced monotheism (Islam) and his mission was continued by successive prophets sent by Allah until Muhammed. Muhammed came to complete the message of Allah to mankind as the final prophet. So there's no surprise there that we find similarities between faiths, especially Abrahamic faiths. The fundamental message that is monotheism has been retained since Adam but each prophet came with different *shari'a* and in each *shari'a*, we find similarities. Muslims believe that all prophets are Muslims.

Micah David Naziri: This is actually an active and classical debate within Judaism. The normative position is that Abraham was the first convert to Judaism; this is supported by the Torah saying that Abraham kept the Torah and *mitzvot* (commandments). Historically speaking, and in terms of classical *halachah* (Jewish law), if one kept the *mitzvot* and circumcised himself, he was viewed as a self-converted Jew. This is supported by Jewish legal works including Talmudic tractate '*Avodah Zarah*, Maimonides' *Mishneh Torah*[1] and the *Shulchan Aruch*[2] which discuss how to deal with the marriage of self-converted Jews into the community.

The Qur'anic Arabic is very specific. Abraham was neither "one who turned away" nor—in the alternative passage of the *'ayah*—he was not a *Yahudi*. Abraham was a convert and a foreigner, an immigrant, a stranger.

A friend: Because we are not totally sure who the children of Israel are and all their descendants, then there must be a Muslim version of the

---

1. Compilation of the Talmud, completed in 1180 CE.

2. *Code of Jewish Law*, written by Yosef Caro in the sixteenth century, Sfat, Holy Land.

fringes as an additional way of serving Allah the most high.

Ben: The normative position is that Abraham was halachically a *Bnei Noah*, which is equated with Islamic *deen,* and thus a Muslim in the sense, **"When it is recited to them they say, 'We believe in it; it is the truth from our Lord. We were already Muslims before it** [the Qur'an] **came' "** (Qur'an, *Al-Qasas* 28:53).

The debate is whether Abraham voluntarily and intuitively kept the *shari'a* of the Torah (see the commentator Rashi[1] on Torah chapter *Vayeshev*), although it is only with Ya'akov that symbolic fulfillment of *tefillin* and other *mitzvot* is actually mentioned.

The term "Islam" is used for both *deen* (basic law) and *shari'a* (covenant). This is not the case with the term "Jew". "*Bnei Noah*" is used for basic law; "Jew", or more properly "Israelite", is used for the specific *shari'a* of Torah.

The debate is that Abraham (pbuh) may have been philosophically "Jewish" in that he may have voluntarily kept Torah laws, but he could not have been a Jew before the covenant that was revealed at Sinai, as the term "Jew" implies covenant.

In this sense Abraham, *halachically* was a *Bnei Noah* and thus Muslim.

Micah David Naziri: Actually, in the United States I have heard rabbis refer to Abraham as the first Jew and the first of the three Jewish patriarchs. In any event, there are many Talmudic discussions about how Abraham kept all of the *mitzvot* of the Torah—both written and oral—including *kashrut* (dietary laws). Resulting from this discussion, the Talmud explains that the angelic visitors in fact never actually ate the non-kosher meal served to them—in the assumption that they were visitors who didn't keep kosher—and that they only made it appear that they ate. Of course, the Qur'an picks up on this Talmu-

1. Eleventh-century rabbi, France, wrote extensive commentary on the Tanakh and Talmud.

dic discussion and confirms it.

Lastly, there are explanations in the Talmud itself that define a "Jew" as "anyone who rejects idolatry"; thus explaining how Mordechai could be both a Benjaminite and a Jew (as stated in the book of Esther). By Talmudic definition of what a Jew is and how one becomes a Jew, Abraham was a Jew.

Zara: In Islam it is explained that the three angels that visited Abraham didn't eat the meat served, not because they didn't keep kosher but because angels just don't eat.

In terms of who was the first Jew, you have to clarify if they are speaking in a general philosophical way or as a matter of Jewish Law.

Sa'im: It seems that Ben Abrahamson's definition of "Jew" is closer to the Islamic understanding. So what exactly, literally does "Jew" and "Judaism" mean in the first place? Does it refer to Judah, the son of Jacob?

Ben: A "Jew" is anyone obligated by the *shari'a* of Moses (pbuh). Put differently, it is anyone who was included in the Covenant at Sinai.

According to rabbinic tradition, the forefathers voluntarily kept the commandments that would be revealed later at Sinai. But this was in the manner of custom. Also when the *midrash* (Jewish traditions) gives some examples of the customs they did keep, it is apparent that they did so, at times, only symbolically.

There is an opinion in the Talmud that anyone who is a monotheist is a Jew. This opinion defines a Jew not as a covenant (*shari'a*) but as a *deen*. In this way Abraham, Isaac and Jacob, etc could be considered "Jews". Using this thinking, all the generations since Moses, all Muslims, and all non-trinitarian Christians are also "Jews".

This minority opinion is not the one used in Jewish law, which holds the forefathers were obligated by the universal *deen* that binds all mankind, and Abraham was the first to observe it properly. In rabbinic terms, they were proper *Bnei Noah (Salamai, Muslamai* in Aramaic). In Islamic terms they were Muslims.

The correct term is "Israelite" not "Jew", and this is the one used in Jewish Law. The term "Jew" began during the first exile when the Jews were sent to Babylon. The tribe of Judah clung most strongly and uncompromisingly to monotheism, so all the Israelites were called "Jews". The first example of this is in the book of Esther, Mordechai was called "a Jew" even though he was not of the tribe of Judah.

Sa'im: Wow, very good explanation. The Qur'an uses the term "Israelites" with the covenant given to Moses at Sinai, and it includes all twelve tribes, not only one. What is your own opinion regarding various Qur'anic terms used for "people before us", like *Yahud, Bani Israel,* and *ahlil kitab* (people of the book)?

Ben: I think the term *Yahud* and *Alazenu Hadu* in Qur'anic usage refers to "Judeans" as they had come to be known during the Hasmoneans and Herodian eras as well as during the Bar Kochba revolts. In this usage it means a mixture of the tribe of Judah and Edomites, as well as members of the government.

The term *Bani Israel* would mean Israelite, in the same sense that Jews use it today. In Jewish law we call ourselves Israel, not Jews.

The term *Nasaara* in early Qur'anic usage refers to "Jordanians", more specifically the tribes of Joseph mixed with the Moabites and Ammonites. They were known as "Aws" and "Kazraj" led by the royal dynasty of Tobiah Ben Netzer the Ammonite, who traced his lineage to both the tribe of Levi and Joseph. They were Hellenist Sadducees, and the first to adopt a form of Christianity, although under queen Zenobia[1] they had also practiced paganism.

The Qur'an mentions the *ahlil kitab* (people of the book) referring to both the *Nasaara* and the *Yahud,* who were both descendants of the citizens of Herods' Judeo-Arab kingdom. One group had accepted a

1. Queen of the Palmyrene empire (located in modern Syria), third century CE

form of Christianity and aligned itself with Rome; the other tried to keep the old Second Commonwealth going and aligned itself with Persia; these were the Sadducees. They both were from "the same stock" and accepted "the same book" yet much conflict was between them.

The term *Sabeans* refers to the monotheist non-Jews who were missionized by Jewish priests in Egypt throughout the reign of the Ptolemies. The most famous was high priest Onias IV. These non-Jews brought sacrifices, took vows, and looked to the Jewish priests (*kohanim, kahins*) as those who could tell the future or warn of an impending attack.

Sa'im: Very informative piece of history. It is remarkable that the terms still apply throughout their generations and up to the modern age.

4. Sunnah/Halachah

Ben Abrahamson: *Sunnah* literally means a clear, well trodden, busy and plain surfaced road. The term *halachah* is derived from the three letter root h-l-ch (הלך)which means "to walk" or "to go"; thus a literal translation means "the way to go."

Umran: And if I am not wrong, *sunnah* pertains only to the practical aspects, right? Some people confuse *hadith* with *sunnah*; however, *hadith* means something which is "said", while sunnah refers to things which are practical in nature.

Ben: It seems to me that *sunnah* is related to *hadith*, the way *halachah* is related to the Mishnah in Judaism. *Sunnah* is derived from *hadith*.

A friend: According to my understanding, *sunnah* is always an act of the Prophet Muhammed (pbuh) while a *hadith* is a report of his statement, act, silent approval, or an incident that took place in his life.

Zaki: How far *hadith* contributes to *sunnah* is disputed and highly dependent on *matn* (context). Classical Islam often equates the *sunnah* with the *hadith*. Scholars who studied the narrations according to their *matn* (context) as well as their *isnad* (transmission) from Muhammed in order to discriminate between them were influential in the development of early Muslim philosophy. In the context of Islamic Law, Imam Malik[1]

---

1. Eighth-century Imam, Arabia. One of the foremost scholars of *ahadith* for whom the Maliki School of Law is named.

and the Hanafi[1] scholars are assumed to have differentiated between the two: For example, Imam Malik is said to have rejected some traditions that reached him because, according to him, they were against the "established practice of the people of Medina".

Zaki: According to the notable Islamic scholar, Javed Ahmad Ghamidi[2], *sunnah* predates both the Qur'an as well as Muhammed, and is actually the tradition of the Prophets of God, specifically the tradition of Abraham. A broad form of *sunnah* was already being practiced by the Christians, Jews, and the Arab descendants of Ishmael when Muhammed reinstituted this practice as an integral part of Islam. *Sunnah* and Qur'an both are equally authentic and the former includes worship rituals like *salah* (prayer), *zakah* (charity), *haj* (pilgrimage), fasting in *Ramadan*, as well as customs like circumcision.

There are seven principles of determining the *sunnah*. If what has been transmitted to the *umma* by the Prophet other than the Qur'an is deliberated upon in the light of these principles, the *sunnah*, like the Qur'an, can be determined with absolute certainty.

A friend: *Sunnah* is "the way," and thank you for sharing the information on *halachah*.

Sa'im: It's a good thing to know there are similar traditions in Judaism. So where does the *halachah* come from? Wow, to think back, Judaism too, very rich in its tradition. How is the *isnad* (transmission) and its authenticity known and protected?

Ben: The Mishnah is a collection of sayings of the sages which reflect the

---

1. One of the four schools of law *(madhabs)* in Islamic jurisprudence. The other three are *Hanbali, Shafi'i* and *Maliki*.

2. Twentieth-century Islamic scholar, Pakistan. Author of the book *Mizan*, in which he outlines the limits for when armed *Jihad* is permissible. Founder of Al-Mawrid Islamic Research Institute in Lahore, Pakistan, and former advisor to Pakistan Parliament.

teachings of the Prophet Moses (pbuh) that were passed down. *Mishnah* is like the *ahadith*. The Mishnah reflects the proper interpretation of scriptural passages, as well as detail that supplements and explains the proper manner in which scriptural commandments should be carried out.

The collection of sayings was standardized in the second century by Rabbi Yehudah HaNasi. However additional sayings surfaced afterwards and they are called *Baraisa*.

This is one half of the Talmud. Because sometimes the sayings are incomplete or contradictory at first glance, there is additional discussion. The second half is called the Gemara, which is the record of legal proceedings where Rabbis worked to clarify and draw conclusions from the Mishnah. I assume this is the same as *fiqh*, although in Judaism it is divided into six time periods: *Tanaim, Amoraim, Savoraim, Geonim, Rishonim,* and *Achronim,* where a decision in a later time period cannot overrule a decision in a previous time period.

The results of these discussions define the proper way to behave in any given situation. This is called *halachah* which means "the way to go" or "well trodden path". By including the answers to many specific cases in the Mishnah, as well as recording all the thinking behind those decisions, rabbis who live in later generations—through humility, fear and submission to God—can understand how to handle situations that had never come up. *Halachah* in this sense is parallel to *sunnah*.

These conclusions are often collected in books that are called codes of Jewish law. The most famous is the *Shulchan Aruch*, which means "a set table" and is the same meaning as *Al-Maeda*.

I believe the word *mishnah* is referred to in the Qur'an in *ayah* 39:23.

This is proper interpretation of scripture, which was transmitted orally. This is because cognitively speaking "understanding" cannot be written down. Over time, examples of this understanding were written down. It is called the Oral Torah and it explains the Written Torah. I believe this is what is referred to by Allah in the Qur'an as the *furqan* (criterion) that was given to the Prophet Moses as noted in *ayah* 2:53.

Eddy: The tablets of the Decalogue (the Ten Commandments) are described in several Torah passages as being handed to Moses. I would see this as a better candidate for the *furqan* in Q2:53. While these are contained in the Torah, also mentioned in the *ayat*, still, the tablets of the Decalogue form something separate and distinct, given to Moses. The idea that the *furqan* parallels the Oral Torah of rabbinicism is in my view rather more difficult to maintain.

Ben: Ibn Kathir[1] explains the term *furqan* in this *ayah* as "the criterion to judge from right and wrong", which would seem to support the idea of further explanation and oral tradition.

---

1. Fourteenth-century Islamic historian of the *Shafi'i* legal school of thought, authored a commentary on the Qur'an entitled *Tafsir al-Qur'an al-'Adhim*, lived in present-day Syria.

5. Mikvah, Baptism and Ghusul

Ben Abrahamson: The roots of all three customs, *mikvah*, baptism and *ghusul* are the same.

Several biblical regulations specify that full immersion in water is required to regain purity after ritually impure incidents have occurred. Most forms of impurity can be nullified through immersion in any natural collection of water. Some require "living water," such as springs or groundwater wells. Living water has the further advantage of being able to purify even while flowing as opposed to rainwater which must be stationary in order to purify. Discoloration or contamination of the water can invalidate the water for immersion.

In Judaism, a *mikvah* (ritual bath) is usually specially constructed as household or other community water sources do not have the quantity and kind of water required. A *mikvah* is used in the following circumstances:

1) by Jewish women to achieve ritual purity after menstruation or childbirth (Leviticus 15:5-10, 19-27)
2) by Jewish men to achieve ritual purity (Leviticus 15:5-10, 19-27)
3) by Jewish men or women after discharges (Leviticus 15:13,16) or leprosy (Leviticus 14:6-9)
4) after contact with a corpse or grave (Numbers 19:19)
5) by Jewish priests when they are being consecrated (Exodus 40:12)

6) after mistakenly eating meat from an animal that died naturally (Leviticus 17:15)
7) for utensils used for food captured in battle (Leviticus) or of non-Jewish manufacture (rabbinic)
8) as part of a traditional procedure for conversion to Judaism (rabbinic)

In Islam, the requirements for ritual bath are the same as Judaism, including the preferred use of "living water," such as springs or groundwater wells and the prohibition of discoloration or contamination. Leniency is given to use tap water where its source is springs or groundwater wells even if it has been stored in retaining tanks before being used. *Ghusul* is required in the following circumstances:

1) by Islamic women to achieve ritual purity after menstruation or childbirth
2) by Islamic men to achieve ritual purity
3) by Islamic men or women after discharges
4) after contact with a corpse or grave
5) for utensils used for food captured in battle or foreign manufacture—there is a *hadith* that requires this, but I do not know if it is practiced by any *mahdab* (legal community).[1]

Andy: Most Muslims do the shower version because Arabia, where Prophet Muhammed was from, has no rivers. So there was a lot of "pouring" the water.

Ben: In Christianity, there are no requirements for ritual bath, although

---

1. There are four *madhabs*, or schools of thought, in Sunni Islamic jurisprudence: *shafi'i, maliki, hanbali* and *hanafi*, each with adherents worldwide. The equivalent in Judaism is *edah*.

based on the accounts of John the Baptist, running river water is preferred (specifically the Jordan river) for Baptism. However, regular
water, spring, standing, or groundwater can be used. Baptism is only
required as part of a traditional procedure for "conversion" (actually
initiation) to Christianity either as a baby (in place of circumcision)
or as an adult to express free-choice acceptance of Christianity.

A friend: In all three faiths, ritual purification is required to validate one's
first ritual prayer with the group. While Jesus himself promoted feet
washing prior to ceremonial gatherings even if one was already ritually pure, this practice has been abandoned wherever a doctrine of
divinity for the Messiah has been adopted.

Ben: So Orthodox Christians practice a form of *wudu*?

A friend: A technical form of it, yes, although the practice has started to die
out among westernized groups.

6. Architecture of Mosques and Synagogues

Starting from top right, going counter-clockwise: Model of Herod's Temple, first century CE; synagogue, third century CE; The Prophet Muhammed's *mihrab*; modern mosque.

Ben Abrahamson: A *mihrab* is a semicircular niche in the wall of a mosque that indicates the *qibla*, the direction towards the *Ka'aba* in Mecca and hence the direction that Muslims should face when praying. The wall with the *mihrab* is the *qibla* wall.

It is often said that word *mihrab* originally had a non-religious meaning and simply denoted a special room in a house. Some have even suggested a room for storing weapons of war. But the Qur'an has a most beautiful explanation.

Then the angels called him [Zakhariya]**, while he was standing in prayer in** *Al-Mihrab* [saying]: **"Allah gives you glad tidings of Yahya** [John] **confirming the Word from Allah, honorable and chaste, a Prophet, from among the righteous."** (Qur'an, *Al-'Imran* 3:39) ...

Then he [Zakhariya] **came forth to his people from the Al-Mihrab. He told them by signs to celebrate Allah's praises in the morning and in the evening.** (Qur'an, *Al-Marya*m 19.11)

Thus, the term *Al-Mihrab* was used by the Prophet Muhammed (pbuh) to denote his own private prayer room. The room additionally provided access to the adjacent mosque, and the Prophet would enter the mosque through this room.

When compared to the corresponding verse in the *Ingel* (New Testament), it can be seen that the *Al-Mihrab* in the above quotes was the Gate of Nicanor, where Zakhariya spoke to the people waiting on the steps below the gate:

And it came to pass, that while he executed the priest's office before God [in the Temple] **in the order of his assignment, according to the custom of the priest's office a lot** [was taken, and it fell to Zakhariya] **to burn incense in the temple of the Lord. And the whole multitude of the people was praying without** [the Gate of Nicanor] **at the time of incense. And there appeared unto him an angel of the Lord standing on the right side of the altar of incense. And when Zakhariya saw him, he was troubled, and fear fell upon him. But the angel said unto him, Fear not, Zakhariya: for thy prayer is heard; and thy wife Elisabeth shall bear thee a son, and thou shall call his name John.** (Luke 1:8-13)

Linguistically, the word *mihrab* may be derived from "to lead to war". However it is possible that it ultimately comes from *ma'arab* which means "west". In synagogues, the Torah Ark (parallel to *qibla*) always points towards Jerusalem. In the Synagogue of Dura-Europos (modern-day Syria) and most synagogues in the Transjordan, the *qibla* faces west.

In the Qur'an (34:14, 38:21-22) the word *mihrab* is used in the same place that *heichal* (sanctuary) is used in the Torah. Indeed many *Sephardim* (Jews from Middle Eastern lands) refer to the To-rah Ark as the *heichal*. In the synagogue in Dura-Europos the shape of the *mihrab* looks like the Gate of Nicanor, as perhaps this was as close to the *heichal* (tall building in front of the altar) as the common people could get.

Thus we see how the *mihrab* follows the pattern of the ancient Torah Ark, which follows the pattern of the Gates of Nicanor, in front of the Temple Sanctuary. This is one more example of how the mosque today reminds us of the beautiful Temple of Solomon, *Masjid Shlomo*.

RIGHT: Herod's Temple, the center of the Judeo-Arab commonwealth. The gate of Nicanor is seen (the small gate in the center). LEFT: An ancient Torah Ark, where the Torah is kept. From a synagogue in Dura-Europos in 256 CE, almost four centuries before Islam. Note that it appears to resemble the Gate of Nicanor illustrated above the Ark.

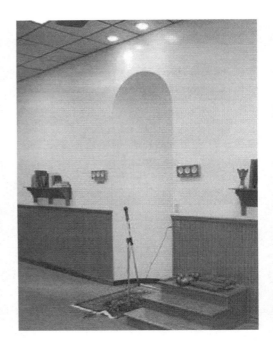

LEFT: The *mihrab* of the Prophet (pbuh). RIGHT: Modern *mihrab*

The form may have been adopted or enhanced, but the function was always there. Most verses equate *mihrab* with *heichal* in all its meanings: palace, place of authority, throne room, private place of prayer, direction of prayer. I remembered a text where *mihrab* was translated as the Altar. "On this day [17th of Hebrew month *Tamuz*] Moses broke the tablets, and the fortifications of Jerusalem began to be destroyed when Persian emperor Nebuchadnezzar besieged them. Further, on this day they put an idol up for worship in Jerusalem, and placed it on the Altar-place [*mihrab*] of the Temple.[1] However, upon comparison with rabbinic texts describing these events, none of them use the Hebrew word *mizbeah* (altar), so *heichal* is probably a better translation. So while the linguistic derivation *mihrab–mikrab–mizbeah* is tempting, the cognitive association of *mihrab–heichal* seems stronger.

---

1. Al Biruni, tenth-century Muslim scholar, Persia; scientist, linguist and historian, known as *al-Ustdadh*, "the Master", for his knowledge of Indian cultures.

I am looking into this derivation: *mihrab–harba–hurva* (ruins)*–hurvat Beit HaMikdash* (ruin of the Temple) as related to *heichal*. Another more direct derivation is *mihrab–(Himyarite)–mekrab* as Temple/Palace*–heichal*.

Note: *heichal* is a different room from the *Kodesh Kodeshim* (Holy of Holies), the former being an ante-chamber or general prayer room. The Holy of Holies concerned Torah commandments relating to atonement and forgiveness of sin, and only the High Priest had access.

Some commentators are thrilled with the hope of brotherhood among Muslims and Jews but at times despair that it has not yet been realized fully.

Ben reassures: The fact that we are having this discussion is one of the signs of the Hour. Muslims, Jews and other believers each with their own *qibla* will come together. As the *hadith*[1] says concerning the collection of those who will follow the *Mahdi* (pbuh), based on the Qur'an verse:

> **And every one has a direction to which he should turn, therefore hasten to [do] good works; wherever you are, Allah will bring you all together; surely Allah has power over all things.** (Qur'an, *Al-Baqarah* 2:148)

Hazzan—Muzzein

Ben Abrahamson: The term *hazzan* in modern terminology refers to a cantor in the Jewish synagogue. He is usually a musician trained in the vocal arts who helps lead the congregation in inspiring prayer. The derivation of the term *hazzan* is obscure. Although many commentators have offered derivations, Rashi said he admits he doesn't know

---

1. *Al Numani* 168, 189, 213, 214

the origin.[1] In this article I attempt to trace the transition of the *hazzan* from watchman and announcer of prayers to sentry, to guardian of the synagogue valuables, to the reader of the Torah, to cantor.

Hazzan as Watchman

The obvious derivation of *hazzan* is the word *chozeh* stemming from the word *chazon* (vision) and means to see from a distance. The original definition seems to have been watchman or overseer.

In the Tel-el Amarna Letters[2] *ziri-basana* or the Field of Bashan was then under the supervision of a *hazzan*, which in the context appears to mean a kind of prefect or even watchman.[3]

The sense of watchman is reinforced by Rashi who interprets the term *hazanei mate* as "guards of the city" in Talmud, *Bava Metzia* 93b. After discussing the city gates of Mehoza, a large Jewish trading town on the Tigris, it is mentioned that the city gates serve only as supports for the "Fort of Turrets". A comparison between this fort and a synagogue which has living quarters for the *hazzan* is made, because they both need a *mezuzah*[4] affixed to their doorposts. (Talmud, *Yoma* 11a)

In discussing all the kinds of watchmen that are in included in the Sabbath boundary of a town, the *hazzan* is included in Talmud, *'Eruvin* 55b:

> Come and hear: The following are included in the Sabbath
> boundary of a town. A sepulchral monument of the size

1, Rashi was an eleventh century Rabbi, France. "I have not heard any explanation (for the word *hazzan*)." —Rashi's commentary on Talmudic tractate *Makkot* 22b.

2. Documents engraved on clay that were found in Egypt and written in Akkadian cuneiform, the writing of ancient Mesopotamia, dated to the fourteenth-century BCE.

3. Sayce, Patriarchal Palestine (1895). p. 95

4. The *mezuzah* is a small scroll containing the *shma* prayer, rolled up and affixed to doorposts of Jewish homes and gates.

of four cubits by four, a bridge or cemetery that contains a dwelling chamber, a synagogue that has a dwelling-house for the *hazzan*, a house of worship that contains a dwelling-house for its priests, horse stalls or storehouses in open fields, to which dwelling-chambers are attached, watchmen's huts in a field, and a house on a sea island.

Announcing the Times of Prayers

Maimonides comments on Mishnah *Yoma* 3:1, "There was a high place in the Temple to which the lookout would ascend [and wait], and when he could see the whole of the east[ern sky] begin to change he would say to them *"barkai,"* which means something like "the light has begun to shine" … He would then say to them, "Yes" and they would then immediately proceed [to begin to unlock the gates and begin the morning service]".

The Talmud is not clear on the meaning of the word *barkai*, saying it may be a contraction of the words *barak hai* (the first light has arrived). I propose that there is a relationship between *barkai* and *barchu*, the Jewish call to prayer that is equivalent to the Islamic *adhan* call to prayer.

During the week, the Temple lookout would announce times of prayers by voice, however the announcement of the approaching Sabbath was done by *shofar* (ram's horn). The Talmud expressly states that this function was done by the turret watchman, the *hazzan* of the synagogue; Talmud, *Shabbat* 35b-36a states:

[T]he School of R. Ishmael taught: Six blasts were blown on the eve of the Sabbath [from the top of a high roof]. When the first was begun, those who stood in the fields ceased to hoe, plough, or do any work in the fields, and those who were near [to town] were not permitted to enter [it] until the more distant ones arrived, so that they should all enter simultaneously. But the shops were still open and the shutters were lying. When the second blast began, the shutters were removed and the shops closed. Yet hot [water] and pots still stood on the range. When the third blast was begun, what was to be removed was removed, and what was to be stored away was stored away, and the lamp was lit. Then there was an interval for as long as it takes to bake a small fish or to place a loaf in the oven; then a *teki'ah*, *teru'ah* and a *teki'ah* were sounded, and one commenced the Sabbath. R. Jose b. R. Hanina said: I have heard that if one comes to light after the six blasts he may do so, since the Sages gave the *Hazzan* of the community time to carry his shofar home. The *Hazzan* of the community had a hidden place on the top of his roof, where he placed his shofar, because neither a shofar nor a trumpet may be handled [on the Sabbath].

**A *muezzin* Calling the Faithful to Prayer
from the Top of a Minaret (1879)**

Town Crier

The Talmud also indicates that the high position of the *hazzan–*watchman was also well suited for communicating other information besides prayers by his voice and the commencement of the Sabbath by a shofar. The *hazzan* would also summon the litigants to a court hearing (Talmud, *Shabbat* 56a) and use fires to communicate the new moon and flags to communicate administrative messages.

Although many of the customs associated with the *hazzan/muzzein* continued, the role of the *hazzan/muzzein* in Islam remained undecided at the time of the Prophet Muhammed's (pbuh) death, including which direction one should choose for the calling, where it should be performed, and the use of trumpets, flags or lamps, all elements at one time of the *muezzin's* role during the *adhan* (Islamic call to worship) (Tabari).

Executor of the Rabbinical Court

One requirement of the ancient role of the *hazzan* as the synagogue lookout was to protect the synagogue from marauders and thieves. To this effect he had to be physically strong, and most cases he would have to be the first line of defense to protect the House of Worship. This physical strength was put to use by the Rabbinical Court when the *hazzan* was required to implement the decision of the court to scourge an offender. At the end of the punishment, the *hazzan* would have to announce in a loud voice: "He administers [the lashes] while the one who recites, says: If thou wilt not observe to do ... the Lord thy God shall make the strokes pronounced" and also "But He, being full of compassion, forgiveth iniquity, and destroyeth not; yea, many a time doth He turn His anger away, and doth not stir up all His wrath."

A modern *hazzan* in a synagogue

Guardian of the Synagogue

It was only natural, due to the instability of the times, that the synagogue lookout should also be entrusted with the safe-keeping of the valuable goods held in the synagogue, especially the Torah scrolls:

> **The High Priest** [then] **came to read. If he wished to read in linen garments he could do so, otherwise he would read in his own white vestments. The *hazzan* would take a scroll of the Law and give it to the head of the synagogue, and the head of the synagogue gave it to the *segan* [second** in command], **and the *segan* gave it to the High Priest, and the High Priest stands and receives it, and reads** [the section]. (Mishnah, *Yoma* 68b)

> **What was the procedure in connection with the portion read by the king? At the conclusion of the first day of the festival** [of Tabernacles] **... they erect a wooden dais in the temple court, upon which he sits; as it is said, at the end**

of every seven years, in the set time. The *hazzan* takes a Torah-scroll and hands it to the synagogue president, and the synagogue-president hands it to the [high priest's] **deputy. He hands it to the high priest who hands it to the king. The king stands and receives it, but reads while sitting.** (Mishnah, *Sotah* 41a)

In the verse **"Accursed is one who will not uphold the words of the Torah, to perform them"** (Deuteronomy 27:26), the Jerusalem Talmud says this is referring to the *hazzan*. The Ramban[1] explains that this is referring to the one who does *hagbah*, holding up the Torah before and after the reading. The *hazzan* has a special obligation to practice what is written in what he literally upholds.

Teaching the Children to Read Torah

Since the *hazzan* was responsible for the bringing out and returning the Torah scrolls, it was only natural that he would supervise the children as they practiced reading from the Torah:

[Just before Shabbat] **a tailor must not go out with his needle near nightfall, lest he forget and go out, nor a scribe with his quill; and one may not search his garments, nor read by the light of a lamp** [lest they come to break *Shabbat*]. **In truth it was said, the *Hazzan* may see where the children rea**d [to arrange the beginnings of the sections], **but he himself must not read.** (Mishnah, *Shabbat* 11a)

The *Fla'ah*[2] claims the word *hazzan* is from the word *hazu*, which means "sees". A *hazzan* is not a visionary, but a teacher. His job is to ensure that each child learns only what is true. The end of the verse Deuteronomy 27:26 says "to perform them". He has to regard each

---

1. Nachmanides, thirteenth-century Jewish theologian, Spain.

2. Rabbi Pinchas HaLevi Horowitz, eighteenth-century Rabbi, Lithuania.

child's actions as the result of his teachings. Woe to a teacher who teaches falsely, that the student puts falsehoods into action.

Reading the Torah, and Later the Prayers, with a Beautiful Voice

In time, the *hazzan* would be the one who would be responsible for prompting the readers of the Torah during services and even reading it himself. In Talmud, *Pesach* 117b, Rabina said:

> **I visited Meremar at** [the academy of] **Sura, when the** *hazzan* **went down** [to the reading desk] **and recited it as the elders of Pumbeditha.**

From this come all the requirements of a good and pleasing voice to inspire prayers.[1]

Another Connection Between Hazzan and Muezzin

The term *muezzin* is sometimes derived from the Arabic word *udun* meaning "ear", which is in turn related to the Hebrew *ozen*. Epiphanius[2] reports that in Cilicia there were three *azanin* (dropping the H for *hazanim*) in the Jewish Community.[3]

As mentioned before, the *hazzan* seems to be derived from the Temple *barkai*. The *hazzan* has a special role in chanting the *barchu* call to prayer that is equivalent to the Islamic *adhan* call to prayer.

But even today, long after turrets and minarets have disappeared from the synagogue, and for many centuries the prayers are announced only to the congregation assembled within the synagogue building, one role stands out that still connects the *hazzan* back to his roots as a synagogue lookout. That is the requirement to be morally upstanding: one who has no sinners among his household and rela-

1. Pesikta D'rav Kahana, Pesikta Rabbati 25, Shibboley Haleket, paragraph 10, *Sefer Hassidim*

2. Bishop of Salamis in Cyprus, 310–403.

3. *Jewish Quarterly Review* (1905) XXVII (O.S.), p. 373 & p. 380 note 2.

tives, with only a good reputation even in his youth. This is not surprising in that the ancient *hazzan* was in an exposed position, required to stand at the top of a Turret or Minaret and wait for the dawn to arrive to announce the prayers.

Islam also shares this concern: After minarets became customary at mosques, the office of *muezzin* in cities was sometimes given to a blind man, who could not see down into the inner courtyards of the citizen's houses, and maintained the utmost moral character of the community.

The *Ka'aba*, Mecca's Focal Point

A friend: Rabbi, you claim "that the *Ka'aba* was rebuilt by Onias IV in 150 BCE based on the pattern of the Temple of Solomon (pbuh)." Would you please direct me to your paper on this thesis?

Ben: I am working on a manuscript "The Quraish as descendants of Onias IV", which explores the possibility that one of the ancestors of the Quraish, the family from which Muhammed hailed, was the High Priest Onias IV, and that initial introduction of Hellenism into some of Islamic culture can be traced to the Ptolemies. The *Ka'aba* may be the "monument on the border of Egypt" mentioned in Isaiah 19 that was rebuilt along with the Temple at Heliopolis.

The main proof I bring is that Josephus[1] claims that Onais IV built his Temple in Heliopolis, based on Isaiah 19:19, which mentions two structures: one in the land of Egypt and the other on the border of Egypt, which during Ptolemy VI Philometor's time was briefly in Arabia. This is supported by architectural similarities between the

---

1. Josephus Flavius was a Jewish historian, first-century CE. Initially led Jewish troops against Rome during the siege that ended with the Temple's fall in 70 CE, then defected to the Roman side and became translator for Roman forces as they completed the siege. Granted Roman citizenship by Emperor Vespasian, whereupon he took the surname Flavius.

Ka'aba and the Temple of Onias as researched by W. M. Flinders Petrie[1] in 1906. This is indirectly supported by Talmudic tractate *Menuchot* which, after discussing the Temple of Onias, goes on to discuss another Temple which had fallen into idolatry "over the Jordan". There is also an alternative rendering of the Prophet's (pbuh) ancestor Adnan as Anan (similar to the names Hanan and Onias).

Additionally, the Elephantine Papyri speak of the tremendous antiquity of their altar in Egypt, and by implication one could suggest that Onias IV chose to rebuild in Arabia in a location that already had a previous ancient tradition of an Abrahamic altar.

I propose that the *Ka'aba* was not originally a house of prayer. It was an altar with a fire burning on top to consume sacrifices in an Abrahamic fashion. At that time, the *Maqaam Ibrahim*, outside the entrance of the *Ka'aba*, would have functioned as a parallel to the Temple "Holy of Holies" and the place of prayer. It was not until sacrifices were discontinued on the altar that it became a room and superseded the *Maqaam Ibrahim*. Thus the *Ka'aba* was based on Solomon's Temple in Jerusalem.

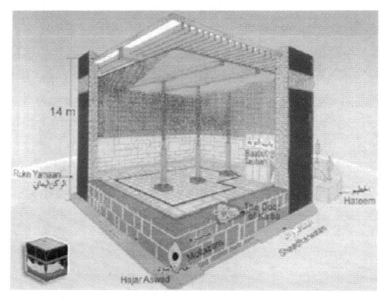

Inside of Ka'aba

---

1. Egyptologist and archeologist, late nineteenth–early twentieth century, England

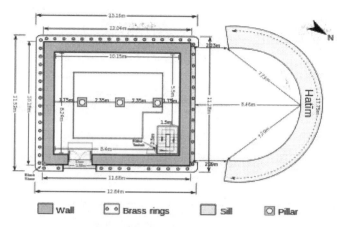

A technical drawing of the *Ka'aba.*

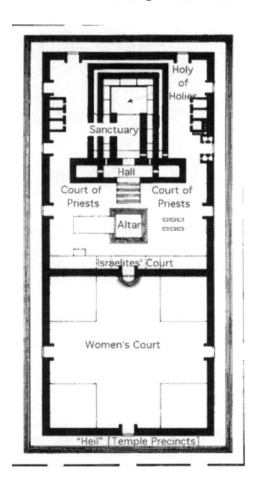

Inside of Jerusalem Temple

Line from Ka'aba in Mecca to Heliopolis in Egypt

The stone foundation of the *Ka'aba* has the same proportions and is roughly the same size as the altar in Solomon's Temple in Jerusalem. Like the altar in Jerusalem, the base foundation of the *Ka'aba* appears to be made of uncut stones. The altar in Solomon's Temple had metal rings to tie down the sacrifices, the *Ka'aba* also has metal rings around its base.

The altar of Solomon had a ramp facing south towards Egypt and Arabia for the High Priest to walk up and bring offerings. The *Ka'aba* had a similar ramp facing north-northwest towards Jerusalem. When the Prophet (pbuh) disbanded sacrifices, the altar was turned into a gate called the *Hattim*.

The altar in Solomon's Temple was surrounded by a columnated courtyard up until Roman times; the *Ka'aba* was surrounded by 360 idols. Around the year 420 CE the Arabian Jews pleaded with Abu Kariba Tubba' to construct a separation between the altar and the idols so that they could pray there. Originally this was made of palm branches, then of a cloth called a *kiswah*, then a wall with a cloth over it, which gives the *Ka'aba* the cube shape that it has today.

Maqaam Ibrahim is a small glass enclosed area outside the entrance and may parallel the Holy of Holies of the Temple. Today it is an octagonal structure, virtually a miniature version of the Dome of the Rock in Jerusalem. The Dome of the Rock is traditionally believed to occupy the location of the Holy of Holies, and is located on top of a large stone outcropping which has been chipped away at throughout the centuries by those wanting to obtain a piece of the holy stone. It is fascinating to note that a square stone was removed from the foundation stone about the same size of the stone found inside the octagonal structure of the *Maqaam Ibrahim* with the footprints of Abraham displayed upon them.

In Qussai's[1] time (420 CE) or later, a courtyard was built around the *Ka'aba*, called by Tabari the place of sacrifices or "kitchen". In Ottoman times a columnated courtyard was built similar in style and structure to the Temple of Solomon. Outside the main entrance of the courtyard of the *Ka'aba* was a large room which functioned as a legislature and judiciary not unlike the Sanhedrin of Solomon's Temple.

Next to the *Maqaam Ibrahim*, the Ottomans placed a large decorated *minbar* (pulpit) for the Friday sermon. This parallels the place where the High Priest used to sit and give his Sabbath dissertation on the Torah reading—the High Priest in Jerusalem would sit on a granite chair while speaking in a semi-prophetic state. This chair was called the seat of Moses (pbuh) and is represented today in the synagogue by the chair of Elijah. This seat of Moses (pbuh) represented prophetic continuity from Moses (pbuh) to the High Priest. I propose this black granite chair was smuggled out together with other Temple

---

1. Leader of the Quraish family.

utensils by the Edumean troops days before the destruction of the Temple by the Romans, and brought to Mecca, and the black stone which is located in the northwest corner of the Ka'aba is the remnants of the chair of Moses (pbuh) and represents the continuation of the prophetic tradition.

In the Temple in Jerusalem, if one stands on the ramp facing the altar, to the left is the Holy of Holies; to your right under the pavement there is an underground system of water cisterns. In the *Ka'aba* as you face the *Hatim,* to the left is the *Maqaam Ibrahim* and to the right is the well of *zamzam.*

The Holy of Holies in Jerusalem was entered through the sanctuary or *heichal.* The *heichal* contained the seven-branched menorah. When Onias built a Temple in Egypt, he decided against using a seven-branched menorah, fearing that this would lead to polytheism. Instead, he affixed a single light on top of his sanctuary surrounded by a gold frame. It was called *manara* or *minaret.* In a related vein, in the first century CE, Helena of Adiabene[1] donated a gold lamp to be affixed at the top of the sanctuary in Jerusalem. Although no light is found above the *Maqaam Ibrahim, minarets* are found outside the courtyard of the *Ka'aba.*

Lastly, the *Ka'aba* is intimately connected with mounts Safa and Marwan which appear to correspond to mounts Scopus and Moriah in Jerusalem. The names are parallel—both scopus and safa mean "to overlook". Mount Scopus is connected to the Mount of Olives which was the destination of the Jewish pilgrimage of the ninth of Av, after the Romans had forbidden all other pilgrimages. The ninth of Av corresponds to the ninth of Dhu al Hijra.

---

1. Also knows as Heleni HaMalka, convert to Judaism and queen of this province in Assyria.

Parallels between the Ka'aba and Temple

Ka'aba	Temple
Hattim	Altar
Maaqam Ibrahim	Holy of Holies
Minbar/Black Stone	Seat of Moses/Granite Chair
Well of Zamzan	Underground Cisterns
Mounts Safa and Maram	Mounts Scopus and Moriah

In summary, I believe that Onias chose to build his monument of the border of Egypt (153 BCE) in the place that had a long tradition of an Abrahamic altar for use by non-Jewish believers. With the fall of the Ptolemeic Empire, this altar fell into idolatry. After the destruction of the Temple in Jerusalem and the closure of the Temple of Onias in Egypt by the Romans, Sadducean Jews came to Arabia with the hopes of using the Abrahamic altar of Onias for the entire Mosaic sacrificial system. The refugees from Palmyra (272 CE) set up a syncretic sacrificial system, which mirrored the sacrificial system in Jerusalem but also included Christian and pagan elements. King Tubba' of Arabia (400 CE) allowed the Sadducean Jews to enclose and purify a portion of the *Ka'aba*. Onias had built his altar for non-Jews to offer sacrifices and never intended that they would fulfill the role of the Temple in Jerusalem.

I propose that the ancestor of the Quraish was Onias (=Hanan/Adnan), so it seems understandable that Allah swt told the Prophet (pbuh) to cease Mosaic sacrifice as had been petitioned by the Sadducean Jews at the *Ka'aba* and return it to its pure Abrahamic roots. It is important to note that rabbinic Jews never supported a sacrificial system outside of Jerusalem.

Dawah is a little uncomfortable with Ben's historical approach,
wondering if looking at religion through a historical lens
diminishes the sacred.

Dawah: Interesting—but, even if the *Ka'aba* was "rebuilt" or "location cho-sen" by Onais IV—it was first built by prophet Adam and then re-built by prophets Ibrahim and Ishmael—aside from what the mod-ern day structure of the *Ka'aba* looks like today ... I could agree that the Quraish were influenced, but Quraish is not Islam.

Ben proposes that a historical approach to understanding religion need not be the exclusive realm of secular intellectuals, nor detract from the sacred. God-fearing people can also utilize the disciplines of history and archeology: The sacred can even be validated and thus enhanced.

Ben: Yes, I agree. I think that Onias IV chose the place that he did because of its long association with the Prophet Abraham (pbuh). I do not think Onias IV was the first to build an altar there. Unlike other historians, such as Wellhausen[1], I argue for the antiquity and Abrahamic origin of the *Ka'aba*.

---

1. See footnote on Wellhausen, chapter 8.

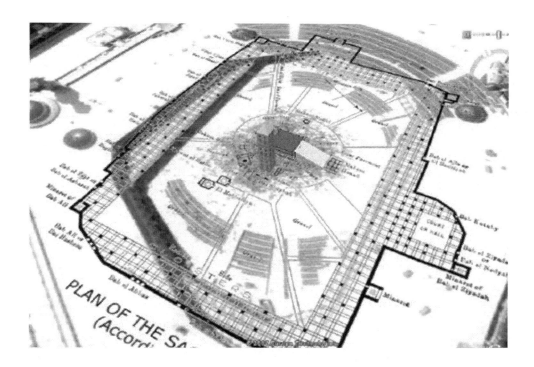

Mecca: superimposed image of Minaret and Altar as in days of Onias on top of the Ottoman *Ka'aba*, which is in turn superimposed upon a modern day picture of the Ka'aba, courtesy of Google Earth.

Minaret and Altar; Same as above from different perspective

Town of Onias, Egypt: Superimposed image of Minaret and Altar as in days of Onias; line from altar to the left goes to Jerusalem.

7. The Messianic Age

Ben Abrahamson: According to Jewish law, a person is declared a prophet by means of the Great Sanhedrin (supreme religious court) in Jerusalem. Since that court was destroyed with the fall of the Second Temple in 70 CE[1], Judaism has given no opinion on Jesus (pbuh) or the Prophet Muhammed (pbuh), only on the movements that were found in their name.

In the Torah, Deuteronomy 18:13-22, the Children of Israel are given instructions how to recognize a Prophet:

1) Must be like Moses (pbuh), morally upright, without sin
2) Must teach the same teachings as Moses (pbuh)
3) If he speaks about the future, his words must be true.

Judaism's main source of teachings about Jesus (pbuh) comes from the church. Most Christians teach that God has a son (surely Allah is above that), the Torah is invalid, the law of Moses (pbuh) no longer needs to be kept, and the Children of Israel have been replaced by the Christians.

These teachings violate the second rule above. The Torah says that its teachings are eternal and that the Law of Moses (pbuh) will never pass away, so Jews cannot accept the "Jesus" of the church.

"Jesus" as taught by the Qur'an is more acceptable to Jewish views,

---

1. The Great Sanhedrin continued to function but with markedly reduced authority from the fall of the Temple until it finally disbanded about 358 CE, at various times relocated to places such as Yavne, Usha, and Tiberius in the Holy Land.

but I have never heard a Rabbi discuss this issue in depth.

There is the additional issue of the claim that Jesus (pbuh) was the Messiah. In Judaism the expectation is that the Messiah will be like King David (pbuh). He will rule Israel and bring peace to the world, which hasn't happened yet. Christianity says that this will happen when Jesus (pbuh) comes a second time, so we will soon see.

Muhammed (pbuh) in Judaism

We are taught that prophecy is not limited to the Jewish people. There were many prophets who were not Jewish, some were Arab. The Torah says:

> **And he said, The LORD came from Sinai, and rose up from Seir unto them; He shined forth from mount Paran, and He came with ten thousands of saints** [prophets]: **from His right hand went a fiery law for them** [*sharia*/covenant]. (Deuteronomy 33:2)

The Qur'an explains it in a most perfect way:

> **To each among you have we prescribed a *shari'a*** [covenant/law] **and *minhaj*** [custom/way]. **If Allah had so willed, He could have made you a single *umma*** [people], **but** [His plan is] **to test you in what He hath given you: So strive as in a race in all virtues. The goal of you all is to Allah; it is He that will show you the truth about the matters in which ye differ**. (Qur'an, *Al Maedah* 5:48)

Thus we are taught that prophets were sent and covenants were made with the nations of the world. These prophets were sent with a divine message, and each covenant is important and binding on its people, not unlike how the Torah is the law and guide for the Jewish people.

Thus from a Jewish point of view, Muhammed could be a prophet. Again the biggest problem is the teachings of his followers. Most

Muslims claim the Torah has been corrupted, and is no longer valid.[1] They claim that the *shari'a* of Moses (pbuh) has been abolished. For a Jew who follows the Torah with all his heart, he cannot accept these claims because the Torah itself says that it is eternal. This causes distance between Muslims and Jews.

Universal Religion

The concept of imposing universal religion on everyone is rooted in Roman imperialism. Under Emperor Constantine, there was a tendency to believe that imperial and military power depended on religious uniformity. This was expressly declared at the council of Nicea in 325 CE.[2] Any time a dictator wanted to consolidate his power, he demanded that every person conform to the same form of worship. Judaism has no tradition imposing one form of worship upon all humanity. Judaism does not recognize "thought crimes" or temporal punishment for wrong beliefs, only wrong actions. The leaders of the time, however, demanded religious uniformity and declared all diverse religious views as unfounded, heretical, and against the empire. In order to demand universal uniformity, it was necessary to abrogate all previous beliefs.

Judaism cannot accept the abrogation of Torah. The Torah was given with great signs and wonders, thunder and the raising up of Mount Sinai (Qur'an, *Al-Baqarah* 2:63). Yet it is claimed that it has been canceled, albeit quietly. So quietly, in fact that there is nowhere in the New Testament, the Qur'an, or the *ahadith* that clearly says the *shari'a* of Torah has been abrogated. The opposite is true. The Torah is confirmed and upheld in the Qur'an and *ahadith,* even during Muhammed's lifetime. (Qur'an, *Al-Maedah* 5:43; *ahadith* collection Abu-

---

1. Rabbinic Jews of today believe that the Septuagint and the Samaritan Torah were altered. Perhaps the Prophet was criticizing these "Torahs", which rabbinic Jews also reject.

2. A council of church fathers met in Nicea, located in modern day Turkey, to affirm belief in the Trinity. This was a response to the Arian controversy, whose followers stated that Jesus was divine but not equal to God.

Dawud 38.4434). So one could question if the concept of abrogation is itself a true teaching or *bidah* (heretical innovation).

To accept that the Torah is still valid and binding, and still recognize Christianity and Islam, is to accept multi-covenantism. Judaism accepts multi-covenantism; these covenants are based on universal basic religion incumbent upon all humankind. We are really all part of the same religion, under different covenants.

If either Christianity or Islam would officially reevaluate claims of the abrogation of the Torah, and present their case before the longed-for future Great Sanhedrin in Jerusalem, Judaism's official stance of silence on Jesus and Muhammed could be reevaluated. Until then, we see that Christianity and Islam are indeed playing a role in bringing monotheism and scripture to the world. Because of this we can assume that their founders are indeed Messengers of Allah swt, but we cannot say how. We are told that in the end of days, the prophet Elijah (pbuh) will come and explain all our questions. The Qur'an, too, says in a most perfect way: "**The goal of you all is to Allah; it is He that will show you the truth about the matters in which ye differ**;" (Qur'an, *Al Maedah* 5:48)

Torah and Talmud

The Qur'an says in a most perfect way:

And remember, We gave Moses the Scripture and the Criterion [between right and wrong]: **There was a chance for you to be guided aright.** (Qur'an, *Al Baqarah* 2:53)

Jews believe that when Moses (pbuh) received the Torah that he was not just given a bunch of words and then left to figure them out. We believe that Moses was given the criterion of how to apply the teachings of the Torah in all future situations. The written words are called "the written Torah" and the criterion of applying those words is called "the oral Torah", preserved in the Talmud. This is what the

Qur'an calls "Scripture" and the "Criterion".

Over time, this understanding was passed down from Moses to Aaron, to Joshua, to the prophets, to the elders, even until the spiritual leaders of today. Difficult cases were brought before the prophets and other leaders. The collection of these legal cases, as well as stories and other teachings, were passed down orally and finally written down in a set of books that we call today the Talmud (which means "learning").

The Talmud is not divinely inspired, but it contains examples of the divine Torah as it was applied and explained by spiritual leaders who had inherited the proper understanding of the Torah. It is believed by Jews that the study of these works, together with pure intention and and a humble heart, will allow a person to reconstruct in his or her mind the proper understanding of the words of Torah.

A commentator: The kingdom of Solomon was founded on witchcraft. Jews charge interest, even though it is forbidden in their Torah.

Ben responds: The sources do not support your views. These views are more heavily influenced by politics than the Qur'an and *al-sunnah* (tradition). Please take the time to learn from a qualified scholar, seek out the sources, read the material in its original Arabic, and practice the characteristics of the Prophet (pbuh):

> **"Shall I not tell you who among you is most beloved to me and will be closest to me on the Day of Resurrection?" He repeated it two or three times ... He said, "Those of you who are the best in manners and character."** (Ahmad; *sahih*)

Another interjects: God says in the Quran, *Al-Araf* 7:3:

> **Follow what has been revealed to you from your Lord and do not follow guardians besides Him, how little do you mind.**

Accordingly, a religion is to be judged based on the sayings of the prophets—the scriptures sent down to them, not on the sayings of the followers. Followers make mistakes but the prophets do not.

Hence brother Ben Abrahamson justifiably said, " 'Jesus' as taught by the Qur'an is more acceptable to Jewish views …"

Likewise, if anyone focuses on the teachings of the scriptures only, he may find more similarities in the monotheistic religions—similarities in the missions of the prophets.

The following verses of the Bible and Qur'an may well be deliberated.

"Think not that I am come to destroy the law, or the prophets: I am not come to destroy, but to fulfill …" (Matthew 5:17). The whole Torah is still inseparably attached to Christian scripture.

And approximately one third of the Qur'an has stories and teachings of Prophet Moses. The Qur'an says:

Say ye: "We believe in Allah, and the revelation given to us, and to Abraham, Isma'il, Isaac, Jacob, and the Tribes, and that given to Moses and Jesus, and that given to (all) prophets from their Lord: We make no difference between one and another of them: And we bow to Allah (in Islam)." (Qur'an, *Al-Baqarah* 2:136)

And remember: We gave Moses the Scripture and the Criterion [between right and wrong]: **There was a chance for you to be guided aright.** (Qur'an, *Al-Baqarah* 2:53).

[Allah] **said: "O Moses! I have chosen thee above** [other] **men, by the mission I** [have given thee] **and the words I** [have spoken to thee]: **Take then the (revelation) which I give thee, and be of those who give thanks."** (Qur'an, *Al-Araf* 7:144).

According to Qur'an, it is the prophet Moses who is endowed with the great honour of speaking to God in person.

These highly revered verses of other prophets and religions are only found in the scriptures—from the prophets of similar mission, not in the interpretation and sayings of the followers.

Another: Rabbi, thanks for the explanation and the Jewish stand about Jesus and Muhammed (peace be upon them). *Jazak'Allah.*

A new friend: Some of us with Christian background believe Jesus was a messiah—a prophet who was trying to get the establishment back on the right track of following God's laws. We believe that Paul invented Christianity and then it spread through the Roman Empire, ignoring the Torah laws as it made itself palatable to new cultures. The Jesus followers were daughters of Judaism and wanted to remain true to the faith. There are some Christians who are now going back to the Torah and starting to reincorporate kosher laws. My prayer is that we can get along rather than fight each other over whose belief is better. Exclusivism fosters division and at this time in our world we need peace, compassion, and love more than ever.

Ben quotes Adnan Oktar: ... "You cannot oppose radical thinking with tanks and rifles and shells. That would lead to bloody, painful times. But once people follow the *Mahdi,* the world will calm down again and become loving and moderate. That is why it is so important to draw attention to Messianic teachings. An atheistic mindest is powerless in the face of radical thinking, terror, war, and suffering."

Adnan Oktar speaks here of the importance of the concept of *Al Mahdi* (pbuh). Rabbinic Jews find the messianic hope of the coming of a real, physical King Messiah to be an essential and necessary part of preparing for redemption.

Ben responds to a friend: I am not trying to say "who is *Mahdi*". I am agreeing with Adnan Oktar that the belief in *Al Mahdi* is important and essential.

Another: I would be extremely thankful if you could please tell us the signs of the coming of such a *Mahdi*, in the light of Bible and Jewish believes. Be blessed.

Ben: The requirements of Messiah according to rabbinic tradition:

- The Sanhedrin will be re-established (Isaiah 1:26).
- Once he is King, leaders of other nations will look to him for guidance. (Isaiah 2:4).
- The whole world will worship the One God of Israel (Isaiah 2:17)
- He will be descended from King David (Isaiah 11:1) via King Solomon (1 Chron. 22:8-10).
- The Moshiach will be a physical man (accomplish all these things in a human lifetime), religious with "fear of God" (Isaiah 11:2).
- Evil and tyranny will not be able to stand before his leadership (Isaiah 11:4).
- Knowledge of God will fill the world (Isaiah 11:9).
- He will include and attract people from all cultures and nations (Isaiah 11:10).
- All Children of Israel will be returned to their homeland (Isaiah 11:12).
- There will be no more hunger or illness, and death will cease (Isaiah 25:8).
- Believers will experience eternal joy and gladness (Isaiah 51:11).
- He will be a messenger of peace (Isaiah 52:7).
- Nations will end up recognizing the wrongs they did (Isaiah 52:13–53:5).

- The peoples of the world will turn to the followers of Messiah for spiritual guidance (Zechariah 8:23).
- The ruined cities of Israel will be restored (Ezekiel 16:55
- Weapons of war will be destroyed (Ezekiel 39:9).
- The Temple will be rebuilt (Ezekiel 40), resuming many of the suspended commandments.
- He will then perfect the entire world to serve God together (Zephaniah 3:9).
- The Children of Israel will all know the Torah (Jeremiah 31:33).
- He will give you all the desires of your heart (Psalms 37:4).
- He will take the barren land and make it abundant and fruitful (Isaiah 51:3, Amos 9:13-15, Ezekiel 36:29-30, Isaiah 11:6-9).

A commentator wonders what happens if ancient scriptures are corrupted: If people follow corrupted scriptures then they will end up considering the false messiah as *Al-Mahdi*.

Ben: Given the quotes from the Torah quoted above, how is that so? It does not follow from the *ahadith* that all those who read the Torah and *Ingil* (Gospel) today will end up considering the *dajjal* (satan) as *Al-Mahdi*. According to the *ahadith*, among the myriads of followers of the *dajjal*, there will be 20,000 Jews from Isfahan, of these only 1,000 will follow him with swords to Jerusalem.

A friend takes issue with the above commentator: God in the Qur'an has revisited all the biblical stories to teach us a moral lesson. And He has enjoined on us *salat* (prayer), *zakat* (charity), *saum* (fasting), and many other things. He said to speak to the *Yehudis* (Jews) and *Nasranis* (Christians) with respect.

The *Tanakh* has an opinion about God, as does the New Testament and the Apocryphal Books. So too does the Qur'an have an opinion about God.

We all take it on faith what our books of authority tell us.

The above commentator defends himself: I never alleged that all Jews or people of the book shall be deceived. I'm reminding people to follow the last message from Allah and understand things from its perspective.

Here we have a party who does not believe in messianism: It should be noted that there is no mention of any Mr Mahdi or Mr Dajjal in the Qur'an. These are just myths made up by people and such a concept can be found in most religions. Each group is waiting for someone to come and save them so that they don't have to work hard.

Ben: No, it's not like that. If a student expects the teacher to enter the classroom at any moment, he makes every effort to be ready when he comes. If the student doesn't think the teacher will show up, he is relaxed in his behavior.

Unconvinced, the above commentator persists: *Mahdi* is a myth. I think the following verse is what Adnan should look into:

> **Surely those who believe, and those who are Jews, and the Christians, and the Sabeans—whoever believes in God and the Last Day and does good, they shall have their reward from their Lord. And there will be no fear for them, nor shall they grieve.** (Qur'an, *Al-Baqarah* 2:62).

The student-teacher example is irrelevant. Such an example is based on fear and implies that an average person is incapable of fixing their own mistakes and is somehow dependent upon another person. Secondly, a student-teacher relationship is preestablished so both parties know the expectations from each other. This is not so in the case of the *mahdi* concept.

Ben: I can absolutely say that the king Messiah is not a myth, and belief in his coming is an essential aspect of rabbinic Judaism. It is clearly stated in the Torah as well as the received, authorized interpretation of many prophecies. It is so central to rabbinic Judaism, that to deny the coming of King Messiah is to exclude oneself from the community of the Prophet Moses. It is considered essential for the community of believers to exhibit proper preparedness by waiting for his coming every day.

Insofar as the *ahadith* and accepted *tafsir* describe the same expectation as we have, of the one who will usher in the Golden Age of *al Mahdi*, I look forward to his coming and encourage those who share this view.

The above commentator is reiterating the positions of an apostate sect called "submitters", who suddenly discovered in the twentieth century that all the oral tradition the Muslims have been using for centuries is a myth. We'd rather go with what is tried, tested, and true.

A friend: Thank you kindly Ben for this post ... always

A new thread, the Messiah's family tree.

Ben: Documentation of the marriages between the Quraish (family from which Muhammed hailed) and the family of the Jewish Exilarch[1] is found in the following books: Abu 'Ubayda Ma'mar's[2] *Kitab al-mathalib and Kitab al-munammaq*, plus Ibn al-Kalbi's[3] book *Kitab mathalib al-'arab*.

According to these sources, Hashim b.'Abd Manaf was married to a daughter of the Exilarch. This information is confirmed in rabbinical

---

1. The Jewish Exilarch, also called *Resh Galuta*, was the temporal leader of the Jewish community in exile, descended from King David.

2. Ninth-century Islamic scholar, and linguist, modern day Iraq b. al-Muthanna (d. 825 CE)

3. Ninth-century Islamic historian and genealogist, modern day Iraq (d. 819 CE)

sources. This would mean that Imam 'Ali[1] was a descendant of King David, and could provide a clue to the similarity between the Imamate (leadership of the Muslim community) and the Exilarch, with the related messianic expectations.

The rabbinic historian Rabbi Sherira *Gaon*[2] writes of the encounter between Imam 'Ali and the head of the Babylonian Academy of Peroz-Shavur:

> Rabbi Yitzchak *Gaon* was in Peroz-Shavur when Ali ben Abu Taleb entered the city, and Rabbi Yitzchak of Peroz-Shavur went out to him and welcomed him with great friendliness. At that time, there were in Peroz-Shavur ninety thousand Jews, who receive Ali ben Abu Taleb with great friendliness.

Yawar: This is amazing information! I of course read that even Jews and Magis wept on the assassination of Imam Ali and now this research confirms the long-standing relationship. Also the claim that ancestors of Imam Ali and Prophet Muhammed were pure monotheists confirms the traditional Sunni position in these matters.

Ben: It would mean of course that *Al Mahdi* would be a descendant of King David.

Yawar: That shouldn't be a problem. All prophets are linked through the same seed.

Another friend: When the caliphate system still existed, was there a distinction between Arabians and Jews?

---

1. Imam Ali was the first male to accept Muhammed's message. He was a cousin of Muhammed and later married Muhammed's daughter Fatima. He served Muhammed both in military and spiritual leadership.

2. *Gaon* means head of the Talmudical Academy; he was the *Gaon* of the Academy at Pumbeditha, Persia. Lived 906-1006 CE

Yawar: Sunni tradition holds that *Al Mahdi* carries the seed of Prophet Muhammed through his daughter Fatima, so more importantly than descent from Imam Ali, it is the progeny of Fatimah who give rise to *Al Mahdi*.

A friend: You asked, "What do you think about my proposal that the institutions of the Imamate and the Exilarchate benefit from a common messianic expectation rooted in prophecies concerning David? Do you see the Imamate and Exilarchate as similar?"

The Imamate goes back much much further than just the period of the exile! If you go all the way back to the book of Genesis, you can see it in the twelve covenantal paradigm beginning with Ishmael's sons and then with the twelve tribes of Israel.

In Abrahamic religions, the number twelve is connected with divine government. Hence you get twelve lesser prophets, twelve judges, twelve Psalms of Asaph, etc. This continues right down to the New Testament era with the eschatonic[1] model laid by the twelve disciples of Jesus.

Ben: Of course the first use of the number twelve is with the twelve tribes. This is taught in rabbinic literature (*midrashim*) to be a microcosm within the Children of Israel that parallels the seventy nations of the world.

Like the seven colors of the rainbow, seven represents the "emotional" attributes of cognition. Any action has ten gradations *(sefirot):* concept, relationships, plan, inclusion, restriction, budget, talents, supplies, action, and completion. Seven emotional attributes paired with ten gradations yields seventy possibilities. It is taught that each of the "seventy nations" of the world has a natural tendency to one of the seventy approaches to understanding.

---

1. End-times, a reference the messianic age

The idea of twelve is related: among the seven "emotional" attributes of cognition, there are twelve pairs.

The book of Genesis spends a great amount of time with genealogies to document the "names" of these approaches and paths, and show how the effulgence of the creative power of Allah sustains creation and expresses itself in different ways. The names identify the way Allah is perceived by different nations due to the natural diversity of humankind. The names given relate to the characteristics of the people.

As with King David, the idea of an Imamate of twelve would be associated with the aspect of completion, which is equivalent to royalty. This is indeed related to the coming of the messiah as well, and in both cases would imply leadership over the "seventy nations" of the world, while acknowledging the diversity of humankind.

But a friend interjects: Rabbi Abrahamson, in our earlier conversation (about King Shapur), you said that in Judaism, a marriage of a Jewess with a non-Jewish man is not allowed. Why in the case of the Quraish family an exception was made?

Ben: Historians have proposed that Adnan, the proginator of the Quraish, was the same as Onias IV, one of the last Sadducean priests that fled to Egypt around 153 BCE. This has some support in that the Sayyid family tests DNA positive for the Cohen gene. If this is true, then the daughters of the family of the Exilarch did not intermarry.

Harry: So, does that means that Quraish descend from the Kohanim, and thus Sayyids as well? Then, when did the Quraish stopped practicing Sadducean Judaism?

Ben: Yes, this is one possible explanation for events. If correct, Sadducean Judaism was abandoned by the Quraish under the reforms of Muhammed.

Harry: Thank you for your information, dear Rabbi. A bit shocking and surprising, to know that the ties between Arabs and Jews are much closer than what I originally thought.

Working Together

Ben: Reported by Abu Hurairah, "You shall not enter paradise so long as you do not affirm belief; and you will not believe as long as you do not love one another. Should I not direct you to a thing which, if you do, will foster love amongst you? Give currency to *as-salamu alaykum* (greeting one another in peace)." (*Sahih* Muslim)[1]

A friend: In other versions, it's "spread the message of peace".

Ben: I thought of this *hadith* when I wrote this comment to a post below: "[T]**he thinking is the rectification of humanity will come when mankind functions together and works together 'shoulder to shoulder' while retaining** [a better word would be *benefiting from*] **our differences."** In the Torah it is written: **"For then will I turn clear language to the Nations, that they may all call upon the name of God, to serve Him shoulder to shoulder"** (Zephania 3:9).

Another friend: Ben Abrahamson, are you a Muslim or a Jew?

Upon discovering that Ben is Jewish, a friend says: WOOOOOOW, I'm really really so amazed! I never saw or heard about a Jew being so nice to Islam/ Muslims. This is really amazing Ben Abrahamson. You're a unique nice Jew.

Ibrahim would like Christians and Muslims to get along better, but some readers counter.

---

1. Collection of *ahadith*–legends

A friend: Ibrahim, I think you should make an even better study as to why Muslims are not cooperating with Muslims. Muslim/Christian conflict is now a thing of the past. Please study the differences between Sunnis and Shias and help bridge the gap between them. It would be the Prophet's greatest pleasure for Muslims to love one another if he were among us today.

Ahmed: I agree.

Ben: I do too.

Faried de Bruyns: Me too.

Eka: *Assalamu alaikum,* peace be upon you.

> *The Facebook® page branches into personal discussions,*
> *as well as historical and theological.*

In May 2013, Ben posted: *Hodu L'Hashem Ki Tov*! Thank G-d I have a new grandson, my daughter and her new baby are doing well. I am blessed with children and grandchildren, *Hamd'Allah!*

> *Facebook® friends sent their congratulations all around.*

Another time, a friend: The Rabbi hasn't posted for a while, is he okay?

Ben: I am fine *Baruch HaShem*, work pressures are making it hard for me to do Facebook® now.

Our friend responds: We will give *dua* that your workload is eased, Ben.

Ben: Many thanks.

PART II

Historical Roots of Islam

8. Origin and Definition
of the Words *Muslim* and *Dhimmi*

Ben Abrahamson: The term "Muslim" was used before the time of Muhammed (pbuh). *Targum* Onkelos[1]. translates "Kenites", who were righteous non-Jews, as *Salamai* or *Muslamai*, which means "those who bring the *shelamim* sacrifice".The term *dhimmi* may derive from the word *edomi*.

Korban Shelamim: Islam in the Bible

In the Torah, there are the five basic categories of sacrifices (*korbanot*): olah, mincha, chatat, asham, and shlamim. Olah and shelamim are voluntary (*n'dava*). The Talmud explains why it is called *"korban shelamim"* —because it makes peace between the priests, the altar, and the one who offers it. During the Second Temple, the people who could offer it included the Children of Israel and the "God-fearers" who would be known as "those who brought the *shelamim*" or the *Muslamim*.

The uniqueness of the *korban shelamim* lies in the fact that it does not come to atone for any given sin and is purely voluntary, acknowledging God for His kindness to us.

One of the main points of dispute in the Talmud is whether a non-Jew can offer the *korban shelamim*. Apparently it depends on the non-Jew who wants to offer the sacrifice. Rabbi Eleazar holds that

---

1. The translation of the five books of Moses to Aramaic by Onkelos, a Roman convert to Judaism, first century CE

the majority of the thoughts of a polytheist are towards idolatry,[1] but this would not be the case of a monotheist *Bnei Noah* or *Ger Toshav* (foreign resident who keeps the seven commandments of Noah). The Rambam[2] holds that a polytheist can offer *olah* if "his heart is turned towards heaven" but not *shelamim*, However, if one gave his offering to an Israelite, it could be offered as a *shelamim*.[3] The *halachah* (practical application of law) during the Second Temple period seems to have been like Rabbi Eleazar.

The notion that a polytheist cannot bring a *shelamim* is discussed further by the Sforno[4]. He cites Na'aman, the captain of Aram, who, when cured from his leprosy by the prophet Elisha, proclaimed his intention for adopting monotheism by saying "For your servant will never again offer a burnt o*lah* offering or any *zevach* sacrifice to other gods, but only to the Lord" (Kings II 5:17). Here too the "*zevach*" following the *olah* refers to *shelamim*.

Discussions concerning Jethro and the sacrifices shed further light on the origin of the word "Muslim". *Yisro* (Jethro) was high priest of Midian and father in Law of Moses. Moses had married *Yisro's* daughter *Tzipora* before his return to Egypt to liberate the Jewish slaves. In the Talmud[5] there is a dispute whether *Yisro* came to Moses before or after the giving of the Torah on Mount Sinai. The Ramban[6] is of the opinion that *Yisro* came before the revelation, while Ibn Ezra[7] is of the opinion that Yisro came a year later. If he came before, he would be a *Bnei Noah* / *Ger Toshav*. If he came afterwards, he would be a full convert to Judaism—*Ger Tzedek*.

---

1. Talmud, *Chullin* 13a.

2. Maimonides, thirteenth-century rabbi and physician, Spain and Egypt.

3. *Ma'asei Korbanot* 3:3, based on Talmud, *Menachot* 73b.

4. Fifteenth-century rabbi and physician, Italy.

5. Talmud, *Zevachim* 116a

6. Nachmanides, thirteenth-century rabbi and kabbalist, Spain.

7. Eleventh-century rabbi and scientist, considered a rationalist, Spain.

In either case, it is apparent that during the period of the Second Temple, there was an entire community of "Children of Jethro" who adopted monotheism but remained distinct from the Children of Israel.

It says in Exodus 18:12, "**And *Yisro*, the father-in-law of Moses, took an *olah* and *zevachim*.**" The term *zevachim* following the term *olah* means *korban shelamim*. Thus Yisro's offering the *korban shelamim* demonstrates his acceptance of monotheism. The Children of Jethro are referred to throughout the Torah as the *Kenim* (Kenites). They lived in Jordan and Northern Arabia.

During the Second Temple, the people who could offer this sacrifice included the Children of Israel and the God-fearers, who would be known as "those who brought the *shelamim*" or the *Muslamim*.

Following this essay, the dialogue begins.

Ben: In the New Testament it is written **"Blessed are the peacemakers ..."** (Matthew 5:9). The Greek word is *eirhnopoioi*, which is usually translated "those who make peace" but could be translated as "Muslims". The Peshita[1] in Aramaic has *ovdei shelama* (workers of peace) which looks very much like Onkelos' *salamai*.

The above expression in Matthew 5:9 is comparable to that in the Psalms: **Blessed is the man who fears the LORD, who finds great delight in his commands.** (Psalms 112:1) **Blessed are all who fear the LORD, who walk in his ways** (Psalms 128:1). These God-fearers are referred to as *yireh shamayim, bnei noah,* or *ger toshav* in Hebrew, *theosebea* in Greek, and *salamai* or *muslamai* in Aramaic.

One can see that the name "Islam" was not given by Muslims themselves, or by others, or by Prophet Muhammed. Neither has the name itself acquired the usage in the course of time. The names "Islam" and "Muslim" are given by Allah Himself.

---

1. Also called the Syriac Vulgate—the Bible used in the Eastern Syriac Christian tradition, written in Aramaic.

This day have I perfected your religion for you, completed my favour upon you, and have chosen for you Islam as your religion. (Qur'an, *Al Maedah* 5:3)

... It is He Who has named you Muslims, both before and in this [Revelation]. (Qur'an, *Al Hajj* 22:78)

Islam is not a new religion, founded by Prophet Muhammed. The term *Muslim* goes back much further than Muhammed. In the Qur'an, it is explained that the Prophet Muhammed's role was to fulfill the original Abrahamic religion.

Full quotes:

Forbidden to you [for food] **are: dead meat, blood, the flesh of swine, and that on which hath been invoked the name of other than Allah; that which hath been killed by strangling, or by a violent blow, or by a headlong fall, or by being gored to death; that which hath been** [partly] **eaten by a wild animal; unless ye are able to slaughter it** [in due form]; **that which is sacrificed on stone** [altars]; [forbidden] **also is the division** [of meat] **by raffling with arrows: that is impiety. This day have those who reject faith given up all hope of your religion: Yet fear them not but fear Me. This day *have I perfected* your religion for you, *completed* My favour upon you, and have chosen for you Islam as your religion. But if any is forced by hunger, with no inclination to transgression, Allah is indeed Oft-forgiving, Most Merciful.** (Qur'an, *Al-Maedah* 5:3)

And strive in His cause as ye ought to strive, [with sincerity and under discipline]. **He has chosen you, and has imposed no difficulties on you in religion; it is the cult of your**

father Abraham. It is He Who has named you Muslims,
both before and in this [Revelation]; **that the Messenger may
be a witness for you, and ye be witnesses for mankind! So
establish regular Prayer, give regular Charity, and hold fast
to Allah! He is your Protector—the Best to protect and the
Best to help!** (Qur'an, *Al-Hajj* 22:78)

A friend: Your most enlightening notes go far to justify my occasional and
arguably anachronistic translation of Islam as *shalom* (peace).

Another: I propose that the terminology Islam and Muslim may have its
origins either in the Jesus' preaching or in the Psalms.

James: Before Muhammed, the Arabians were worshiping rocks. That's
why he established the Islamic faith, to raise their consciousness to
the level of belief in God.

Ben counters: We see in the very etymology of the word *Muslim* that this is
not the case. Your claim echoes that made by the German revisionist
school of Wellhausen in the late 1800s, with which I strongly disagree.[1]

---

1. Julius Wellhausen was a nineteenth-century biblical scholar, Germany. His work in
biblical criticism became the foundation for subsequent secular biblical critique. He
proposed that the five books of Moses was a redaction of four independent documents,
written during different epochs, later edited together. He stated that each name for
God indicated a separate author. Both the timing of his proposed epochs have been
questioned, as well as the theory that each name of God indicates a different author;
archeological discoveries indicate that other ancient texts from peoples who dwelled
near the Israelites also used multiple names of God in a single document. Wellhausen is
known to have been aware of these discoveries. He espoused the evolution of religion,
and has been said to have applied Darwinism to theology. It has been said that his
evolutionary approach paved the way for concepts of superior culture and superior race.

Gambo: To an independent and honest investigator it matters concerning the origin and nature of scriptures; there is absolutely no significant difference between the Holy Bible and the Holy Qur'an. Both came from the same source. In fact the Bible is the source from which the Qur'an depends whenever a quotation or evidence is necessary. Misunderstandings arise not from the scriptures themselves but from those who profess to interpret them.

Ben invites his friend to look at Scripture: Please find in the Qur'an or *ahadith* (traditions) a precise definition of what the requirements are for a Muslim.

A friend offers:

> **Whoever submits his face in Islam to Allah while doing good will have his reward with his Lord. And no fear will there be concerning them, nor will they grieve**. (Qur'an, *Al-Baqarah* 2:112)

> **When** [Abraham's] **Lord said to him, "Submit", he said "I have submitted** [in Islam] **to the Lord of the worlds." And Abraham instructed his sons** [to do the same] **and** [so did] **Jacob,** [saying], **"O my sons, indeed Allah has chosen for you this religion, so do not die except while you are Muslims." Or were you witnesses when death approached Jacob, when he said to his sons, "What will you worship after me?" They said, "We will worship your God and the God of your fathers, Abraham and Ishmael and Isaac— one God. And we are Muslims** [in submission] **to Him."** (Qur'an, *Al-Baqarah* 2:122-133

She concludes: Abraham was neither a Jew nor a Christian, but he was one inclining toward truth, a Muslim (in terms of submitting to Allah).

Dhimmi

A friend: What are the similarities and differences between *ger toshav* and *dhimmi*?

Ben: I have proposed the origin of the word *dhimmi* was "Edomi" or Edomites, who were the largest community of foreign residents ever assimilated into the community of Israel during the Second Temple period (500 BCE–70 CE) under the laws of *ger toshav.*

I believe the the concept of *dhimmi* was originally based on *ger toshav.*

- Both describe the rights and obligations of foreign residents in a host nation.
- Both recognize a common law that binds both the minority and majority.
- Both absolve the minority from religious law of the majority.
- Both recognize the duty of the majority to protect the minority, enable them to obtain employment, and provide for their widows and orphans.
- Both impose a kind of tax in recognition of the sovereignty of the state.
- Both exempt the minority from military service.

However the two systems evolved differently. While the concept of *ger toshav* recognized the foreign resident as a "proper citizen" with a valid religion (having a share in the world to come), the institution of *dhimmi* did not implicitly validate any other religion besides that of the majority.

Another difference had to do with the payment of the tax (*jizya*). Due to various *ahadith* (traditions) as well the *tafsir* (commentary) on the verse **"his hand will be to all, and (their) hand to him, above the face of his brothers,** [they will pay for their] **dwelling"** (Genesis 16:12), the word "above" was interpreted to mean that the payment of the tax was not just recognition of sovereignty, but also a recognition of superiority of the state and the national religion.

Although there were guidelines on how much or how little to tax the *dhimmi,* and how much or how little to humble them, this system was frequently abused often on a local level by ambitious governors and tax collectors.

A friend: Thanks for your answer. Concerning the Edomites, there are contradictory historical sources concerning the conversion of the Idumeans, who may be the Edomites. Josephus[1] implies that their conversion was forced, including circumcision[2] which implies full conversion (*ger tzedek*). According to Strabo[3] they converted out of free will[4] which implies accepting the *ger toshav* (righteous gentile) status.

Were the Idumeans halachically *ger tzedek* or *ger toshav*?

Ben: I believe that the Hasmonean kings were more interested in enlarging their territory and keeping the peoples from revolting than they were in following Jewish law. In an attempt to reconcile Josephus and the Talmudic accounts, I understand that king Yohanan Hyrcanus[5] wanted to incorporate the Edomites into the Jewish nation and religion. Because forced conversion is not permitted, he resorted to a legal loophole of declaring the Edomites "slaves to the king" and then released them, effectively forcibly converting them to Juda-

---

1. Jewish historian, first-century CE, Roman citizen.

2. Antiquities 13.257-258.

3. Greek philosopher and historian, first-century CE.

4. Geographica 16.2.34

5. Hasmonean king of Judea from 134–104 BCE. Judea had been devastated by the Seleucid siege; Yohanan was determined to revitalize the nation and did so through military campaigns that would expand the borders of the devastated state, this may have been the impetus behind his desire to expand the definition of "who is a Jew". His policies alienated traditional Jewish factions.

ism. The rabbinic Jews did not recognize this legal fiction concerning those Edomites who did not follow Jewish law. They distinguished between *ger tzedek* and *ger toshav*.

Qur'anic Islam did not appear suddenly upon a pagan landscape, as claimed in the nineteenth century German revisionist school of thought. We have seen Qur'anic texts and *ahadith* attesting to Islam's ancient monotheistic roots. In the following chapters we will see historical evidence of its ancient roots as well.

9. Jewish Sects in Last Days of Second Temple Commonwealth

Herod's Temple, the center of the Judeo-Arab commonwealth. The gate of Nicanor is seen (the small gate in the center).

A friend asks: Can you please narrate the history of divisions between the sects in Judah and Palestine during the Second Temple period? The Pharisees, the Sadducees, the Essenes. What were the scriptural bases for the ideology of each and which one was nearest to the ideology of the Levites and Cohanim, those allowed in the inner sanctuary of the holy of holies in the First Temple period?

Ben: Our major source for the Second Temple period is Josephus and the New Testament, although various Greek historians as well as the books of Maccabees augment our understanding. The major sects were the Pharisees, Sadducees, and Essenes, as well as Herodians, Zealots, and Sicarii. They have their roots in the four Persian Jewish governors that were sent to rule the area in the fifth century BCE that had once been under Solomon's (pbuh) kingdom before the Babylonian exile. The four governors were: Zerubavel, Sanballat, Tobiah and Gashmu.

1) Zerubavel ruled in Judea. His followers eventually split into the Pharisaic and Sadducean sects. He was responsible for religious worship for the entire Trans-Euphrates. All the other governors had to pay taxes to him to support Temple worship in Jerusalem. He required the nobles to divorce their foreign wives who kept idolatrous and polytheistic practices.

2) Sanballat ruled the coast and was in charge of military colonies from Egypt and Arabia to what is now Lebanon. His people, the remnants of the Northern Kingdom of Israel, mixed with local residents and sought to have their own independent base of worship. After Alexander the Great, this was set up in Mount Gezirim. While originally allied with Egypt, they prospered under

the Seleucids[1], populated Asia Minor and heavily intermarried with the local population. Their religious leadership was not involved in the general population. His followers were known as Shomronim, or Samaritans.

3) Tobiah ruled the Transjordan and was in charge of collecting taxes and tribute for the Persian king. Precursor of Sadducees and Essenes, his base was in Iraq Al-Amir in Jordan. His immediate family sought to intermarry with the line of prophets, including Zechariah. He used a system of doves for speedy communication between Jerusalem, Jordan and Persia. His people were the remnants of the tribes of Joseph mixed with local natives. The religion that developed under him was based on what they thought were the characteristics of Joseph: the use of doves as a means to obtain "word from heaven", foretelling the future, reading stars, and embracing groups known as the "children of the prophets". They developed a monastic movement, living in the desert and caves, seeking prophetic revelations. His followers were known as the *Notzrim*, one group of this was the Essenes.

4) Gashmu ruled the Arabian Peninsula and was in charge of managing its trade routes. Claiming to be a descendant of the Queen of Sheba, he followed a form of Abrahamic monotheism, and contributed to the support of the Temple in Jerusalem. His followers were known as Sabeans (TSaBiuN) which some derive linguistically from the word *"ger ToSaBiN"* or *ger toshav* (resident).

---

1. The Seleucid Empire was the Near-Eastern division of Alexander the Great's empire following his demise, favored hellenism, fourth-to-first century BCE

Three of the four groups above are mentioned by Allah swt in the Qur'an:

> **Those who believe, those who are Jews, and the *Nasaara* [Christians] and *Sabeans* [righteous gentiles], all who believe in Allah swt and the Last Day and act rightly, will have their reward with their Lord. They will feel no fear and will know no sorrow.** (Qur'an, *Al-Baqarah* 2:62)

The Samaritan religion was limited in scope, so the Tobiad religion began to spread both north into Damascus and south into Egypt and Arabia. Supported by the Ptolemaic and then the Seleucid monarchies, their religion was a mix of Judaism and Hellenism. This had great success with the Ptolemies in Egypt, who contributed to the entire rebuilding of the Temple in Jerusalem, and a great missionary effort ensued. Eventually the Tobiads set their sites on control of Jerusalem itself, as they felt had been prophesied to their forefather in Zechariah 6:12. Through a marriage of a daughter to the grandson of Zaddokite priest Shimon HaTzadik, they introduced Shimon, Onias and lastly Alcimus into the High Priesthood. With this newfound power they introduced Greek culture and traditions. This, in turn, provoked rebellion by the traditionalists and nationalists. The Jewish Hellenists later became known as Sadducees.

Eventually rebellion turned into open warfare when the Syrian forces tried to raid the Temple treasury. Syrian forces invaded, invoking martial law and prohibiting Jewish customs; this lead to the wars of the Maccabees and the ousting of the Zaddokite, Oniad priesthood. Onias IV fled to Egypt and continued his missionizing movement there. This is based on the Prophecy in Isaiah 19:19, which says that there would be an altar in Egypt (Heliopolis) and a monument on the border of Egypt (Mecca). These altars were run by Zaddokite/Oniad priests, but the people who brought offerings were non-Jewish monotheistic believers.

The anti-Greek reaction, supported by the new rising power of Rome, led to the formation of the Pharisaic party, which claimed to represent the true chain of tradition that had returned with the Babylonian exiles from Persia. This party participated in the wars against the Syrians. But when the Hasmonean rulers themselves began to adopt Hellenism, confrontation erupted. One confrontation with Hasmonean king Alexander Yannai resulted in the crucifixion of 1,000 Pharisaic leaders. Pharisaism ceased to be a political party and became a popular conservative movement.

In the meantime, the Tobiads had split into two parties: those who supported the Ptolemaic (Egyptian) monarchy and those who supported the Seleucid (Syrian) monarchy. The Ptolemaic Tobiads lost power and withdrew to the deserts and caves. Their religion thrived and John the Baptist, as well as the Essenes, were probably members of this group. They resented the Hasmoneans who allied with wealthy Hellenist Sadducees. They waited for the return of the Teacher of Righteousness (Onias IV), the restoration of the Zaddokite priesthood, and a Messiah who was a descendant of Joseph.

The Hasmoneans, with the sanction of Rome, embarked on a period of expansionism. They tried to rebuild the entire Solomonaic Empire of the Trans-Euphrates. They met with limited success, but the Hasmonean Alexander Yannai conquered the Edomites and what was left of the Ammonites and Moabites. He made them his "slaves" and using a Jewish legal technique he freed them, forcing them to become Jewish converts. This was opposed by the Pharisees and was one of the factors leading to the confrontation mentioned above. What this did mean was that Judeans and Idumeans (Edomites) were now mixing freely in Jerusalem.

In the meantime, one branch of the Ptolemaic Tobiads managed to regain power. Antipater had been educated in Rome and became an advisor to the Hasmonean king Hyrcanus. When civil war broke out between Hyrcanus and Aristobulus, Rome intervened and Pompey restored Hyrcanus as a puppet king but gave the Edomite Antipater the real authority. Eventually his son Herod came to power, and he embarked on a campaign to fulfill the prophecy of Zechariah 6:12. Herod gloriously reconstructed the Temple. He waged war in Arabia, trying to bring it under his control, and he negotiated with Rome for control of greater lands to the north and east of Israel. Herod's Judeo-Arab kingdom saw the Temple in Jerusalem become the center of culture and religion for the whole area. Those who saw him as messiah were called the Herodians.

Meanwhile the Ptolemaic Tobiads embarked on a revivalist movement, and a rejection of the Roman influence imported by the Herodians. This in turn sparked corresponding revivalist movement among the Pharisees. While there were differences in theology between the *Notzri* philosophy of the Ptolemaic Tobiads and the "traditions of the fathers" of the Pharisees, they generally were sympathetic to each other. Herod being rejected as the Messiah, the scene was set for the appearance of the Messiah, son of David.

The beliefs of each group varied:

1) The Pharisees were at various times a political party, a social movement, and a school of thought beginning under the Hasmonean dynasty (140–37 BC) in the wake of the Maccabean Revolt, as a rejection of Greek polytheistic influence. The Pharisees believed that God gave Moses both the commandments as well as the knowledge of how they should be applied. This oral tradition was codified and written down from about 200-600 CE in what is known as the Talmud, in both the land of Israel and Persia. As reported in the Christian book of Acts, the Pharisees were generally sympathetic to the *Notzrim*. The Pharisees also maintained that an afterlife existed and that God punished the wicked and rewarded the righteous in the world to come. They also believed in a messiah who would herald an era of world peace.

2) The Sadducees were elitists who wanted to maintain the priestly caste, but they were also liberal in their willingness to incorporate Hellenism into their lives, something the Pharisees opposed. The Sadducees rejected the idea of the Oral Law and insisted on a literal interpretation of the Written Law; consequently, they did not believe in an afterlife, since it is not explicitly mentioned in the Torah. The main focus of Sadducean life was rituals associated with the Temple. After the destruction of the Second Temple by the Romans, the Pharisaic leadership gradually relocated to Persia. The Sadducean leadership gradually relocated to Egypt and Arabia. None of the writings of the Sadducees survived, so the little we know about them comes from their Pharisaic opponents. In the Gospel account of the crucifiction, the book of Acts, and Josephus, the Sadducees are portrayed as the most zealous persecutors of the Christians. Eventually almost the entire Sadducee population of Asia Minor converted to Christianity. A descendant of Tobiah in Edessa (Sanliurfa Turkey), is credited for allowing the Apostle Thaddæus to preach to Asia Minor.

3) The Essenes are proposed to be an offshoot of the Ptolemaic Tobiads, called the *Notzrim*. It has been suggested that the reason that the Essenes are never mentioned by name in the New Testament is because the proto-Christians were "Essenes". In this sense the terms *Notzri* and perhaps even Nazereth would not just indicate a town but would indicate a religious group associated with Tobiads, tax collecting, doves, monasticism, and spending time in the desert to be "led by the spirit".

4) The Zealots and Sicarii. When the Herodians (Idumeans) and other Hellenists faced conquest from Rome, they

encouraged insurrection. After the utter defeat in the
First Revolt, which also resulted in the destruction of the
Temple, Rabbi Gamliel suppressed any further revolt.
After his passing, Rabbi Akiva, a Pharisee of Edomite
lineage, gave his approval to Bar Kokhba to revolt against
Rome. Eventually the Pharisees saw the hopelessness of
the situation and began to sue for peace. Bar Kokhba's
troops killed Rabbi Eleazar and Pharisaic support for the
revolt was withdrawn. The Romans slaughtered most of
Bar Kokhba's troops in Beitar, although a few held out in
Masada. The survivors of the zealots fled, some to Egypt
and many to Arabia. The Romans closed Onias' Temple
in Egypt to prevent it from becoming a rallying point for
further revolt. The Romans made a foray into Arabia,
perhaps to destroy Onias's Temple in Mecca, but they
were thwarted by the desert.

5a) The Herodians were also an offshoot of the Ptolemaic
Tobiads; a minority of academics have suggested that
Paul was a Herodian. Some actual descendants of Herod
were given minor positions by Rome outside of Israel.
Aristobulus fled to Jordan and set up a kingdom there,
but Rome destroyed that city. He and his family fled
south to Arabia, eventually to intermarry with the royal
family of Himyar, revitalizing a dying dynasty, and
creating the first of the Tubba' kings who would play a
role for the next 400 years in Arabia.

5b) A minor descendant of the Tobiads, an officer in the
Roman army, Vaballathus (Wahballath) was made ruler
of a Syrian outpost called Palmyra. His family received
the Roman citizenship under an emperor of the Severan
dynasty. Eventually his grandson Lucius Septimius
Odaenathus took advantage of chaotic conditions in

Rome to claim to be Emperor of an Eastern Roman Empire. He did not forget his Tobiad roots and was referred to in the Talmud as "Ben Netzer (*Notzri*)". When Palmyra was crushed by Rome in 270 CE, the refugees fled to Yathrib. There they were welcomed by the Himyarite king Shamir Yuhar'esh II Tubba', 275 CE. These polytheistic Arab-Jews and Yemenites would later be referred to as the Aus and Kazraj.

5c) Lastly, we read of the Jewish prince "Tobiyah" described by Moses of Khorene who is said to have introduced Thaddæus, and thus Christianity, to Edessa (in modern day Şanliurfa, Turkey). This Tobiyah is said to be the ancestor of the Armenian-Georgian royal family of Bagratuni and by some accounts the basis of their claim to "descent from Kings of Israel"

A friend: Interesting. I shall have to look and see if you have other "notes."

Sa'id: Shalom, Rabbi, thanks for your article, very interesting indeed, and also thanks for accepting me as a friend, be blessed.

Ben: *Wa aleikum salaam wa rahmatullah.*

Ali: *Was salamu ala manit taba al huda.*

Muhammed R: *Jazak' Allah h'airan.*

Faried: May Allah reward you dear Rabbi. So many questions, only after I have tried to answer for myself. Thank you so much!

10. Jewish Sects in Arabia at the Dawn of Islam

Ben Abrahamson: Scholars Al Jahiz[1] and Ibn Hazm[2] record that the Jews of Arabia were *"Al Saduqiyyh*: This sect associates itself with a person called Saduq (Zadok). Differing from all other Jews, they regard Uzayr (Ezra) as the son of God."[3] Additionally they were priests and officiated at the *Ka'aba*, according to Tabari.[4]

I propose that because the Prophet Muhammed (pbuh) did away with the priests, altars, and sacrifices of Jahilliya, the Sadducees of Arabia, especially the leadership—the Kahins (Cohens)—opposed this policy as much as the polytheists.

According to Tabari, Jews founded Yathrib (later called Medina). They were displaced by the arrival of the Aws and Khazraj, but they continued to own the palm groves and orchards in the area.

Hisham: There are some hints in the *sira* and the *hadiths* indicating that they settled there because they knew the last Prophet would come to that city.

Ben validates this point: This is what the two rabbis of Yathrib told Abu Kariba Tubba', when he threatened to destroy Yathrib.

---

1. Ninth century Muslim theologian, present-day Iraq.

2. Eleventh century Muslim theologian, Spain.

3. Ibn Hazm's book: *Kitab al-Fasl fi al-Milal wa al-Ahwa wa al-Nihal.*

4. Muslim historian, ninth-century Persia.

Loyalty between Jews and Arabs at the Dawn of Islam

Ben: Mukhayriq was a Jewish man from Bani Tsalabah who owed many farms and date palm gardens. Before the battle of Uhud, he heard there will be battle between Meccan polytheists and the Muslims. Mukhayriq told the Jews to support the Medina Charter. When some protested because the battle was taking place on Sabbath, Mukhayriq replied that helping Muhammed (pbuh) does not disgrace the Sabbath. Afterward he prepared his sword, went to the battle of Uhud, fought the polytheists, and was killed.

Bani Tsalabah is sometimes translated as "the crucified ones". This is not a reference to the crucifixion mentioned in the New Testament. Instead, this is a reference to the children of Mar-Zutra II, the 30th Exilarch (493-520 CE). Mar-Zutra II was the reigning descendant of King David (pbuh) in exile. He was crucified, together with his father, on the bridge of Mahoza by King Kovad I. He had been accused of collecting taxes and trying to organize a militia to defend the Jewish community during the Mazdakite revolts[1] and general chaos in Babylon (Persia).

Mar-Zutra II's son, Mar-Zutra III, who was born on the same day as his father's death, was raised secretly. He did not attain the office of Exilarch. In 520 CE, aged eighteen, he traveled to the Holy Land where he became head of the Academy of Tiberias under the title of *"Resh Pirka"*. Several generations of his descendants succeeded him in this office, and apparently some of his descendants—such as Mukhayriq—ended up in Medina.

A question: What is the source of this account?

Ben: The Islamic scholars Ibn Ishaq[2] and Tabari.

1. Mazdakites claimed to follow a reformed form of Zoroastrianism which included concepts of communal property that are said to be proto-socialist.

2. Eighth-century Islamic scholar, Arabia.

Most of the native Jews in Arabia were Sadducean. Rabbinic Jews were rare and only came into contact in any great numbers after the conquest of Babylon. The relationship between Islam and each of these groups varied considerably.

Jews are required by Torah law to be absolutely honest in business transactions and likewise to uphold contracts and treaties (Deuteronomy 25:13-16). If upholding a mutual defense treaty has the potential to save lives of the community, either directly (by defending the community against attackers) or indirectly (by assisting the members of another community who defend them in return), then it is permissible, and even required, to violate the Sabbath. (Leviticus 18:5)

An enthusiast for open mindedness says: The message of oneness of God is more important than the messenger or the prophet.

Ben: I don't see how it is possible to say this. The basic message of Noah (pbuh), Abraham (pbuh) and all the prophets (pbu them) was the same: *Tawhid* (Oneness of Allah), belief in the Last Day and good deeds. But without *shari'a/brith* (covenant) and *fiqh/halachah* (law), I don't see how it is possible for a given community with its specific needs and nature to arrive at a proper form of worship that includes *tawid*, proper belief, and good deeds without the proper vessels of *shari'a* and *fiqh*.

Maya: Salam Rabbi, what is Samaritan Judaism? They claim that their Torah is the exact Torah as given by the Prophet Moses at Mount Sinai. So what is the difference between their Torah compared to the others?

Ben: *Wa aleikum salaam wa rahmatullah.*

We must ask, when the Qur'an mentions the "Yahud", to whom is it referring? The Qur'an says the Yahud worship Uzayr [Ezra] as the son of God.[1] The Qur'an also says the Yahud changed the wording of the Torah. An example given is:

> **"... distorting** [the word] **with their tongues and taunting about religion; and if they had said** [instead]: **We have heard and we obey.** (Qur'An, *An-Nisa* 4:46)

Of all the Dead Sea Scrolls there are four families. approximately 6 percent of the fragments matched the Masoretic (rabbinical) text (MMT), 5 percent agreed with Samaritan (SP), 5 percent agreed with the Septuagint (G), and the rest were written in a dialect of Qumran or non-aligned. It should be noted that all of the scroll fragments found in the Judean desert (outside of Qumran, but belonging to the same time period) agreed with the Masoretic text exactly.

The proto-Samaritan (SP) family of texts is most interesting, because although it does not mention Mount Gerizim, it shares many features of the Samaritan Pentateuch. It is not a single text like the Masoretic text but rather a family of similar texts. The differences include changes that reflect the philosophical tradition of Alexandria, or what we have come to know as a Sadducean tradition:

1) Anthropomorphisms (references to God in human terms) are reworded.

2) Quotes from Deuteronomy are duplicated in the earlier books so that the verses which say "I said to you at that time ..." Deuteronomy 1:9, 9:20, etc are literally fulfilled.

3) Verses are changed to be more rational, for example "we will obey and we will hear" (Exodus 24:7) is reworded to "we will hear and we will obey". This reflects the

---

1. The Qur'an (9:30) has a verse stating that the Jews called a certain Uzair the son of God, a claim denied by Maimonides as being contrary to Judaism's strict monotheism. Muslim scholars have clarified that this verse refers to a small group of Jews.

Sadducean view that rational derivations of the Torah
have an equivalent standing as the Torah itself. The
Pharisaic and later rabbinic authorities greatly objected to
this rationalist view.

Ninth-century Islamic scholar Al Jahiz refers to a Jewish group
termed Saduqiyya (Saducees), which was found in Yemen, Syria,
and Byzantine territory. He says its name stems from "a man whose
name was Zadok [the student of Antigonus of Sokho], and that they
held that 'Uzair was the son of God." Ibn Hazm records "Al Saduqiyyh: This sect associates itself with a person called Saduq (Zadok).
Differing with all other Jews, they regard Uzair (Ezra) as the son of
God.[1]

So it is obvious the "Yahud" of the Qur'an were Sadducees and
the "corrupted Torah" of the Qur'an refers to the Sadducean Torah,
Samaritan Pentateuch vorlage[2].

Historically it appears that the Qur'an was not referring to rabbinic Judaism, which was almost unknown in Arabia, or to the Masoretic text that rabbinic Jews use.

Omar: You stated, "Historically it appears that the Qur'an was not referring
to rabbinic Judaism, which was almost unknown in Arabia, or to the
Masoretic text that rabbinic Jews use."

I agree. The Qur'an has its own definitions of terms which may
not be the same as that of the historians, and it's always important to
examine the text to see which group or faction the Qur'an is talking
about in light of history.

In a similar but related matter, I was actually trying to figure out
what the Qur'an means by the terms *Taurat, Zaboor,* and *Injeel* (Gospel)
and whether, for example, *Taurat* is referring to the whole *Tanakh* or
just the five books of Moses.

---

1. Ibn Hazm's book: *Kitab al-Fasl fi al-Milal wa al-Ahwa wa al-Nihal*

2. Vorlage means prior version of text.

I presumed that the *"Injeel"*, (assuming it was a revelation that was in book-form), would most likely have been written by God in the "first person voice" and revealed in the Aramaic tongue.

Benito: Rabbi, do you have any more info about Uzair being referred to as the son of God?

Ben: There are comments by Islamic scholars Ibn Rabban, Ibn Qutayba, Al Ya'qubi, Al Tabari, Al Mas'udi, Al Maqdisi, Al Baqillani, Al Biruni and Ibn Hazm, who all speak highly both of Ezra and the tradition that claims that because he was able to memorize the Torah exactly without error, he was considered a "son of God" by one group of Jews, not literally, but as a sign of respect. Only Ibn Hazm refers to the Torah as a forgery, and he does not attribute it to Ezra but rather a wicked Jew who lived around his time.[1]

This has led me to propose that a different Ezra was intended: that the Uzair of the Qur'an is actually Nehemiah ben Hushiel, the son of the Jewish Exilarch and the symbolic head of the Persian troops during their invasion of the Holy Land on their way to capture Egypt in 610 CE. There was much speculation about Nehemiah ben Hushiel, and it would have been fresh in the minds of the people of Arabia at the time of the *Hijra*. Perhaps it was he was dubbed "Uzair/Ezra".

Malik proposes that rabbinic Judaism was present in Arabia: Certainly there were interactions between the rabbinic Jews and the first Muslims. The rabbis are mentioned in *ayats* 5:44, 5:63, and 9:31. So it was not only Sadducean Judaism in the beginning of the Muslim era. In fact *Surah-al-Kahf*[2] speaks of stories that were revealed

---

1. This was forty years after the return from Babylon, approximately the time that Nehemiah excluded the Samaritans from the Jewish community. They then set up their own altar, according to Josephus.

2. The chapter in the Qur'an about the cave, in which believers in one God sought refuge in a cave from being persecuted for their monotheism.

specifically to answer rabbinical objections, such as the story of *Khidr*.[1]

Ben: We can't learn that from the word *rabaniyuna* alone. The word Rabban was a title of respect. For example 'Ali al-Tabari was called Ibn Rabban, which some thought this meant his father was a Jew, when in fact Rabban repeatedly refers to his Christian past in his introduction to his book *Radd 'ala l-Nasara*. It has been shown that he was a Nestorian Christian with the title Rabban.

   Surah-al-Kahf discusses stories which are out of character with rabbinic (Talmudic) Judaism, and not found in our literature.

Malik: But the story of *Khidr* and *Al-Kahf* was revealed as a response by the Prophet to questions asked by rabbis to verify his prophethood. And these cannot be confirmed from the *Tanakh*, they can only be confirmed from the Talmud. What about the connection between *Al-Khidr* and Elijah/Pinchas?

   The Qur'an actually concedes to the Talmud over the *Tanakh* in fact, as seen by how it cites the story of the mountain over their heads. Many Qur'anic stories like Solomon's command over the *jinns*[2] are only found in the Talmud.

Ben: I agree that rabbinic Judaism had its representatives in Arabia. I just think they were a small minority.

Malik: While we are on this topic, what is your view on how the Samaritans, representing the northern state of Israel, had Mt. Gerizim as their holy of holies while the southern state of Judah had it in Jerusalem? Then there are the Jews of Elephantine (southern Egypt) who also had their own temple as well.

1. The chapter in the Qur'an about Moses meeting the *Khidr*, or servant of God who was claimed to be immortal.

2. Spirits who have free will and can take on human form

Ben: Back to the sixth-century BCE, as I understand it, there were four
Jewish governors set up by Persia to tax and administer what was
once Solomon's (pbuh) kingdom. Sanballat, Tobiah, Zerubavel, and
Gashmu.

Sanballat's territory was the coast, from Egypt (including Elepha-
tine[1]) to Tyre. Tobiah's territory was the Transjordan. Zerubavel was
the area around Jerusalem and the south. Gashmu was the Hijaz and
Sinai. In addition Sanballat was given responsibility for the Persian
troops, Tobiah for taxation, Zerubavel for Temple worship, Gashmu
for mining, ores and incense.

Cyrus enforced a single Temple in Jerusalem that all governors
would support financially but only Zerubavel would administer.
This generated resentment.

When the prophet Nehemiah replaced Zerubavel, part of his reforms was to insist that the Children of Israel divorce their foreign
wives. Those who did not agree were "erased from the book of genealogies" and would no longer be considered Children of Israel.

Even though they were prohibited from being part of the adminis-
tration of Temple worship in Jerusalem this did not prevent Sanballat
from setting up independent altars in Egypt, Mount Gerizim, and
elsewhere. What we know as the Samaritans was only one group of
Sanballat's followers who practiced an independent sacrificial form
of Judaism.

Letters from the Elephantine were addressed to Sanballat as well
as to Jerusalem.

Tobiah on the other hand never established competing cultic centers but explored his "Josephean" heritage and established monastic
centers whose members would spend time seeking angels, interpreting dreams, and collecting taxes.

The discussion of "People of the Cave" is related to stories of Syrian origin. It appears to refer to an actual community of scholars in

---

1. An island in the Nile river

Edessa.

If *Dhul-Qarnayn*[1] had some relationship to Alexander the Great (with which I think you disagree) as many Islamic scholars have suggested, it would also point to a Hellenistic/Syrian connection.

The question about the nature of *ruach* (spirit, wind) also appears to be influenced by Hellenestic and perhaps even Christian questions about the nature of *ruach*.

In all, much more content related to these questions can be found in Syria than in Babylon. The Syrian Jews, as well as those in Asia Minor, largely subscribed to the rational, hellenized, "Sadducean" form of Judaism.

The Sadducees believed that Moses (pbuh) received a revelation and not a book. This is the reason they were not as careful about the exact wording of the Torah, but stressed its meaning as they understood it. The proto-Samaritan texts differ from each other and make a family of texts rather than a single text.

Malik: Are there any specific citations to verify that Sadducees believed in revelation rather than scripture, perhaps from Sadducean sources?

Ben: There are virtually no sources that survive written by self-described Sadducees. All our information comes from people who have described them (Josephus, the New Testament, the Talmud, etc) and assumptions made about the identity of the people of Qumran and *ahadith* like the one above. I use the term "Sadducees" as I believe it was intended by the Talmud. I use it to mean hellenized Jews who tended towards rational thought and philosophy, intellectually equalizing, discarding the concept of a received interpretation— even if these Jews would not call themselves Sadducees.

My point here was not to pin down Sadducees so much as to say it was foreign to rabbinic (Talmudic) thought. The equalizing tendency, rejection of a received interpretation, and the embracing of private

1. A heroic protective figure in the Qur'an

interpretation is illustrated in the following quote from the Talmud:

Jewish king Alexander Yannai, of the Hasmonean dynsasty, asked a Sadducee leader, Eleazar ben Poira, how he should punish the Sages whom he believed affronted him. The Sadducee replied, "Trample them under foot." Taken aback, the king then asked, "And what will happen to the Torah?" The Sadducee blithely answered, "It will be wrapped up and laid in a corner, and all who wish to study it, let them come and study" (Talmud. *Kiddushin* 66a).

Evan: Fascinating discussion. Thank you on all sides.

11. The Arabian Kingdom of Himyar

'Iraq al Amir near Amman Jordan, built by Tobiah the Ammonite, governor of Transjordan, fifth-century BCE.

Ben Abrahamson: Wars in fifth- and sixth-century Arabia between the Sadducean Jews and Roman Byzantine Christians, with each side vying to convert the Arabians, created fertile ground for the Prophet Muhammed to declare a return to Abrahamic roots. The Prophet's message was thus in defiance of kingdoms competing for both spiritual and temporal allegiance. Muhammed promised his followers salvation, not by choosing sides but by following the original monotheism of Abraham.

Let's look at the historical backdrop of this pivotal time in history.

Historical Background

The Arabian kingdom of Himyar spanned three centuries, from the second century CE until the fifth century CE.

I believe that Herod and the later Tubba kings of Arabia descended from Tobiah, governor of ancient Judea, sixth century BCE.

Just as Mount Gerizim was the religious center of the Samaritans, who were governed by Sanballat, a Jewish governor in the fifth century BCE, 'Iraq al Amir was the religious center for Tobiah's people, who were called the *Nasaara*. *Nasaara* is the term used in the Qur'an for Christians.

In 270 CE, the Palmyrenes migrated from the area known today as Syria to Himyar. Their influx revitalized the aging Himyar dynasty. During this period, the kingdom of Himyar conquered the kingdom of Sheba, located in or near Yemen. They developed the trade routes from the Red Sea through Medina in Arabia to Petra in Jordan and along that Silk Road to the east.

The Tubba' kings built a series of minarets which acted as fire beacons along the Silk Road. These relayed religious or political messages to the east within a day. The Tubba' kings maintained the *Ka'aba* at Mecca, thereby supporting the priesthood of the Quraish.[1] The sacrifices and holidays at the *Ka'aba* attracted pilgrimages from all across Arabia. The Tubba' kings oversaw the pilgrimage from Arabia to Jerusalem on the ninth of *Av* to mourn the destruction of the Jewish Temple. At least one Tubba' prince was buried in Beit Shearim in the Galilee, Israel with all the great princes and rabbinic scholars of Israel.

Beginning in the fourth century CE, local trade began to fail for several reasons: inter-tribal warfare, the Nabetean revolt in the area between Arabia and modern-day Jordan, and the loss of control over the naval trade routes after the Byzantine conquest of Egypt, Syria and *Hijaz* (western Arabia). Most of Himyar's income had derived

---

1. The Quraish is the tribe from which the Prophet Muhammed is descended.

from taxes on caravans of the Silk Road, and not from local trade. The tribes of Arabia thus became disunited and scattered.

This period witnessed much disorder and turmoil. Foreign and civil wars cost the people of Sheba their independence. During this era, the Aksumites from Ethiopia invaded the Arabian cities of Tihama and Najran in 340 CE, exploiting Himyar's intra-tribal conflict. The Aksumite occupation of Tihama and Najran lasted until 378 CE, whereafter the kingdom of Sheba expelled the Aksumites.

In 450 or 451 CE the Ma'rib Dam, located in modern day Yemen, burst, causing a great flood. Thousands were displaced. Himyar was thus further weakened and nearly collapsed. The Tubba' kings were left with mostly a title and functioned not much more than wealthy businessmen.

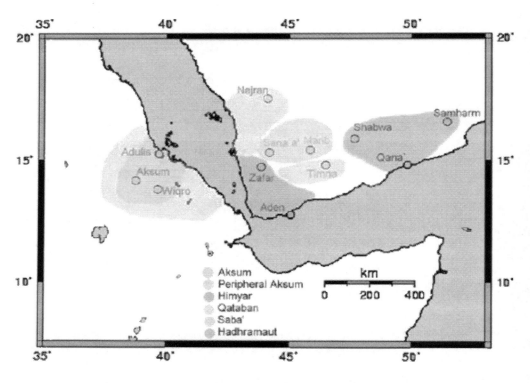

Map of Saba and Himyar—present-day Ethiopia and southern Egypt to left of Red Sea, present day Arabia to the right

Judaism and Christianity in Arabia

The Tubba' kings were interested in commerce. They jealously guarded the routes and left day-to-day management of the kingdom to their counselors, who came from the tribe of Lakhmids. The Tubba' kings embraced Sadducean Judaism which had some Samaritan and Tobiad influences. This form of Judaism rejected the oral tradition preserved in the Talmud. This stood in stark contrast to rabbinic Judaism with its Pharisaic roots, which emphasized oral tradition and was prominent in Persia and the land of Israel. Meanwhile, the Lakhmids had gradually allowed the introduction of Byzantine Christianity into Arabia.

In the fifth century CE, Arabia found itself between the competing empires of Christian Byzantium of the Eastern Roman empire and Zoroastrian Persia. Neutrality and good trade relations with both empires was essential to the prosperity of the Arabian trade routes, both of which had allies and even established colonies in Arabia. But this policy of tolerance was leading to the disintegration of the kingdom.

About the year 500 CE, the king of Himyar, Abu-Kariba Assad Tubba', undertook a military expedition into northern Arabia in an effort to eliminate Byzantine influence. The Byzantine emperors had looked to the Arabian Peninsula as a region in which to control the lucrative spice trade and the route to India. Without actually staging a conquest of the region, the Byzantines hoped to establish a protectorate over the Arabians by converting them to Christianity, which would provide commercial advantages as it did in Ethiopia. The Byzantines had made some progress in northern Arabia but had little success in the areas of Himyar that had Jewish influence.

Now we turn our focus to Persia, where events in the Persian Jewish community would greatly influence events in Arabia.

Attempts at Jewish Autonomy in Persia
Influenced Similar Attempts in Arabia

During this time in Persia, the Mazdakite religion, a form of Zoroastrianism, was flourishing. The Mazdakites persecuted Jews and Christians, rioting in various Jewish towns in villages, kidnapping children to convert to their religion.

Exilarch[1] Mar Zutra II requested from Persian King Kovad (r488-531 CE) the right to autonomous self defense against the Mazdakites. This was denied. Mar Zutra II then raised an army including an elite group of 400 soldiers for the defense of the Jewish community. Having been denied autonomy, he declared independence. He succeeded in maintaining an independent state for seven years (513-520 CE), collecting revenue even from the non-Jewish population.

King Kovad vanquished the Exilarch's state; he accused Mar Zutra II of mis-using tax money for personal use. The king crucified Mar Zutra II, only twenty-two years of age, together with his father Mar Hanina on the bridge of Machoza, his capital, 520 CE. His infant son, Mar Zutra III, was carried to Israel, where he later founded a new line of *nasi'im* (religious leaders).

Connection between Attempts at Jewish Autonomy
in Persia and Events in Arabia

The king of Himyar was Abu-Kariba. His grandson, Shamir al-Janah had been sent to India and married the daughter of the Jewish Exilarch Huna V (r465-470). From this union Dhu Nuwas was born, nephew of Mar Zutra II. Upon the failure of his uncle Mar Zutra II to create a Jewish state in Persia, Dhu Nuwas returned to Arabia, killed

---

1. The Exilarch was the political head of diaspora Jewry. The daughter of Exilarch Huna VI married Mar Hanina, the head of the Talmudical academy. Their son was Mar Zutra II. He was a minor when Huna VI died in 508, so a rival claimant named Pachda was appointed as regent to the Exilarchate. When Pachda died with no male heir, Mar Zutra II became the next Exilarch.

the Lakhmid ruler, sacked the Byzantine colony of Najran, and attempted to rally all Arabia to his cause. He was the first to introduce rabbinic Jewish customs to Arabia. By adopting the more conventional version of Judaism, he hoped to claim the rights and honors of a Tobiad ruler of the Transjordan, from the "Nile to the Euphrates". He styled himself "The King of all the [Twelve] Tribes".

The Byzantines pressured the Jews in Tiberias to stop Dhu Nuwas, and provided ships to Abyssian troops to invade Himyar. Dhu Nuwas was killed in the ensuing battle, and this brought to the end the last remnants of the Second Jewish Commonwealth, four hundred and fifty years after the destruction of the Second Temple. The ambitions of Dhu Nuwas the Tobiad, who traced his lineage and rights to Joseph the interpreter of dreams, to rule the Transjordan were left unfulfilled.

The above is an excerpt from "Yosef Dhu Nuwas, a Sadducean King with Sidelocks" by Ben Abrahamson

Chaos in Arabia thus set the stage for Muhammed's ministry. The Prophet stood up to threats of damnation from warring sides and declared a return to the Abrahamic faith, what we also call Noahism.

> **Follow the messenger, the gentile prophet** [Muhammed], **whom they find written in their Torah and Gospel. He exhorts them to be righteous, enjoins them from evil, allows for them all good food, and prohibits that which is bad,** *and unloads the burdens and the shackles imposed upon them.* **Those who believe in him, respect him, support him, and follow the light that came with him are the successful ones."** (Qur'an, *Al-Araf* 7:157)

A friend: I have no doubt that the capital of HaDramaut in Yemen is the very same HaTzramut detailed among the descendants of Shem's grandson *Ever*.

David Ben Abraham: Thanks for this wonderful post! Nestorian records do, indeed, mention that Dhu-Nuwas' mother was a "Jewish captive from Nisibis". I have always found this interesting. Where is your source taken from, where you wrote: "Abu-Kariba's grandson Shamir al-Janah, who had been sent to India, married the daughter of the Jewish Exilarch Huna V (r465-470)." Where is it that we learn that she was the daughter of the Jewish Exilarch, Huna?

Ben: This is written up in some detail by Tabari. Additional support for this claim is Dhu Nuwas' title to be "king of all the tribes" and the Byzantines' use of the *nasi* (leader) in Tiberias, who would have been his cousin, to pressure him to stop his campaigns. Correlating the research of Graetz[1] with Tabari yields the conclusions that I present above.

   The name Dhu Nuwas itself means "lord of beautiful sidelocks (*peyot*)" which was a Persian rabbinic custom and not known in Sadducean Arabia, which is why it made such a lasting impression that it should become his cognomen. The white dove of Tubbu' / Tobiads is still displayed on the "Ark of the Covenant" that was captured from Dhu Nuwas in 525 CE and brought to Axum in Ethiopia.

David Ben Abraham: Very interesting. However, I am not sure that it is possible to conflate the historical account left to us by Tabari with the scholarly work left to us by Graetz. There should always be more solid evidence when making an affirmative statement that Abu-Kariba's grandson, Shamir al-Janah, married the daughter of the Jewish Exilarch Huna V. Are there records showing that the daughter of the Jewish Exilarch Huna was, indeed, taken captive and sold to a Yemeni king? Was she originally brought to Yemen from Nisibis? These facts are wanting.

---

1. Nineteenth-century Jewish historian, Poland. Authored *The History of the Jews,* which was groundbreaking as he wrote about Jewish history from a Jewish perspective.

Ben: Yes I agree. This is of course, research in progress. This period is difficult, because the available evidence is lacking to prove any theory. The technique I use is based on comparative study across the religious boundaries of the confessional corpora. It is interdisciplinary literary approach based on historigraphical evidence and supplemented by archaeological evidence where available. But at best, lacking "hard evidence" it will always remain a theory.

I am trying to track down details concerning possible written correspondence between the *nasi* in Tiberias and Dhu Nuwas, as well as the circumstances surrounding the burial of the Tubban kings of Himyar in Beit She'arim, hoping to shed light on the relationship between the Tubba's and the family of the Exilarch. Later marriages with Exilarch's family and the Quraish are detailed in Abu 'Ubayda Ma'mar b. al-Muthanna's (d. 210/825) *Kitab al-mathalib*, and another work *Kitab al-munammaq* and also, Ibn al-Kalbi's (d. 204/819) book *Kitab mathalib al-'arab*.

David Ben Abraham: Your passion for understanding the past history of Arabia (Tabari, Ibn-Hisham, Al-Hamdani, Ibn-Khaldoun, etc.) is commendable. I will do my best to share with you the information that is known to me. Hopefully, we will be able to glean more information from these ancient sources, along with those that you have already mentioned. There is much still to learn. *Yishar koach* (good job)!

12. Constitution of Medina

The Agreement that Muhammed (pbuh) made with tribes that dwelled in Medina is a crucial point in understanding Muslim-Jewish relations. Was this document only relevant to the circumstances of the day, or did it apply to future generations as well? Who were the tribes that the constitution was made with? Idolaters? Sadducean Jews?

Ben: The *Sahifat al-Medinah* (Constitution of Medina) exists in two recensions (versions), one of Ibn Hisham (d. 833) by way of Ibn Ishaq (d. 767),[1] the other of Abu `Ubayd (d. 838) from al-Zuhri (d. 742). The Constitution of Medina is also found in other books, but these would still seem to rely upon the recensions of Abu `Ubayd and of Ibn Ishaq.

A simple reading of the document leaves one with the impression that it was meant as a blueprint for a politico-religious community, uniting Muslims and Jews under the protection of God (*dhimmat Allah*) so that they might fight "in the way of God" (section 17). Many Oriental scholars, perhaps influenced by Wellhausen and nineteenth century German historical revisionism,[2] approach the text taking for granted antipathy towards the Jews assumed to be found in the Qur'an and Muhammed's biography (*sira*), while minimizing both the part of the Jews and of religion.

---

1. Islamic scholar Ibn Hisham of Arabia and Egypt edited the biography of Muhammed that was written by historian Ibn Ishaq.

2. See footnote on Wellhausen, Chapter 8.

The most prominent Jewish tribes in the *sira* are Nadir, Qurayza, and Qaynuqa`. At the time of the Constitution's writing, Muhammed was getting along with these major Jewish tribes, even declaring Jews and Muslims as an *Umma Wahida* (one nation) with a unified judicial system.

If Muhammed had intended treachery against the Jews at the time of writing the Constitution, he would have specifically mentioned the names of these three most prominent tribes. Instead, he mentioned minor Jewish clans, and some even not by name.

Wellhausen and Wensinck[1] assume that the three major Jewish tribes must have been intended. It is true that the Prophet later fought these tribes, and so the revisionists postulated treachery on the part of the Prophet and asserted that the document did not represent a real agreement with the Jews. However, subsequent warring does not prove retroactive treachery.

This is an example of how the meaning of an authentic historical document can change based on the context that the modern scholars read into it.

Hisham: I read the document in Arabic, and I do agree that one perceives Muhammed's peaceful intentions to create an *Umma Wahida*. However, don't you think that maybe the Jews of Medina didn't get the point? So the antipathy of the Prophet towards them (if there was any) was a result of this inability of Medina's Jews to see the bigger picture?

Ben responds that antipathy towards the Jews was read into the text by German revisionists: Unfortunately, and perhaps ironically, many modern Islamic historians follow Wellhausen and his revisionist school of thought. Welhausen claimed two things: treachery on the part of Muhammed and that the Constitution was a limited political agreement with the tribes of Medina.

---

1. Nineteenth-century German revisionists

However, the tribes mentioned in the Constitution did not live within Medina. The revisionists' tendency to downgrade the agreement to an "exclusively political unity" that "served purely political ends" seems to go against the text. The very first line stresses that the believers and those who follow them are "a single community" (*umma wahida*), a phrase which is used several times in the Qur'an to denote a people who were, are or could have been, one community under God. It is generally thought that they lived near Medina but outside it. The Constitution does not make a strong point of where they lived. For instance, the Banu Qurayza, a Jewish tribe in Medina, lived in fortresses called *utum*, in plains stretching to Medina. The names Nadir, Qurayza, and Qaynuqa` are not expressly mentioned. Yet because of assumed antipathy by the German revisionists, they are read into the text to the point that Welhausen says, "[the Prophet pbuh] had in view the expulsion of the Jews even at the moment of its writing".

Hisham points out: The Prophet refused to even wink at a companion because he considered it a way of lying and said to him: "**A Prophet would never have treacherous eyes.**" Let alone sign a treaty as important as this one with intentions of betrayal.

The *Sahifat al-Medinah* discusses Jews and Muslims, both "sharing the same religious orientation". The recension of Abu `Ubayd says "the Jews ... are a community of believers *(umma min al-mu'minun)*" as opposed to the reading of Ibn Ishaq: "the Jews ... are a community with the believers *(umma ma`a al-mu'minun)*".

Ben: The concept of *mu'min* (believer) in Arabic as well as *ma'amin* (believer) in Hebrew means one who trusts in Allah. However, a related meaning is that *mu'min* carries the connotation of one who provides security, and is trustworthy and reliable. It is not just one who trusts in God but is himself trustworthy. Thus in Arabic, as in Hebrew, the recognition of who is a believer is tied to concepts of a secure community. It is in this sense that it the word *mu'min* was used in *Sahifat al-Madinah*; it is this sense which is essential to peacemaking in the Middle East.

> **O Mankind! We created you from one male and one female, and made you into different nations and tribes only so you may know (*lita'arafu*) each other. Verily the most honoured of you in the sight of God is the one who is most righteous. Truly God has complete knowledge of all things, and is fully aware.** (Qur'an, *Al-Hujurat* 49:13)

The word *lita'arafu* has the connotation of to "acknowledge" and "recognize" and is related to the root *bil-ma'rufi,* which means to be fair, honorable, and behave in a kind manner.

> **Unto this, then, summon** [O Muhammed]. **And be thou upright as thou art commanded, and follow not their lusts** [for you to be like them], **but say** [to the people of the book]: **I believe in whatever scripture Allah hath sent down, and I am commanded to be just among you. Allah is our Lord and your Lord. Unto us our works and unto you your works; no argument between us and you. Allah will bring us together, and unto Him is the journeying.** (Qur'an, *Ash-Shura* 42:15)

13. The Conquest of Jerusalem 614 CE
A Historical Reconstruction Based on Sebeos

*Wars between Persia and Roman Byzantium created chaos and hopes
for religious redemption. This was the backdrop of Muhammed's
ministry, who declared that redemption comes not from choosing sides
but from a return to the original teachings of Abraham.*

King Khosrau of Persia Invades Westward

Ben Abrahamson: In the year 614 CE, the Sassanid king of Persia, Khosrou
 Parviz, invaded Asia Minor and Syria. He claimed that his purpose
 was to avenge the murder of his father-in-law, the Roman Byzantine
 Emperor Maurice, who had been killed by the usurper Phocas. In
 reality, king Khosrau had his eye on Egypt, which was under Byzantine rule. Egypt was in rebellion against Phocas, and if Khosrau
 could conquer Egypt, he could make peace with Phocas. All that
 remained between Persia and Egypt was Syria-Palestine. Khosrau

developed a plan: He could gain Egypt, settle his domestic problems, and gain the Jews as a powerful ally if he declared the Jews entitled to reclaim their ancestral homeland. The Jews may or may not succeed, but they would keep the Roman Byzantines busy as he concentrated on Egypt.

Jewish Exilarch Nehemiah Leads Persian Troops

In 608 CE, Khosrau had placed the son of the Jewish Exilarch, Nehemiah ben Hushiel, as the symbolic leader of the Persian troops. Nehemiah was a mystic so Khosrau knew he would not interfere in military affairs. Promising to re-enact the military feats of bygone years, the Exilarch drafted a Jewish army said to have consisted of 20,000 men. In return Khosrau allowed the reopening of the leading Jewish academies Pumbedisa (607) and Sura (609); later Khosrau wrote to the Roman Byzantine Emperor Phocas, "Do not deceive yourself with your vain hopes, for how can that Christ who was unable to save himself from the Jews [but was crucified instead] save you from me [and my Jews]? For [even] if you descend to the bottom of the sea, I shall stretch forth my hands and seize you. And then you will see me under circumstances which you would rather not."

Hearing news of the Exilarchs' march in full splendor at the head of the combined Judeo-Persian forces, Jews expected the miraculous. In Antioch, Syria, the Jews rioted, killing the Christian Patriarch. In Arabia, they rioted and killed the Christian representative in Yemen. The book of Zerubavel attributes these events to the miraculous work of the prophetess Hefzibah. Within a few years, Phocus' armies were put to rout in succession: Khosrau reached both Edessa (modern Urfa, in Asia Minor), and Aleppo and Antioch in Syria. Khosrau set the Exilarch up with a full court in Edessa. In the twentieth year of king Khosrau's reign [610], Persian general Shahen raided the western areas, reaching Caesarea in Israel. While the Christian inhabitants of the city departed, the Jews submitted to Shahen. He remained in that city for one year. Everything was going according to Khosrau's plan: Persia would conquer Egypt, then Persia would make peace with Phocas.

General Heraclius Becomes Byzantine Emperor

Then the unexpected happened. When the Byzantine ministers saw that Phocas could not protect Egypt, they sought help from the African governor, the powerful Exarch of Carthage. He sent his son, General Heraclius, to Constantinople with a strong fleet. Heraclius had been one of Byzantine Emperor Maurice's key generals in the war with Persia in 590. With the support of Priscus, one of Emperor Phocas' top military leaders, the patriarch Sergius and the Green political faction, Heraclius overthrew Phocas and personally executed him. On October 5, 610, Heraclius I was crowned Emperor (r610-641). Thus, this leader of a rebel province had become the Emperor of Roman Byzantium. This was not according to Khosrau's plan. According to Islamic historians, this happened the year Muhammed was appointed to Prophethood.

When Heraclius took power, the Byzantine Empire was in a desperate situation and he considered moving the capital from Constantinople to Carthage. He dispatched messengers with great treasures and edicts to king Khosrau requesting peace. King Khosrau, however, did not listen. He said: "That kingdom belongs to me, and I shall enthrone Maurice's son, Theodosius, as emperor. [As for Heraclius], he went and took the rule without our order and now offers us our own treasure as gifts. But I shall not stop until I have him in my hands." Taking the treasure, Khosrau commanded that his envoys be killed and he did not respond to his message.

The moral excuse for which Khosrau had started the war was no longer valid after the deposition and execution of Phocas. If the object of his war really had been to avenge the murder of his ally, Byzantine Emperor Maurice, he would have made peace with the new Emperor Haraclius after Phocas' demise, but Persia continued to fight.

In 612 CE, to counter the Persian choice of the Jewish Exilarch,

Heraclius summoned the priest P'ilipikos to military service. This P'ilipikos was the son-in-law of Emperor Maurice and had long served in the military. Then, he had cut his hair and donned priestly garb, becoming a soldier for the church. Heraclius forcibly made him general and dispatched him to the East with a large army. This gave the war the color of a holy crusade.

Heraclius was a brilliant general and he ranked among the greatest of the Byzantine emperors. His reforms of the government reduced the corruption which had taken hold under the disastrous reign of his predecessor Phocas, and he reorganized the military with great success. He developed the idea of granting land to individuals in return for hereditary military service. This arrangement ensured the continuance of the Empire for hundreds of years and enabled Heraclius to reconquer lands taken by the Persians, ravaging Persia along the way.

Residents of the Holy Land Unite with Persia against Byzantium

After the Persian conquest of Caesarea in 610 CE, the entire area of Israel willingly submitted to Persian King Khosrau. A contemporary historian wrote: "The remnants of the Hebrew people took in hand their native zeal [The translation is uncertain: perhaps "manifesting desire for their homeland"] and wrought very damaging slaughters among the multitude of believers." At that time, the army of the king of Persia was stationed at Caesarea. The Jews and Persians were joined by Benjamin of Tiberias, who enlisted additional Jewish soldiers plus residents of Nazareth and the mountain cities of Galilee. They marched on Jerusalem with the Persian division commanded by Shahrbaraz (Rhazmiozan). Later they were joined by Jews of southern Israel. Supported by a band of Arabs, the united forces surrounded Jerusalem in July, 614 CE.

Conquest and Disaster at Jerusalem

Shahrbaraz encouraged the inhabitants of Jerusalem to submit voluntarily. The noble citizens of Jerusalem submitted, offering gifts to the general and princes, and requesting that a loyal *ostikan*, governor, be stationed to preserve the city. This governor was none other than Exilarch Nehemiah ben Hushiel. Thus, five years after his appointment to lead the conquest of Israel and the "ingathering of the Jewish nation", the Exilarch Nehemiah was made ruler of Jerusalem. He was a strong young man, handsome and adorned in royal robes. He began the work of rebuilding the Temple by sorting out genealogies to establish a new High Priesthood. The Jews were exuberant, but an uneasy, explosive, tension was in the air.

Several months later a riot occurred in the city. A mob of young Christians united and killed Nehemiah and his "council of the righteous". They dragged their bodies through the street and dumped them over the city wall. Then the whole Christian population rebelled against Persian rule; a battle took place among the inhabitants of the city of Jerusalem between Jew and Christian. The Christians grew stronger and killed many of the Jews. The remainder of the Jews escaped and joined the Persian army in Caesarea.

Persian General Xorheam then assembled his troops and sieged Jerusalem, warring against it for nineteen days. Digging beneath the foundations of the city, they destroyed the wall. On the nineteenth day of the siege, the Persian and Jewish forces took Jerusalem. According to Christian sources, they put their swords to work for three days, slaughtering almost all the people in the city, then burning the place down.

According to Christian sources, 35,000 Christians were taken alive, among whom was a certain Christian Patriarch named Zak'aria who was custodian of the Cross. A century later, Christian sources claimed that the Jews purchased Christian slaves in order to slaughter them. The Jewish soldiers spoke about the Staff of Aaron, the "Rod of Hefzibah", which they claimed would bring victory in battle. The Christians called it "the remnant of the Holy Cross". The Persian soldiers pressed the clerics to reveal the location of this treasure, executing some. Finally the clerics pointed out the place where it was hidden. The Persians took it into captivity and also melted the city's silver and gold, which they took to the court of the king.

According to Christian sources, Persians and Jews swept through

Israel, destroyed many monasteries, and expelled or killed the monks. Bands of Jews from Jerusalem, Tiberias, Galilee, Damascus, and even Cyprus, united and undertook an incursion against Tyre, having been invited by the 4,000 Jewish inhabitants of that city to surprise and massacre Tyre's Christians on Easter night. The expedition failed, as the Christians of Tyre learned of the impending danger, and seized the 4,000 Tyrian Jews as hostages. The Jewish soldiers destroyed the churches around Tyre, an act which the Christians avenged by killing 2,000 of their Jewish prisoners. To save the remaining Jewish prisoners, the besiegers withdrew.

According to Jewish sources, the immediate results of these wars filled the Jews with messianic expectation. Many Christians converted to Judaism. A famous monk in Sinai embraced Judaism of his own free will, and became a vehement assailant of his former belief. The Judaic nation was free from the Christian yoke for about fourteen years; and they seem to have deluded themselves with the hope that Khosrau would assign Jerusalem and a province to them in order that they might establish a Jewish commonwealth.

Persecution of Jews in Byzantine Lands and Khosrau's Response to the Sack of Jerusalem

The Byzantine response was swift. The largest ever meeting of Merovingian Bishops, the Fifth Council of Paris in Gaul (France), took place to counter this Jewish insolence. They decided that all Jews residing in the Byzantine Empire who held military or civil positions must accept baptism together with their families. Massive anti-Jewish persecutions began to occur throughout the Roman Byzantine Empire.

Reports of the sack of Jerusalem terrified Khosrau. He did not intend for things to go this far. He issued an order to have mercy on prisoners, to build a city and settle them there, establishing each person in his former rank. His betrayal of the Jews culminated in his command that the Jews be driven from the city. At the time, Persian Jewish troops were stationed outside the Eastern Gate of the Temple Mount.

The distrust between the Jews and Khosrau reached its height, as the Jews accused Khosrau of plotting the assassination of Nehemiah. This discord between the allies ended in the deportation of many Jews to Persia. Nehemiah's brother Shallum was sold into slavery until his redemption a full ten years later.

Effect of Wars between Persia and Byzantium on Arabia

Within a year after the Persian conquest of Jerusalem, Persian troops overran Jordan, Israel, and the Sinai Peninsula, reaching the frontiers of Egypt. Arabia was split between those who supported Persia and those for Byzantium. In Mecca, Muhammed had declared his support for the Byzantines. His followers were thus opposed by the chiefs of the Quraish, who were Muhammed's family and supporters of Persia. The conflict had reached such a state that in 615 CE, a substantial number of Prophet's followers fled Arabia and took refuge in the Christian kingdom of *Habash* (Ethiopia), which was an ally of Byzantinium.

The Byzantines were losing ground. In Asia Minor the Persians pushed them back to Bosporus, and in 617 CE, they captured Chalcedon (modern Kadikoy) just opposite Constantinople. As a gesture to the Byzantines, Khosrau granted amnesty to prisoners. He ordered Jewish soldiers to leave Jerusalem and forbade Jews to settle within a three-mile radius of the city, and placed Christian archpriest Modestos over the city as governor.

Disillusioned with Persian promises, the Jewish soldiers did not heed Khosrau and continued to encamp outside golden gate.

By 619 CE, Egypt had passed into Persian hands and the Persian armies had reached as far as Tripoli. The Byzantine Emperor sent an envoy to Khosrau, praying that he was ready to have peace on any terms, but Khosrau replied, "I shall not give protection to the emperor until he is brought in chains before me and gives up obedience to his crucified god and adopts submission to the fire god." However, Khosrau, as a gesture to the Byzantines, withdrew his protection over the Jewish troops encamped outside the Golden Gate. The Byzantines then violently slaughtered the trapped Jewish regiment outside Golden Gate and left the bodies to rot. As many as 20,000 were killed. The Golden Gate was sealed. In Arabia, the year it was called "the Year of Sorrow". It was during these events that the Prophet had his "Night Journey" vision, flying from Mecca to Jerusalem on a winged animal.

Byzantine Emperor Heraclius, unsatisfied with Persian gestures, went on a rampage killing every Jew found in Israel. Men, women and children were killed without mercy, sparking the author of "The Prayer of Shimon bar Yochai" to bemoan how quickly the priests granted forgiveness to the soldiers after committing such attrocities. By 622 CE, the Emperor Heraclius had assembled an international army against the Persians. He had retaken Judea from the Sassanid Persians and the Jewish cause looked hopeless.

Signs of the Coming of the Prophet

With the death of Nehemiah ben Hushiel, the Jewish nation tried to grapple with the meaning of these events in terms of their literary heritage. They would come to the Golden Gate to pray. According to Jewish tradition, the Messiah of Joseph was destined to die before the arrival of the King Messiah of David, so Nehemiah must have been the Messiah of Joseph. This meant that the King Messiah was sure to follow. However, before the King Messiah could appear, he would be preceded by Elijah the Prophet. Their leaders said "A Prophet is about to arise; his time draws near. We shall follow him; and then we shall slay [our enemies] with [divine] slaughter ..." As the common people became aware of the Prophet, "they spoke one to another—surely know that is the same Prophet whom the Jews [Cohanim, Priests] warn us about."

Prophet Daniel had prophesied that there would be seventy weeks of years until the Temple would be rebuilt; 490 (seventy times seven) years had passed from the destruction of Bar Kochba's armies until this year (622 CE). Bar Kochba was a failed Messiah; now the true Messiah would arrive.

A warrior with "the helmet of deliverance on His head" and clad in armor.

He will don garments of vengeance [as his] **clothing and will put on a cloak of zealousness.**

He will fight the final battle of *Gog u-Magog* [the final wars that catalyze the advent of the Messiah] **and against the army of Armilos** [meaning here Heraclius].

Parents hoping that their child might be this Messiah might name him after Daniel, *ish HaMuDot*, Man of Delights—*muHaMuD*.

In 620 CE, the Prophet Muhammed, aware of these successive developments, and the renewed opposition of the Quraish, set out for Tayif (sixty or seventy miles to the east of Mecca). He ministered to the Arabian tribes. In opposition to Sadducean Jewish traditions, he stressed resurrection from the dead, and the importance of prayer five times a day.

After being unsuccessful in trying to convince them of his message, he was met by Addas, a young Christian boy at the outskirts of the city, who embraced Muhammed's message. Here Muhammed is said to have encountered the souls of those slaughtered at the Golden Gate. These "souls of the Garden", or *jinn*,[1] accepted Muhammed's message. The Qur'an states:

And when [the Lord] **turned towards you a party of the Jinn who listened to the Quran; so when they came to it, they said: Be silent; then when it was finished, they turned back to their people warning** [them]. **They said: O our people! we have listened to a Book revealed after Moses verifying that which is before it, guiding to the truth and to a right path.**

The commentators say these *jinn* were Jewish. In short, the Jewish souls were willing to accept his message. Thus began Muhammed's leadership.

---

1. Similar to the word *gan* in Hebrew, which means garden

Mahmoud Abo AlSamen: Islamic sources confirm that Caliph Umar was determined to construct Al-Aqsa Mosque, that's why he removed the garbage located there, but not to give it to the Jews. Didn't he tell Ka'ab Al-Ahbar[1] "you imitated Judaism!"? Do we have any Islamic sources to back up this interesting story?

Ben: No. Only Sebeos[2] and various documents from the Cairo Geniza.

Mahmoud Abo AlSamen: Do we have any Islamic sources related to the Exilarchs?

Ben: Yes, almost all the information about the Exilarchs from this period comes from Islamic sources.

Mahmoud Abo AlSamen: Concerning the treaty known as the "*Al-'Uhdah Al-'Umariyah*",[3] I don't accept its historicity, because I know that Caliph Umar I, Umar Ibn Al-Khattab,[4] invited the Jews to come back to Jerusalem and didn't ban them as some sources suggest.

Ben: I favor the opinion of those scholars who attribute *Al-'Uhdah Al-'Umariyah* to Umar ibn Abd al-Aziz[5] of a later date.

Mahmoud Abo AlSamen: Do the sources differentiate between a Jewish leader from an Exilarch who is entitled to rule all Jews in exile? Or do they just point to them as "Jewish leaders" with no elaboration?

---

1. An early convert to Islam, Al-Ahbar was a Jew from Yemen who accompanied Caliph Umar on his campaigm to Jerusalem and directed him to build a place of worship on the Temple Mount.

2. Seventh-century bishop and historian, Armenia.

3. Umar's declarations against the Jews

4. Seventh-century ruler of Muslim world and one of the *sahaba* (companions of Muhammed)

5. Eighth-century caliph

Ben: Islamic sources specifically call the Exilarch by the term *Reish Jaluta* derived from the Hebrew title *Reish Galuta*. Look up the history of the
Exilarch Bostanai. Most of the primary sources about him are Islamic.

See also the book of Abu 'Ubayda Ma'mar b. al-Muthanna[1] called
Kitab al-mathalib and another work *Kitab al-munammaq* and also Ibn
al-Kalbi's[2] book *Kitab mathalib al-'arab*. These works document the numerous marriages between the Quraish[3] and members of the "noble
house" of the Jewish Exilarch.[4,5]

Mahmoud Abo AlSamen: *Al-'Uhdah Al-'Umariyah* is clearly attributed to
the Caliph Umar I, Umar Ibn Al-Khattab, in our sources. There are
three narrations as far as I know. The longest and most complete
account is narrated by Al-Tabari[6] with a discontinuation of *Isnad*
(transmission) of about 100 years. It clearly says " ... Allah's servant
Umar Ibn Al-Khattab *Ameer Al-M'umineen* ..."[7]

A shortened story appears in the history of the Shi'ite historian
Ya'qobi[8] that refers to "Umar Ibn Al-Khattab" alone with no *Ameer
Al-M'umineen*—as he doesn't believe he was a legal Caliph.[9] The third

---

1. Eighth-century Islamic scholar and linguist, Persia

2. Eighth-century Islamic historian and genealogist, modern-day Iraq

3. Family from which Muhammed hailed

4. Michael Lecker of Hebrew University discusses this in his article, "A note on early
marriage links between Qurashis and Jewish women", in *Jerusalem Studies in Arabic and
Islam* (1987).

5. The sources I used were from Goldziber, Renseignements de Source Musulmane sur
la Dignité du Resch-Galuta, in R. E. J. 1884, pp. 121-125. A quote connecting the Exilarch
with the martyrs at *Karbala* is given on page 123.

6. (Tabari 3\607)

7. *Ameer Al-M'umineen* means Commander of the Believers and refers to a caliph,
religious and political leader of Muslim state.

8. Ninth-century Muslim geographer

9. Ya'qobi 2\147

is narrated by Ibn Habban, and I didn't look it up. I've read many Islamic studies discussing the authenticity of this document, which all arrive at the conclusion that it cannot be attributed to Caliph Umar I, Umar Ibn Al-Kattab.

Exilarch Bostanai (Khouli Al-Asbahi) appears a lot in Shi'ite resources to have been involved in many of the violent events during the *fitna* (civil war). He is said to have killed Caliph Yazid Ibn M'uawiyah in 683 CE, while Sunni sources say that Al- N'uman Ibn Basheer is the one who killed Yazid.

Can I know what the exact word is for "Exilarch" in Arabic?

Ben: The exact Arabic term for Exilarch was *Ras al-jalut*. According to Graetz there were two lines of the Exilarch after 642 CE, a deposed militant line that led to Abu Isa al-Isfahani,[1] and a line of scholars that was supported by the Caliphate that began with Bostanai.

Mahmoud Abo AlSamen: Many thanks, brother.

Some help in keeping the names straight:

- *King Khosrau—Sassanid King of Persia, enticed Jewish allegience by promising to help them reclaim the Holy Land.*

- *Emperor Maurice—Roman Byzantine King, usurped by Phocas*

- *General Heraclius— Roman Byzantine general under Maurice, usurped Phocas and crowned emperor 610 CE*

- *Nechemia ben Hushiel— Son of Jewish Exilarch, inherited the exilarchy, general of Persian troops under Khosrau, assassinated in Jerusalem by Byzantines, 614CE*

- *Pilipikos—Priest and later general under Heraclius*

---

1. Self-proclaimed Jewish prophet, eighth-century Persia

14. Different Languages for Different *Ummas*

Holy scriptures are written in Hebrew, Aramaic, Arabic, Greek,
with different dialects thereof. Diverse languages are vital in
relating to the various needs and natures of the peoples being
addressed—they are part of our divine diversity. And—who were
the "lost sheep of Israel"?

A friend asks: Why wasn't the Torah given in Arabic through an angel like the Qur'an?

Ben: In my opinion, I wouldn't think that one would expect either the Torah or the *Injeel* (New Testament) to be in Arabic because they were given to different *ummas* (peoples). The Qur'an says:

> **We sent not a *rasul* [Law Giver] except to teach in the language of his own people, in order to make things clear to them. Now Allah leaves straying those whom He pleases and guides whom He pleases: And He is exalted in power, full of wisdom.** (Qur'an, *Ibrahim* 14:4)

It would make sense that the Torah was given in Hebrew and the *Injeel* in Greek because otherwise the *umma* to which it was sent would not understand it.

Had We sent this as a Qur'an [in the language] **other than Arabic, they would have said: "Why are not its verses explained in detail**? (Qur'an, *Fussilat* 41:44)

As far as whether scripture is written in first person, second person, or third person, this would depend on the nature of the revelation. In both *ahadith* (traditions) and the Torah it is taught that the level of Moses' revelation was such that he was not taught through an angel. Thus the Torah writes in second person, **"And the Lord said to Moses, saying, speak to the Children of Israel saying ... ."** There is a rabbinic teaching that each revelation is given to an *umma* exactly according to its needs and character. The language, form, style, and content of the revelation exactly match the path required for the *umma* to accomplish its mission.

I am reminded of this rabbinic teaching when I read the *ayah*:

And among His Signs is the creation of the Heavens and the Earth, and the variations in your languages and your colours, verily in that are Signs for those who reflect.
(Qur'an, *Ar-Rum* 30:22)

The word "signs" comes from a Semitic root which also means "Letters [of the alphabet]" as well as "wonders" or "miracles".

Judaism teaches that there is only one Book in Heaven. But when it was given at Mount Sinai it was translated to seventy languages (all the languages of the world). And each *umma* is responsible for the version that they received by the hands of the Prophet (pbu them) that was assigned to them. As Allah says most perfectly:

To every people [is given] **a *rasul*** [law giver]: **when their Law Giver comes** [before them] **the matter will be judged between them with justice and they will not be wronged.**
(Qur'an, *Al-Yunus* 10:47)

The rabbinic version of this teaching is encapsulated thus:

**And he said, The LORD came from Sinai, and rose up from
Seir unto them; He shined forth from mount Paran, and
He came with ten thousands of saints** [prophets]: **from
His right hand went a fiery law for them** [*shari'a*/covenant].
(Deuteronomy 33:2)

As well as:

**God cometh from Teman, and the Holy One from mount
Paran, selah. His glory covereth the heavens, and the earth
is full of His praise ... He stood, and measured the earth: he
beheld, and drove asunder the nations; and the everlasting
mountains were scattered, the perpetual hills did bow: His
ways are everlasting.** (Habakuk 3:3,6)

The word "measured" in Hebrew is the same word as "character-
ized", and "drove asunder" is related to "excesses" so this verse is
understood to teach: "He stood, and characterized [the nations of]
the earth: He saw the excesses of the nations; and the everlasting
mountains were scattered, the perpetual hills did bow [they were
given a path to overcome their bad traits]: His ways are everlasting
[His scripture will never change]."

I understood the *"umma"* of the Prophet 'Isa (Jesus) to be among
the Greek-speaking Christians.

Abdul: If Jesus (pbuh) was sent to Children of Israel, the *Injeel* had to
be in Hebrew, because it was given to the same people, making
them lawful those things which were unlawful for them before
(*Al-Imran* 50), that means Torah, Psalms, and *Injeel* were for the
children of Israel and must have been in Hebrew. Qur'an says

this most acurately because the Qur'an's position towards the children of Israel is very clear, and we have to accept Qur'an as whole:

> **Verily this Qur'án doth explain to the Children of Israel most of the matters in which they disagree.** (Qur'an, *An-Naml* 27:76)

SK: All languages are the same and created by Allah. No nation could be superior for their particular points regarding their language.

The discovery of the manuscript of Book Of Ayob proves that Arabic is the mainstream Semitic language and perhaps much older than Hebrew. Allah knows best.

Eka: Moses spoke in Hebrew, Jesus spoke in Aramaic-Hebrew, and Muhammed spoke in Arabic-Quraish.

Ben: There is support for the theory that Jesus (pbuh) spoke Greek in his sermons. Some of the indications are:

- In the New Testament, three independent witnesses recorded Jesus' speeches. The probability that they would make almost exactly the same translations from Aramaic into Greek is small.
- Peter and John were recognized as "uneducated and untrained men" (Acts 4:13); certainly they did not have special training in the Greek language beyond that of the middle classes, and yet they were able to write in Greek. James, the brother of Jesus, was most likely a carpenter like his father, certainly not one of the social or political elite, and yet he composed a letter in Greek to other Jews less than two decades after the crucifixion.
- The occasional appearance of Aramaic words in the Gospels

lends proof that Jesus did not usually speak in Aramaic. If Jesus usually spoke Aramaic, then why would only a few of these words appear in the Gospels and noted as translations from Aramaic to Greek, if all of his words were translated from Aramaic to Greek?

- There is also the account of the conversation between Jesus before Pilate. In these accounts Jesus speaks to Pilate, and Pilate speaks to Jesus, the priests, and the crowds. There is no mention of an interpreter, and many of the exchanges would not lend themselves to the use of an interpreter. As a Roman, Pilate spoke Latin, but this language was probably not spoken by Jesus, the priests, or the crowd. It also seems unlikely that Pilate had learned Aramaic or Hebrew. Greek would be the natural medium of communication for Pilate to use with the people of Judea.

- John 20 records a meeting between Jesus and Mary after the resurrection. In the middle of the conversation John writes, **"She turned and said to Him in Hebrew, 'Rabboni!' (which means Teacher)"** (v. 16). In the midst of a conversation recorded in Greek, John makes a point of noting Mary's use of Aramaic. It seems safe to conclude that the rest of the conversation actually occurred in Greek.

- In John 21:15-17 a conversation takes place between Jesus and Peter, which involves the interplay of three pairs of near-synonymous Greek terms. These pairs cannot be reproduced in Aramaic or Hebrew. Similarly, the wordplay in Matthew 16:18 is lost in Aramaic or Hebrew. How can this added complexity be explained if these texts are the product of translations?.

- In John 7:35: **"The Jews said to one another, 'Where does this man** [Jesus] **intend to go that we will not find Him? He is not intending to go to the Dispersion among the Greeks,**

and teach the Greeks, is He?" Presumably Jesus would teach the Greeks in Greek, so these Jews must have thought he could speak Greek.

Omar: More likely Aramaic than either Hebrew or Greek. Greek was used by the hellenized Jews (like Saul/Paul), who overwhelmingly appeared to have rejected his message.

Ben: Most people of that period spoke Aramaic and Greek. But Reverend Aaron Tresham, in a survey of the literature, makes a pretty good case that Greek was the language used in Jesus' (pbuh) public sermons.

Omar: There is far more evidence demonstrating it was Aramaic, including the spread of the earliest church among Aramaic speakers, not Greek.

All that came later, with Paul. And there were major rifts as a result.

Leah: "The earliest church of Aramaic speakers (and presumably writers) was lost to history." What about Maronites and Assyrians?

Omar: We have records of their existence, and their conflict with Paul and his Hellenistic version of Christianity, ie, opening it up to non-Jews. The Book of Acts describes the conflicts in the early church. All of these early Christians were Jews, or non-Jews who converted to Judaism, in order to become Christian. The Talmud itself references these groups numerous times, ie, Ebionites and Nazarenes.

So we have lots of evidence of their existence. What we do not have is the scriptures that they used, which are definitively not the New Testament documents we have today, which were indeed drafted in Koine Greek.

To Leah: Syriac is a dialect of Aramaic. It's not necessarily the

Aramaic that Jesus spoke. And unfortunately even their scriptures are derived from the Greek originals, retranslated back into Aramaic.

The original Aramaic theological community is only known through *midrashim*[1] and now through archeology.

Ben: Can you elaborate?

Omar: There are grammatical clues which show an Aramaic origin, not in the scripture, but in the quotations, which were later popularized in Koine.

Ben: Okay, those are linguistic clues. What about *midrashim* or archeology? Do you discount the possibility of a Greek speaking Jesus (pbuh)?

Omar: If he spoke it, he wouldn't have done so fluently in my opinion given his background and social standing.

Also, if we extend the Essene hypothesis further (that he was relating to the Essenes in some way), then preaching in Greek would actually be objectionable.

Malik: "Greek was used by the hellenized Jews (like Saul/Paul)." This idea that Paul uniquely was a hellenized Jew is nonsense. All of second temple Judaism was hellenized, including the factions that denied any such influence.

The question of Jesus' primary language would be settled if we knew what people in Nazareth in the first decades of the first century CE were speaking. Unfortunately, this knowledge is more elusive than we might like. There is evidence, however, that points to the use of Aramaic in the Galilee, the region where Nazareth was located. Such evidence includes inscriptions, contracts, and other ancient writings. It makes sense that residents of Nazareth spoke Aramaic, given the fact that Aramaic became the official language of the Gali-

---

1. Jewish traditional legends

lee from the sixth-century BCE onward. Thus, it seems likely that ordinary residents of the Galilee, including Nazareth, spoke Aramaic as their first language. This was the language of common discourse among Jesus' family and friends.

A few scholars believe that people in Nazareth spoke Hebrew as their primary language. This is possible, but unlikely. Hebrew may well have been used primarily among some people in Judea (south of the Galilee), among Jewish separatists (those who wrote the Dead Sea Scrolls), and among Jewish theologians, but even among these people Aramaic is prevalent. But we have no strong evidence for the common use of Hebrew in Nazareth and the surrounding region of Galilee.

Omar: You said, "All of second temple Judaism was hellenized, including the factions that denied any such influence." They may have had Hellenic influences, but to say they were hellenized is a far cry. Qumran practices would be a deliberate and definite trend in the opposite direction.

Ben: I have proposed that the Essenes were one branch of the Tobiads. The Tobiad family of Jordan, at least according to Josephus, split into a Greek hellenized branch (under Joseph) and an Aramaic-speaking, monastic branch (under Hyrcanus) just prior to the appearance of the Essenes.

Omar: It's fair to say that many of the verses of the New Testament make better sense in Aramaic than in Greek.

I'll give an example. In Mark Chapter 2, when Jesus was being rebuked for picking grain on the Sabbath, he replied **"The Sabbath is made for man, not man for the Sabbath. Therefore, the Son of Man is Lord of the Sabbath."**

Anyone reading this passage in Greek would notice that the word 'therefore' is redundant in this passage. It doesn't actually need to be there in the first place.

The mystery is solved when we read it in Aramaic. In the Aramaic language, the word for "man" and "son of man" is the same. The word is *barnashah*.

When we read it in Aramaic, it goes something like this: 'The Sabbath was made for *Barnashah*, not *Barnashah* for the Sabbath. Therefore, *barnashah* is Lord of the Sabbath.''

Now that makes more sense.

Ben: "There is evidence, however, that points to the use of Aramaic in Galilee" — There is also evidence that points to Greek use in the area around the Sea of Galilee, especially around Beit Shean. According to the New Testament, many people "from the Decapolis" came to hear Jesus (pbuh) speak, and Greek would be a natural choice. I understand that the theory is not that Jesus (pbuh) spoke Greek from day to day, but that he preached in that language.

Malik: So would the language of revelation to the children of Esau be Greek or Aramaic? I would argue Aramaic, for the language of the Tobiads as well, since Greek is not semitic.

Thus, Aramaic should be the language for the *Injeel*, correct?

Ben: I would think that there is pretty good case to say that anyone who holds that the New Testament as we have it today is accurate, would be forced by internal evidence within those documents to conclude that Jesus (pbuh) spoke Greek occasionally, if not exclusively during his public sermons.

Do you think that the "Greeks" and "Jews" of the New Testament refer to ethnicity or spoken language? If I were to claim that the "Greeks" of the New Testament were really hellenized, Greek speaking, intermarried Jews, is there a verse or text that would disprove this?

Ben responds to a friend who proposes that the Torah was revealed in Arabic: The Torah says:

Then you shall declare before the LORD your God: "My father was a wandering Aramean, and he went down into Egypt with a few people and lived there and became a great nation, powerful and numerous." (Deuteronomy 26:5)

The authorized commentaries understand the above verse to mean that the Israelites became a "nation" because they remained "distinct". Rav Huna said in the name of Bar Kapparah: Because of four things Israel was redeemed from Egypt: They didn't change their names or their language, they didn't speak slander, and they did not intermarry (Midrash, *Vayikra Rabba).*

There is a *hadith* that says "Narrated Abu Huraira: The people of the Book used to read the Torah in Hebrew and then explain it in Arabic to the Muslims. Allah's Apostle said [to the Muslims], 'Do not believe the people of the Book, nor disbelieve them, but say, "We believe in Allah and whatever is revealed to us, and whatever is revealed to you" ' (*sahih* Bukhari, Book 92, *hadith* 460).[1]

Although not conclusive, this *hadith* says "The people of the Book used to read the Torah in Hebrew" without a hint that they were reading a translation.

We need not agree to enjoy our spirited discussions!

Ahmed: *Mash'Allah,* loved reading all your comments every one *jazak'Allah*!

Ben: Here is a quote from the Talmud supporting the idea that Galileans spoke Greek (in addition to Hebrew):

The Galileans were not exact in their language. For instance, a certain Galilean once went about inquiring, "Who has *amar*?" "Silly Galilean", they said to him, "do

---

1. *Sahih* Bukhari is a collection of *ahadith.*

**you mean an 'ass' for riding, 'wine' to drink, 'wool' for
clothing or a 'lamb' for killing?" A woman once wished to
say to her friend, "Come, I would give you some fat to eat"
but that what she actually said to her was, "My castaway,
may a lioness devour you."** (Talmud, *Eruvim* 53b)

The examples of dropping letters that don't exist in Greek apparently show Greek influence.

More on the idea that Jesus spoke Greek: Christian tradition has it that the parents of Mary, Anna and Joachim, were natives of Sepphoris, at the time a Greek speaking hellenized town. The town was destroyed after it revolted at the death of Herod the Great in 4 CE. The inhabitants of Sepphoris are assumed to have been buried four kilometers south, in a cemetery which is now located under the town of Nazareth. The "Nazareth Stone" is an inscription in Greek found during the Nazareth excavations dated to 41 CE, probably issued by the Emperor Claudius. It prohibits moving or modifying tombs for the "cult of ancestor worship".

The funerary art of Palmyra may indicate that "ancestor worship" could have been part of the religion of the Tobiads.

JM: The original followers of Jesus were probably both Greek and Aramaic speakers. The Galilee was bilingual at the time of Jesus.

Ben: The question I asked above, could Jesus' sermons have been given in Greek to reach the widest audience? That is to say, the Gospels are—for the most part—not a translation from Aramaic but a record of the actual words spoken in Greek.

Irshad Alam: Jesus's ministry was limited to the Israelites. New Testament: "I've come to save none but the 'lost sheep of the house of Israel'." The Qur'an also says it.

Ben: There were Edomites who were forced to convert to Judaism, who were intermarried with the tribes of Ephraim and Menasseh (some of the lost tribes, the "lost sheep of Israel"). Because their conversion to Judaism was forced, I propose that Jesus released them from their so-called obligation to the Mosaic covenant and said they only had to the keep "the religion of Abraham (pbuh)" or what we call today Noahism.

To Irshad, you write "Jesus's ministry was limited to the Israelites"—but the New Testament says that the Jesus' ministry included converts and intermarried people: "**And do not think you can say to yourselves, 'We have Abraham as our father.' I tell you that out of these stones God can raise up children for Abraham** [referring to the followers around him]" (Mathew 3:9).

Jesus' ministry is described in the Qur'an:

And [appoint him] **a messenger to the Children of Israel** [with this message]: **"I have come to you, with a Sign from your Lord, in that I make for you out of clay, as it were, the figure of a bird, and breathe into it, and it becomes a bird by Allah's leave: And I heal those born blind, and the lepers, and I quicken the dead, by Allah's leave; and I declare to you what ye eat, and what ye store in your houses. Surely therein is a Sign for you if ye did believe;** [I have come to you] **to attest the Law which was before me. And to make lawful to you part of what was** [before] **forbidden to you; I have come to you with a Sign from your Lord. So fear Allah, and obey me. It is Allah Who is my Lord and your Lord; then worship Him. This is a Way that is straight." When Jesus found unbelief on their part He said: "Who will be My helpers to** [the work of] **Allah?" Said the disciples: "We are Allah's helpers: We believe in Allah, and do thou bear witness that we are Muslims."** (Qu'ran, *Al-Imran* 3:49-52)

As a historian, I find the references to clay remind me of the To-rah's references to the "potters of Jordan" called the *Notzrim*. The dove was also the dynastic symbol used by the Tobiads in their religion called *Notzrim*, and the dove was seen as a sign of the "Holy Spirit". When the Prophet 'Isa (pbuh) found unbelief on the part of the Children of Israel, the "helpers" declared their submission. The word there is *ansar* which is also related to *Notzrim*. The Tobiad *Notzrim* were tribes from the Children of Israel who had intermarried with the Ammonites, Moabites, and Edomites. They had been expelled from the nation of Israel by Nehemiah (pbuh) but later were forced to convert to Judaism (against the advice of the Pharisaic Rabbis) by Hasmonean King Alexander Yannai. Thus these *Notzrim* were part of the House of Israel, the Lost Tribes of Israel, but they were not fully considered Jews—Children of Israel.

Technically speaking, the "lost sheep of the house of Israel" refer to intermarried children of Israel who were excluded by proclamation of Prophet Nehemiah (pbuh) and thus not considered Jewish:

And they made proclamation throughout Judah and Jerusalem unto all the children of the captivity, that they should gather themselves together unto Jerusalem; and that whosoever came not within three days, according to the counsel of the princes and the elders, all his substance should be forfeited, and himself separated from the congregation of the captivity. (Ezra 10:6)

But this theory is irrelevant to topic at hand, the language of the sermons that he spoke. There were many of the House of Israel who spoke Greek. See my comment above where I discuss Aaron Tre-sham's M.Div. Th.M. research, where in a survey of the literature, he makes a case that Greek was the language used in Jesus' (pbuh) public sermons.

Allah says:

We sent not a Law Giver [*rasul*] **except** [to teach] **in the language of his** [own] **people, in order to make** [things] **clear to them. Now Allah leaves straying those whom He pleases and guides whom He pleases: and He is Exalted in power, full of Wisdom.** (Qur'an, *Ibrahim* 14.4)

Had We sent this as a Qur'an [in the language] **other than Arabic, they would have said: "Why are not its verses explained in detail?** (Qur'an, *Fussilat* 41:44)

So, doesn't this mean that since the Qur'an wasn't revealed in Hebrew, the Children of Israel would say, "Why are not its verses explained in detail?"

It appears that each *umma* must follow the revelation of the Prophet that was assigned to them, who spoke in their language.

PART III

Islam Today

15. The "Doctrine of Abrogation"

Ben felt compelled to respond to an article that characterizes Islam
as intractably violent.

Ben Abrahamson: On December 12, 2012, Daniel Pinner wrote a response to the Turkish Muslim political and religious commentator Sinem Tezyapar, who wrote an optimistic article under the headline "Islam Mandates Abiding by Peace Agreements". While he lauds her vision of how Jews and Muslims can coexist in peace, he disagrees that her vision is in accordance with the Qur'an and Islamic teachings.

One of his main objections concerns the "Doctrine of Abrogation". He says that because the Qur'an was revealed over the course of twenty-three years and contains numerous seemly contradictory verses, Islamic exegetes resolved these contradictions by asserting that later texts superseded previous ones. He makes his argument by saying that the ninth *sura* (chapter) was written last, and because it was written during a time of war, it "contains no mercy", and thus reflects the "true" (negative) tone of Islam.

I object to this description on the grounds it is both misleading and incorrect. It is not a fair characterization of Islam or Islamic exegesis. First of all, "abrogation" is not an adequate translation of the term *naskh*. In Arabic the word comes from a root which means "to remove" (2:106, 22:52) as well as "to transcribe" (45:29,7:154). It is similar to the Hebrew word *nusakh* which derives from a root which means "to remove" as well as "to formulate" (as in *Nusakh Ashkenaz* or *Nusakh Sefard*). *Naskh* is not a historical exercise of determining which *suras* came first or last—indeed there is not even complete agreement of the order of the *suras*—rather it is a way to explain seeming contradictions between verses or between traditional practices. Early scholars listed as many as 200 changes, although later scholars concluded there were as few as seven examples of *naskh*.

Just like the rabbinic writings explain seemingly contradictory verses by explaining each verse in its appropriate context, Islamic scholars use a similar method to resolve seeming contradictions. For example, Islam recognizes the Mosaic revelation but regards itself as its own unique covenant, with customs that differ from the Mosaic. The change in direction of prayer from Jerusalem to Mecca, the change in fasting on Yom Kippur to fasting on Ramadan, the prohibition of drinking wine, etc. are most definitely not abrogations in the sense that these former practices are no longer worthy. Instead, God explains that for the Islamic community some of these practices have been reformulated *(naskh/nusakh)* differently. While the form may be different, for example the direction of prayer, the essential principle is the same. Indeed the Qur'an says:

> **To Allah belong the east and the West: Whithersoever ye turn, there is the presence of Allah. For Allah is all-Pervading, all-Knowing.** (Qur'an, *Al-Baqarah* 2:115)

Naskh applies to only the customary parts of God's revelation. It does not and cannot apply to the basic fundamental tenets of religion, such as mercy, kindness, and justice. The commentator Tabari explains:

> God alters what was once declared lawful into unlawful, or vice-versa; what was permitted into prohibited and vice-versa. But such changes can occur only in verses conveying commands of form, positive and negative. Verses cast in the absolute and conveying narrative statements can be

affected by neither *nasikh* [abrogating material] nor *mansukh* [abrogated material].

Allah did aforetime take a covenant with the Children of Israel: **and We raised up from among them twelve chieftains. And Allah said, "I am with you. Surely, if you perform the prayer, and pay the alms, and believe in My Messengers, honour and assist them, and loan to Allah a beautiful loan, verily I will wipe out from you your evils, and admit you to gardens with rivers flowing beneath; but if any of you, after this, resisteth faith, he hath truly wandered from the path or rectitude. But because of their breach of their covenant, We cursed them, and made their hearts grow hard; they change the words from their [right] places and forget a good part of the message that was sent them, nor wilt thou cease to find them ever bent on [new] deceits, except a few of them."**

Yet pardon them, and forgive; surely Allah loves the good-doers. (Qur'an, *Al-Maedah* 5:12-16)

Qatada ibn al-Nu'man said *"al-din wahid wa al-shari'a mukhtalifah"* (religion is one, *shari'a* is diverse).[1]

Both Judaism and Islam teach there is only one *deen* which is acceptable to Allah. Islam calls this the *deen* of Islam or just *deen*. Rabbinic Judaism calls this the *deen* of the Prophet Nuh/Noah (pbuh). This general religion is obligatory upon all mankind. No other religion is acceptable before Allah. This is the teaching of all the prophets (pbu them) and there is no distinction between them.

Allah sends prophets to different *ummas*, each with a different *shari'a* (Qur'an, *Al Maeda* 5:48), or what we call in rabbinic Judaism a "covenant". He could have made us one *umma* with one *shari'a,* but He chose not to. Instead the goal of all of us is Allah and we are to compete as if in a race for virtue.

---

1. Qatada was one of the *sahaba,* companions of Muhammed.

In this way a proper Jew is a *Musawi* Muslim, a proper non-idolatrous Christian is an *'Isawi* Muslim, etc.

End of published response to Pinner article.

Ben continues discussion with friends: There are many parallels here to rabbinic jurisprudence. *Sunnah*—oral tradition—parallels *mishnah*. *Fiqh*—law in daily life—parallels *halachah*. *Madhab*—legal community—parallels *edah*.

One difference perhaps is the approach to law. This article describes *fiqh* as an attempt by righteous jurists to approximate God's law, which in turn may or may not be enforced by the sovereign of the state. Rabbinic law also recognizes normative pluralism in "orthodox" belief (divides into schools of thought), but as far as enforcement goes, it recognizes two courts, the heavenly court and the earthly court. While the rabbinic jurist is required to clarify the implementation of God's law, in both civil and religious matters, the main judgment is left up to God alone to decide. The sovereign is limited to enforce the subset of those laws which are required to maintain civil order.

Salman: After a detailed study of this topic, it is my understanding that there is no abrogation in the Qur'an. Such a concept has no support from the Qur'an itself. We read in the book:

> **This is a book whose verses have been perfected**. (Qur'an, *Hud* 11:1)

> ... **the words of God are unchangeable.** (Qur'an, *Yunus* 10:64)

The problem comes from the mistranslation and misinterpretation of verses 2:106 and 16:101 where the Arabic word *ayah* is mistranslated as a "verse" of the book. The fact of the matter is that the word *ayah* has four meanings in the Qur'an itself:

1) It could mean a miracle from God as in: "**And We supported Moses with nine profound *Ayah's* [miracles].**" (Qur'an, *Bani Isra'il* 17:101)

2) It could also mean an example for people to take heed from as in: "**And the folk of Noah, when they disbelieved the messengers, We have drowned them and set an *Ayah* (example) of them for all people.**" (Qur'an, *Al-Furqan* 25:37)

3) The word *ayah* can also mean a sign as in: "**He said, 'My Lord, give me an *ayah* [sign].' He said, 'Your *ayah* is that you will not speak to people for three consecutive nights.'**" (Qur'an, *Ta Ha* 19:10)

4) It can mean a verse in the Qur'an, as in: "**This is a book that We have sent down to you that is sacred, perhaps they will reflect on its *ayat* [verses].**" (Qur'an, *Sad* 38:29)

Now if we consider verse 106 of *sura* 2, we can easily spot that the word *ayah* in this particular verse could not mean a verse in the Qur'an. It can mean any of the other meanings (miracle, example or sign) but not a verse in the Qur'an. This is for the following reasons:

1) The words "cause to be forgotten" could not be applicable if the word '*ayah*' in this verse meant a verse in the Qur'an. How can a verse in the Qur'an become forgotten? For even if the verse was invalidated by another (as the interpreters falsely claim) it will still be part of the Qur'an and thus could never be forgotten.

2) The words "We replace it with its equal" would be meaningless if the word *ayah* in this verse meant a Qur'anic verse, simply because it would make no sense for God to invalidate one verse then replace it with one that is identical to it!

3) If the word *ayah* in verse 106 meant a miracle an example or a sign, then all the words of the verse would make perfect sense. The words "cause to be forgotten" can apply to all three meanings and that is what actually happens with the passing of time. For example, the miracles of Moses and Jesus could have been forgotten. We believe in them because they are mentioned in the Qur'an.

Similarly the words "We replace with its equal or with that which is greater" is in line with the miracles of God. God indeed replaces one miracle with its equal or with one that is greater than it.

A divine book cannot have any contradictions (4:82) so when the meanings of verses are in conflict of each other, we need to take a closer look at the expanded meaning of each word and the context of the verse as well as the chapter into account.

In my understanding, the concept of abrogation was floated in order to support the contradictions found in the books of *hadith* written 250 years after the death of Muhammed.

Ben responds: *Masha'Allah.* We have a similar teaching.

In Torah exegesis, we have a tradition that no verses are abrogated. There is the principle that "when two biblical passages [appear to] contradict each other the contradiction in question must be solved by reference to a third passage." This usually means both statements are true within their own context.

So strive as in a race in all virtues. The goal of you all is to Allah; it is He that will show you the truth about the matters in which you are different. (Qur'an, *Al-Maedah* 5:48)

16. Our Inherent Unity

Adnan Oktar and Ben discovered each other's message of brotherhood based on our commonalities; Ben was Mr. Oktar's guest in 2010.

Ben Abrahamson: Being here this evening reminded me, since all the time I talk about history, that 2,000 years ago the Jewish kings expanded the Temple Mount, *Haram Al-Sharif*. Basically there were three courts. There were the courts for the priests, the courts for the Israelites and the courts for the nations. They made the courts for the nations very large to provide space for the *yireh shomaym*, the Fearers of God. They should come from Arabia, from Parthia, from Persia, from Syria; there should be Bedouins. All of them should come together with the Jews during the Sukkot (Tabernacles) holiday and they should all pray together in what we call in Hebrew the *Chag*, or in Arabic it's called the *Hajj*. They would all pray together and worship together in beauty and holiness.

In some small way this evening, we are seeing the children of the children of these people who worshipped together, sitting together at this table, together with unity and speaking words of God and promoting the devout faith in each other. This is what we call in Judaism *Bnei Noah* Teachings, which I've talked about with everybody here. And I hope that Messiah will come quickly; together we'll celebrate in Jerusalem all in peace and devotion.

When Herod became king of Judea, he enlarged the area of the Temple Mount to allow for over a million Jewish and non-Jewish pilgrims during the course of the Tabernacles holiday.[1]

During the holiday, Jews and non-Jewish *Bnei Noah* would circle the Altar seven times, outside of the *soreg* (fence) that separated the court of the Israelites from the court of the nations.

Pilgrims join processions of hundreds of thousands of people, who simultaneously converge on Mecca for the week of the *Hajj* and perform a series of rituals: Each person walks counter-clockwise seven times about the *Ka'aba*.

When Alexander the Great died in 323 BCE, he left no heir to the throne. His general Ptolemy Lagi was awarded Egypt, Palestine, Arabia, and Peterea.

Ptolemy II held onto most of the territories conquered by his fa-

---

1. *Jewish Antiquities*, Book 15, Chapter 11, 382-387.

ther, though his control was tenuous at times. Nubia came under his partial domination and the Arabian Peninsula was part of his sphere of influence. Ptolemy II re-excavated the canal connecting the Nile and the Red Sea and established colonies on the Arabian Peninsula. This enhanced the status of Egypt in East Africa and Arabia and added to the country's prosperity.

When the Roman ambassador Popillus Laenas supported Ptolemy VI Philometor (reigned 180-145 BCE) over the Seleucids, Ptolemy reasserted his dynasty's claim to Arabia.

Ptolemy VI Philometor soon lost control of that area, but we know that Mark Antony in 35 CE, reaffirmed the claims of Ptolemaic Egypt when he gave Cleopatra VII, daughter of Ptolemy Auletes, Cyprus, the Cilician coast, Phoenicia, Coele-Syria, Judea, and Arabia. Ptolemaic garrisons were again stationed in Arabia.

Ben's appearance on Mr. Oktar's show prompted further discussion.

A question: Dear Ben, thanks for the note. Do you have any literature study related to the similarity of counterclockwise direction between Abrahamic pilgrimage ritual and revolution of the planet?

Adnan Oktar has an interest in the relationship between religion and science, so perhaps we can learn something that maybe there is a hidden message from Allah to humans through this ritual.

Ben: The "metaphysical" reason I have heard is that a person looking at the people will see them going from left to right, which represents strictness to kindness.

A response: Judaism and Islam are not simply two separate religions with no relation to one another, nor two faiths that grew from common biblical soil. Judaism and Islam have a relationship that is noted in the Torah between Jews and *Gerei Toshav*, and in the Second Temple

Era between Jews and Theosebes, and indeed in Medina under the leadership of Muhammed between Jews and Muslims as an *Ummatan Wahidatan* (One Nation) [30]. The time has come to return to that precedence, and stand side by side in co-worship, dialogue, and remembrance of what the Oneness of *Ha'Shem `Elyon/Allah ta`ala* truly means.

> **Allah swt did aforetime take a covenant with the Children of Israel; and We raised up from among them twelve chieftains. And Allah swt said, "I am with you. Surely, if you perform the prayer, and pay the alms, and believe in My Messengers, honour and assist them, and loan to Allah a beautiful loan, verily I will wipe out from you your evils, and admit you to gardens with rivers flowing beneath; but if any of you, after this, resisteth faith, he hath truly wandered from the path or rectitude. But because of their breach of their covenant, We cursed them, and made their hearts grow hard; they change the words from their [right] places and forget a good part of the message that was sent them, nor wilt thou cease to find them ever bent on [new] deceits, except a few of them."**

> **Yet pardon them, and forgive; surely Allah swt loves the good-doers**. (Qur'an, *al-Maedah* 5:12-16)

Ben: Back to the thread topic. I find it interesting that most comments focus on the "curse" part of this *ayah*, rather than the forgiveness part. When I read this *ayah*, it was the end that struck me so powerfully; that even those who had gone astray, Allah swt seeks their repentance not their destruction.

The analogy that I have been taught is that it is similar to building a great house. You cannot do that with just one kind of person. You need brick layers, carpenters, electricians, plumbers, etc. Each one should be an expert in his field, devoting all his time and energies to building his professional skill. You wouldn't want an electrician to start laying bricks. The house can only built if they cooperate together, when they recognize their need for each other, encourage and support each other.

This is what I think of when I read the last words in Qur'an, *Al-Maedah* 5:48.

> **So strive as in a race in all virtues. The goal of you all is to Allah; it is He that will show you the truth about the matters in which you are different.**

A commentator says: I agree. Thanks for your comments. We need all different sorts of people in this world. It is easy for the politicians and corporate executives to become arrogant and forget who is actually enabling them to survive. I'll look up that *surat* (verse). Thanks.

Another asks: You wrote "If Allah had so willed, He could have made you a single *umma* [people], but [His plan is] to test you in what He hath given you: so strive as in a race in all virtues ... ." If you remember I too asked you a similar question—what would you say about those who were born in a family who are not from *Ahle Kitab* (people of the book) and then later researched on their own and chose the path they found is the perfect one? Or what would you say about an atheist who later started believing in the supreme power? According to you one should not leave or shun the predestined fact that he was born in the family of a particular religion.

Ben: An *umma* generally contains people who were born into it but not exclusively. Many people have joined the *umma* of the Prophet Moses or Muhammed (pbuh).

A friend asks: What is your understanding of this *hadith*: It is narrated by Saaiduna Ali Radiallahu Anhu that Muhammed once said:

> **He who possesses sufficient provisions and means of journey for the performance of *Hajj* [pilgrimage] and yet does not do so, let him die the death of a Jew or a Christian.** (Sunan Tirmizi)

Ben: If someone belongs to the *umma* of the Prophet Muhammed and has been assigned the obligation to perform the *hajj*, yet does not do so, he is acting as if he belongs to another *umma*. He is cutting himself off from his *umma*. There is a similar concept in Judaism, if one eats leavened bread on Passover, he cuts himself off from his *umma*.

A friend: The first man on earth, *Hazrat* Adam (the honorable Adam) was a Muslim. I believe in Adam, Noah, Idris (Enoch), Yahya (John the Baptist), Ibrahim, Moses, Jesus—peace be upon them all. Everyone— the people of the divinely revealed books, Psalms, Torah, Gospel, and Qur'an—all people must believe and take their religion as Islam and as revealed to Prophet Muhammed, the last of all the prophets.

> **Do they seek other than the religion of Allah even though to Him submitted all creatures in the heavens and the earth, willingly or unwillingly? And to Him shall they all be returned.**

> **Say, "We have believed in Allah and in what was revealed to us. We have believed in what was revealed to *Ibrahim* [Abraham], *Isma'il* [Ishmael], *Ishaque* [Isaac], *Ya'qub* [Jacob] and the descendants, and in what was given to Moses and Jesus and in what was given to the prophets from their Lord. We make no distinction between any of them. We have submitted to Allah."**

And whoever seeks a religion other than Islam, it will never be accepted of him. In the Hereafter he will be among the losers. (Qur'an, *Al-Imran* 3:83-85)

Some wonder how Ben can have such a high regard for Qur'anic Islam yet remain steadfast in observing traditional Judaism.

A question: Shalom Rabbi: It seems you have high regards and respect for the Prophet Muhammed. Would it be too much to say you do believe in him? I cannot comprehend why you are not a follower of the Prophet just yet.

Another comment: I have tried to understand your statement regarding Islam as a divine faith. If Islam is a divine faith it means Prophet Muhammed has perfected the *shari'a* of Prophet Moses and all the prophets before him. Therefore we tend to believe the *shari'a* of Moses is void. Is it not?

A commentator: Ben Abrahamson, surely you know that Islam is the true religion and that the followers of Muhammed are the representatives of God on earth. The Qur'an is the final revelation from God and the people of the book are to follow it. Mr. Abrahamson, I invite you to the true religion, the way of all the prophets and the way most beloved to Allah, Islam.

Ben responds: *Salaam Aleykum.* My ancestors stood at Mount Sinai, when "Allah held the mount over our heads". They swore to uphold and keep the covenant of Torah for all time. Who am I to break this oath?

The Torah says repeatedly that the children of Israel should keep the *shari'a* of Torah for all their generations, and not anywhere in the Qur'an or *hadith* was this command rescinded for the Children of Israel.

When some wicked Jews came to the Prophet Muhammed for lighter judgment for adultery, Allah said in a most perfect way:

> **And why do they come to you for a decision while they have the Torah, in which is the Decision of Allah; yet even after that, they turn away. For they are not believers. Yet they turn back after that, and these are not the believers.** (Qur'an, *Al-Maedah* 5.43)

A commentator disagrees: "The only religion accepted with Allah is Islam" is in the Qur'an. Islam includes believing in Prophet Muhammed and in Qur'an.

Ben: Islam as a *shari'a* includes believing in the Prophet Muhammed and in the Qur'an. But there were people called Muslims even before the Qur'an. Rabbinic commentary says that *Shu-ayb* (Jethro) was of the *Bnei Noah* (righteous non-Jew). The children of Jethro were known as "God-fearers" and "Kenites". *Targum* Onkelos (the translation of the five books of Moses to Aramaic by Onkelos in the first-century CE) translates "Kenites" as *Salamai* or *Muslamai.*

> **When it is recited to them they say, "We believe in it; it is the truth from our Lord. We were already Muslims before it** [the Qur'an] **came."** (Qur'an *Al-Qasas* 28,53)

This refers to Islam in the sense of *deen* (general laws that apply to all *ummas*). In this sense a proper Jew is a *Musawi* Muslim (Muslim who follows Moses), a proper non-idolatrous Christian is an *'Isawi* Muslim (Muslim who follows Jesus).

Depending on what you think of supersessionism, otherwise known as replacement theology, then everything else follows.

Islam, what we call the *Bnei Noah*, was the basic religion of all mankind starting with Adam.

The faith, as we are taught, is based on the Ten Commandments, except for three that are specifically related to the children of Israel.

1 I am י – ה – ו – ה your God.

2 You shall have no other gods before me—You shall not make for yourself an idol.

3 You shall not make wrongful use of the name of your God.

4 Remember the Sabbath and keep it holy.

5 Honor your father and mother so that you will live long in the land that I will give you.

6 You shall not murder.

7 You shall not commit adultery.

8 You shall not steal.

9 You shall not bear false witness against your neighbor.

10 You shall not covet your neighbor's wife. You shall not covet anything that belongs to your neighbor.

The first law refers to the name of Allah in Hebrew. The fourth law refers to keeping the Sabbath. The fifth law refers to the land which the Children of Israel will inherit.

This leaves Seven Laws, which we believe are the foundation of proper religion, something that the entire world will accept during the end of days, when the *Mahdi* (messiah) comes.

The Qur'an says it in a most beautiful way:

Those who believe, those who are Jews, and the Christians and Sabaeans [righteous gentiles], **all who believe in God and the Last Day and act rightly, will have their reward with their Lord. They will feel no fear and will know no sorrow.** (Qur'an, *Al-Baqarah* 2:62)

And it is clear that there were Muslims before the Qur'an as it is written:

When it is recited to them they say, "We believe in it; it is the truth from our Lord. We were already Muslims before it came." (Qur'an, *Al-Qasas* 28:53)

To each among you have we prescribed a *shari'a* [law] **and** *minhaj* [custom]. **If Allah had so willed, He could have made you a single** *umma* [people], **but** [His plan is] **to test you in what He hath given you: so strive as in a race in all virtues. The goal of you all is to Allah; it is He that will show you the truth about the matters in which ye differ;** (Qur'an, *Al-Maedah* 5:48)

And:

To each is a goal to which Allah turns him; then strive together [as in a race] **towards all that is good. Wheresoever ye are, Allah will bring you together. For Allah hath power over all things**. (Qur'an, *Al-Baqarah* 2:148)

The Jews and Christians who follow the basic law of Islam / *Bnei Noah* will have nothing to fear. Surely it is a "race for virtues", we should "then strive together [as in a race] towards all that is good."

Thus I agree with you that all mankind must become Muslim /

Bnei Noah. They must keep the seven commandments.

We appear to differ concerning *shari'a* (covenant) and what laws we must observe.

As I explained in more detail in other posts, in sixth-century Arabia both the Sadducean Jews and Roman Byzantine Christians were claiming that the Arabians had to convert to their religion to merit eternal life. They did this to force the population to take sides in the war between Byzantium and Persia. The Sadducean Jewish leaders covered up Noahidism, ie, that one could be a perfect believer and not take on the *shari'a* of Torah. That is why you will see the word "covered up" connected with *tahrif.* The word abrogation means absolvement, ie, the Arab tribes were absolved from having to keep the *shari'a* of Torah because it was incorrectly applied to them. As the Qur'an beautifully states:

> **Follow the messenger, the gentile prophet** [Muhammed], **whom they find written in their Torah and Gospel. He exhorts them to be righteous, enjoins them from evil, allows for them all good food, and prohibits that which is bad,** *and unloads the burdens and the shackles imposed upon them.* **Those who believe in him, respect him, support him, and follow the light that came with him are the successful ones.** (Qur'an, *Al-Araf* 7:157)

It doesn't mean that the former *shari'as* were nullified and made void. It means that Muhammed was restoring the Noahide covenant, releasing the Arabians from the "shackles" of the imposed *shari'a* of Moses or Jesus.

A friend interjects: Rabbinic Jews of today follow the Torah as preserved in the five books of Moses and recited with great devotion every Sabbath. There have been other Jewish "scriptures" which rabbinic Jews themselves rejected: the Septuagint, in which Jews were forced to translate the Torah into Greek in the second-century BCE and which was seen as a calamity by rabbinic Jews; the Samaritan Bible, which changed the order of the wording of key verses; the Sadducean sect, which did not alter the written Torah but did reject the oral tradition.

Hisham, while acknowledging the passages in the Qur'an that accept Jews and Christians as true believers, still supports universal Qur'anic Islam for all:

> **Say, "O People of the Scripture, come to a word that is equitable between us and you—that we will not worship except Allah and not associate anything with Him and not take one another as lords instead of Allah." But if they turn away, then say, "Bear witness that we are Muslims [submitting to Him]." (Qur'an, *Al-Imran* 3:64)**

And also if they refuse to take the Qur'an as their book and Islamic *shari'a* as theirs, then at least they should apply the laws in the Torah and the *Injeel* (Gospel, for Christians).

> **And let the People of the Gospel judge by what Allah has revealed therein. And whoever does not judge by what Allah has revealed—then it is those who are the defiantly disobedient. (Qur'an, *Al Maedah* 5:47)**

However, that does not mean it condones the Jews and says it's fine if they just ignore Qur'an and carry on with their Torah. Please, read the subsequent *ayah* [number 48] and understand the word *muhayminan* in that *ayah*. It is crucial to put things into context.

Another commentator states: Many Jews today condemn *shari'a* but they make the mistake of taking it out of context. Jewish law can seem downright draconian for non-Jews if taken out of context as well.

Ben: Concerning the actions of people who deviate from proper religion, who espouse violence, prejudice and other characteristics, I do not think these characteristics are fitting of true believers.

I hope in some small way by showing the common historical sources of Islam and Judaism, to increase understanding in these matters. Psalm 115:9-11 says:

> **Israel, trust in the Lord; He is their help and their shield. House of Aaron, trust in the Lord; He is their help and their shield. Those who fear the Lord, trust in the Lord; He is their help and their shield.**

In this verse King David speaks about three groups: the Children of Israel, the Priesthood, and the God-fearers. In rabbinic Judaism the God-fearers are called *Bnei Noah*, which the Targum Onkelos translates as *Salamai*, or *Muslamai* (Muslims). The Priests form one circle of believers, the Children of Israel form another circle, and the God-fearers/*Bnei Noah*/proper Muslims form another circle. We are all required to do our part and encourage each other to be stronger, more devout believers with all the best characteristics. In this way, the deviators will become nothing **"and in a little bit** [of standing for good] **the wicked will become nothing"** (Psalms 37:10).

This is not any easy task. My teacher is Rabbi Benamozegh (1822-1900) who said: "Although I write [about the beautiful relationship between Judaism and Islam] only in hopes of winning ideas to my readers that I believe to be true, but if I were to fail, despite everything, more or less completely, it will suffice to throwing a seed which, I firmly believe, sooner or later to bear fruit."

We pray and long expectantly for the *Mahdi* to come, when differences will be explained and understood and a global age of peace will be brought to the world!

17. Oral Tradition in Judaism & Islam
Authority and Who Decides

Ben Abrahamson: In Islam, the *fiqh* (*halachah* in Hebrew, law in daily life) on women's clothing is that it must:

1. Cover the entire body, only the hands and face may be visible.

2. Hang loose so that the shape of the body is not apparent.

3. Not resemble man's clothing.

4. Not resemble non-believing women's clothing.

5. Not consist of bold designs which attract attention.

6. Not chosen solely to gain reputation or increase status.

7. See-through material is forbidden.

Judaism has similar laws. Similar laws apply to men as well.

Adam: Brother Ben, these *fiqh* rules are largely derived from the *ahadith* (traditions). It is the belief of many scholars that the *ahadith* contain Jewish, Christian, Arabian and Persian influences. Therefore, I believe many Jewish laws and others have infiltrated into *fiqh*, but have nothing to do with Islam. In fact, the covering of women according to these *fiqh* contradicts the Qur'an on many levels. There are other seventh-century traditions that Muslims today practice that Jews have long ago done with.

Ben: In Judaism, it is our understanding that Jewish law reflects the application of the proper understanding of scriptural verses. This understanding was handed down in an unbroken chain from Sinai to the present day. We don't believe that religion evolved.

In Islam, *ahadith* and *sunnah* also appear to be a similar encapsulation of the proper understanding of divine teaching. Their influence on *fiqh* cannot be easily dismissed.

I am not aware of seventh-entury Jewish traditions that Muslims today uphold that Jews have long ago done away with.

Raya: The Qur'an clearly states that *hijab* is an obligation; read *surat* (chapters) *Al Nisa'* and *Al Nur.*

Salman: *Ahadith are optional.* All these *mullahs* (clergy) lived in the eighth-ninth century and their understanding was influenced by the society of their time. Their opinions are not relevant today.

The entire world cannot uphold the traditions of medieval Jewish and Arab culture.

Hadith books as well as old Jewish scriptures are unreliable as due to their many inconsistencies and contradictions. They are not law but people can follow them if they want to. They are not binding.

The word *hijab* is not even used in the Qur'an. There is no head or face cover required anywhere in the Qur'an. In 24:31, women are enjoined to cover their chest (which is common sense anyway) and nowhere is a covering for the head or face suggested.

Khimar simply means a "cover" so it is up to the individual woman to determine how she wants to cover herself. A Saudi woman may want to cover her face, but a Canadian woman may decide otherwise. This is how the verse becomes universally applicable for all times.

A friend defends Islamic practice: Wearing *hijab* is not mere tradition, it's clearly written in Al Qur'an.

Ben: All four *madhabs,* (legal communities, *Edah* in Hebrew) Hanafi, Shafi'i, Maliki and Hanbali as well as Ja`fari require *hijab.* See *surat An-Nisa* 4:59 and *Al-Ahzab* 33:58–59, as clarified by the *ahadith sahih* al-Bukhari 6.60.282, 7.65.375, *sahih* Muslim, 8.3334, and *sunan* Abu Dawud 32.4090, 32.4091.[1]

It seems clear to me that the *sahaba* (companions of Muhammed) who received teachings directly from the Prophet (pbuh) have a fuller understanding of the meaning of the revelation than those who are farther down in the chain of narration—or not in the chain at all.

The *ahadith* were preserved and transmitted orally before they were written down.

Salman: Those are just someone's opinions, not law. It is not written in the Qur'an that women must wear a head cover.

Ben: *Hanafi, Shafi'i, Maliki, Hanbali* and *Ja'fari madhabs* are not "just some-one's opinions." They reflect understandings and applications of law. If every Muslim interpreted the Qur'an according to his own personal stream of thought, what would become of Islam?

Salman: Nothing would become of Islam. Such an idea that every human being must think and believe the same way is against common sense and all logic. Such an idea is marketed by the clergy of most religions because they are insecure and afraid of the intellectual freedom that others may exercise in order to decide matters of faith for themselves.

How do you expect the understanding of one group of people at one point in time of history to be applicable for all people and all times to come for the rest of the world?

---

1. The terms *hadith* and *sunan* are similar—legends, traditions.

Ben: I do not believe that the proper understanding of scripture, passed on by the righteous of our faith, originated in their own heads. The understanding may require clarification at times, but its proper application can meet every need of today's innovations and culture until the end of the world.

Shirah: Dear brother, the law on women's clothing between our two faiths is the same!

HL: Judaism has the same laws? I never saw that.

Raya: Brother HL, if you have never seen Jewish women wearing modest clothing, then this does not mean that it is not part of Judaism's laws. I can tell you that I was blessed *alhamduli'Allah* to meet Jewish sisters who truly respect and follow the Jewish religion. Thanks for allowing me to share my humble opinion with you.

A friend: Never thought I'd see the day when a Jewish man defends Islam and knows more about Islam than a Muslim. I side with Rabbi Ben on this one. You're an inspiration. May Allah bless you and all of us.

Is tradition—ahadith and sunnah—not necessarily obsolete but just a matter of personal choice?

Salman clarifies his position: The proper application of seventh century concepts and beliefs in the twenty-first century may be beneficial on a case-to-case basis.

I fail to understand how they become a law and binding upon all humans.

What if the religious commentators were wrong? Were they not humans that were capable of making mistakes? How can I consider people from another century whom I have never met as "the most righteous of the faith"?

Ben: In the case of Islam, by a solid chain of tradition, compatibility with known truths, and exemplary lives. Both Islam and Judaism agree on the concept of *yeridat hadorot*—that previous generations were on a higher spiritual plane than later ones. The *sahaba* were thus on a higher plane than modern clergy. We do not believe that religion evolves in the sense of improves over time.

We say (Deuteronomy 6:4) that one must serve God with all one's heart, soul, and strength. Rationalism is one important part of this. But the human being is so much more than just "rational thinking".

First, the understanding/interpretation that these righteous leaders inherited is an integral part of Scripture. It did not originate with them; they did not make it up or figure it out. A word can have no meaning if it is not interpreted. A word and its meaning are an integral part of each other. A word can be written down, "meaning" cannot. "Meaning" can only be applied.

Salman: The Qur'an that tells us that it is a fully detailed and explained scripture in its own.

> **Qur'an is the best *hadith* (39:23) and no other *hadith* after this is from God (45:6, 77:50).**

> **Qur'an is the best *tafsir* [commentary] (25:33) and is nothing more than the reminder for all people (81:27).**

> **The book is fully detailed (6:114).**

Are you in denial of these clear cut verses in favor of cultural traditions? Any rituals, practices or beliefs held dear by people are simply a result of cultural traditions and not a matter of law.

Raya: Brother Salman, there are many issues that are not described in detail in the Qur'an. That is why we have the *ahadith* to explain them. For instance, in the Qur'an, Allah proclaims the obligation of prayer ... but it does not specify how to pray. That is when we look at the *ahadith*, in order to learn about the details of prayer. The same thing applies to the *hijab*.

Ben: Salman, what you are doing is changing the regularly accepted meanings of "book" and "complete". The Qur'an anticipates its need for *ahadith*, as we will see below.

You believe that the Qur'an is complete with regard to everything, needing no binding elaboration, and that the correct interpretation of the Qur'an is whatever you feel. It follows that if the Qur'an does not plainly say something, then one does not have to do it. This leaves one free in many areas to pursue whatever interest they wish in any way they desire. Most believers have difficulties with this approach. Let's look at the two key aspects of this.

First of all, in regard to the meaning of *kitab* (scripture) and personal interpretation: the meaning of a book is determined by its author, not its reader. The Arabic words are best understood in their meaning, context, and implication by those who were closest to its revelation and applied its teachings in their lives. We receive a chain of tradition from them.

The Qur'an itself says:

Be obedient to Allah, the messenger, and those of power [*amr*] amongst you. (Qur'an, *Al-Nisa* 4:59)

This verse commands obedience to three entities. One, acting on the Qur'an is obedience to Allah. Two, acting on the *ahadith* is obedience to the messenger, the prophet Muhammed (pbuh). Three, acting on the rulings of the jurists completes the obedience to the *sahaba*. If obedience to only the Qur'an was necessary, this verse would not have mentioned obedience to three things.

Here is another quote that supports the importance of tradition/ *ahadith*:

Our Prophet teaches them the book [ie, the Qur'an] ***and*** **wisdom**. (Qur'an, *Al-Baqarah* 2:129)

If there was no need of additional elaboration, why did this verse mention wisdom along with the Qur'an?

And take what the Messenger gives you; and whatever he prohibits you from, stay away from it. (Qur'an, *Al-Hashr* 59:7)

If accepting only the Qur'an was necessary, this verse would've read, "And whatever We give you, take it; and whatever We prohibit you from, stay away from it." So, we can deduce from this verse that everything we receive from the Prophet (pbuh) (be it the Qur'an or even *ahadith*) must be taken completely.

He who obeyed the messenger *[ahadith]* **has obeyed Allah** [Qur'an]. (*Qur'an*, Al-Nisaa 4:80)

Since the Qur'an and *hadith* are both regarded as revelation, acting upon the latter is obedience to Allah.

The Holy Prophet [referring to *ahadith*] **prohibits impure things on them**. (Qur'an, *Al-A'raf* 7:157)

This verse establishes that prohibition is also learned from the *hadith*, otherwise the verse would have mentioned Allah and not the Prophet Muhammed. The prohibition of consuming the flesh of dogs and donkeys are from *hadith* and not explicitly mentioned in the Qur'an.

Indeed We have revealed the Qur'an and We alone are its protectors. (Qur'an, *Al-Hijr* 15:9)

The Qur'an teaches that Allah is the protector of the Qur'an's words, meanings, commands, and all of its secrets. This is why its reciters (*qaaris*), scholars (*aalims*). and judges (*mashaikh*) will be forever found until the Day of *Qiyaamat* (the day of judgment). The *hadith* is a medium for the protection of these treasures. If this wasn't the case, the words of *salah* and the practice of *zakat* would be protected but not their commands and secrets. Bear in mind that *salah* and *zakat* can also mean "to dance" and "to wash clothes" respectively amongst other meanings. In short, the greatest means of protecting the Qur'an is the *hadith*.[1]

Secondly, your interpretation of "complete" is not according to *tafsir* (commentary). You are limiting the scope of the Qur'an to its literal reading, and no more. According to the *tafsir* of all the standard *madhabs*, all utterances of the Prophet Muhammed (pbuh) which are part of the *deen* are from Allah. The content and words he spoke by means of *wahi* (revelation) is known as Qur'an, while the content which was from Allah swt but whose wording was the Prophet's (pbuh) is known as *hadith*. The Qur'an is called *wahi-e-jali* (the manifest revelation) while the *hadith* is called *wahi-e-khafi* (concealed revelation).

Ben goes on the challenge Salman.

Ben: Look at what you yourself are doing. I think you are creating your own interpretation of these verses. You are creating your own *madhab*.

Salman: I am not creating anything. I simply quoted verses which are fully detailed and explained in all respects possible.

---

1. From the book *Ek Islam* by Mufti Ahmed Yaar Khan Naeemi Ashrafi.

When the book is the "fully detailed" and "best *tafsir*" in itself, this means that any rituals, practices, or beliefs held dear by people are simply a result of cultural traditions and not a matter of law.

Nothing we have missed from the Book. (Qur'an, *Al-An'am* 6:38)

Ben: This is your own invented *tafsir*, your *madhab*, your justification for following the *hadith* as rigidly or as lax as you wish do.

Salman: The book is either complete or it is not. If it is not complete, as you have claimed, then 6:114-115, 25:33, 45:6, 77:50 and many similar verses are wrong.

So you do not think that the Book is fully detailed and best explained in all aspects of guidance? A simple yes or no would be sufficient.

Ben: We have been through this before, let us agree to disagree.

Alya: Salman, Islam has two sources of legislation, Qur'an and *hadith*. We are to follow these sources and *ahadith* of the six books, they are:

- Sahih Bukhari, collected by Imam Bukhari (d. 870), which includes 7275 *ahadith*.
- Sahih Muslim, collected by Muslim b. al-Hajjaj (d. 875), includes 9200 *ahadith*.
- Sunan al-Sughra, collected by al-Nasa'i (d. 915)
- Sunan Abu Dawood, collected by Abu Dawood (d. 888)
- Sunan al-Tirmidhi, collected by al-Tirmidhi (d. 892)
- Sunan ibn Majah, collected by Ibn Majah (d. 887).

These are completely reliable and authentic.

Salman: The books that you have mentioned are from the Sunni religion. These are rejected by Shias, and Shia books are rejected by the Sunnis. They also claim that their books are extra legislation besides the Qur'an while during all this, Qur'an stands on its own when it claims: "**These are the revelations of God, We recite them to you with the truth.**" So, in which *hadith* after God and His revelations do they believe?"

Cala supports Salman:

> **Among the people, there are those who uphold baseless *hadith*, and thus divert others from the path of God without knowledge, and take it in vain. These have incurred a shameful retribution**. (Qur'an, *Luqman* 31:6)

Salman: I would like to share some verses for everyone to read:

> **God is the only source of law and the Book is complete and fully detailed** (6:114, 6:38)

> **Qur'an is the Best *hadith*** (39:23) **and no other *hadith* after the Qur'an is from God** (45:6, 77:50)

> **Qur'an is the best explanation in contrast to all other sources claimed to be from God** (25:33).

There is no mention of any *hadith* or *sunnah* related to a Prophet anywhere in the Qur'an. It is interesting to note that God compares his book with all man-made *ahadith* and then criticizes them. God has criticized religious scholarship in 9:31, and we find such a concept in the Bible as well where Jesus criticized the religious scholars.

Hikmah simply means wisdom or intelligence. It has no connection with any external source of information. Per the Qur'an, *hikmah* was given to all prophets.

To obey the messenger is to follow the message he delivered. This is simple enough yet we see that there is a plethora of books and stories attributed to the messenger by each one of the unlimited number of "rightly guided" sects we have in business today.

To me, it is illogical to consult scholars and loads of other books when God's word is easy, fully detailed, and without any contradiction or nonsensical narrations.

Use of dictionaries or lexicons is a good idea as they give us an idea of the meanings of words. The root of the word protects the meaning and hence understanding it becomes easy.

Mike: Salman, I agree with you on most issues and our hearts are in a similar place. I can relate quite well to your idea that, "it is one thing to respect and study with scholars, but it is another to take them as all source of understanding and guidance".

However, I am not completely sure I agree with the statement that "God's word (ie, Qur'an) is easy and fully detailed". I feel that knowledge and wisdom comes from reading as many books as one can, as well as choosing the right ones. In addition, wisdom can come from speaking to people of sound reason and intelligence and not just reading the Qur'an. Our understanding of Qur'an can also benefit from consulting with Jewish and Christian historians and scholars. Developing wisdom requires more than just studying sectarian *hadith* texts or just the Qur'an.

Ben: Salman, did you see my second post on this thread? If the Qur'an is complete unto itself then what is the *hikmah* referring to in *surat* Al-Baqarah 2:151?

> **Similarly, to complete My Blessings on you, We have
> sent among you a Messenger** [Muhammed] **of your own,**

> **reciting to you Our Verses** [the Qur'an] **and sanctifying you, and teaching you the Book** [the Qur'an] **and the** *hikmah* [*ahadith*–traditions, and *fiqh*–jurisprudence], **and teaching you that which you used not to know**.

It is not scripture, but it was sent by Allah and teaches Muslims that which they used not to know.

Yaqub sides with Salman: Qur'an is absolutely complete. *Hikmah* doesn't mean *hadith* or Islamic law. *Hikmah* is the capacity of person to understand Qur'an.

Ben: If *hikmah* in this context is the capacity of a person to understand the Qur'an, then why does it use the word *wayu allimukumu* (and teaches you) *l-kitāba wal-ik'mata*. How can one teach "capacity to learn"?

Mike wants it spelled out better: Ben, I also do not think of the reference to *hikhmah* (wisdom) in that verse to be just the *hadith* text and the method of interpreting it. I think of *hikmah* as a more general awareness rather than something written down. As far as I can tell, this wisdom was with some of the companions, the *Ahlul Bayt* (Shia), and in the *hadith* text (Sunni).

If a text was meant, then more should have been said explicitly in the Qur'an about it being a book. Also, both the Prophet (pbuh) and the rightly guided caliphs should have done more to collect this additional source of wisdom in book form. Instead we find it was collected more than a century later with a mixture of contradictory statements, without guidance from the Prophet (pbuh) or the rightly guided caliph's on how to separate them. By definition, such a tool in the practice of religion, is a *bidah*—a heretical innovation—without the example of the prophet or the caliphs.

Ben: The traditions were preserved orally before they were written down. Please show examples of the true and false statements that you mention.

In *surat* Al-Baqarah 2:269 a different verb is used—*yu'tī l-ik'mata* (to grant [the] wisdom), unlike 2:151, which says *wayu allimukumu* (and teaches you) *l-kitāba wal-ik'mata*

Yaqub: There isn't any different word in both *ayat* (verses). The word is *el hikmet*.

Ben: But the verb is different, to *teach* wisdom is different than to *grant* wisdom.

If one can be so bold as to compare this to rabbinic teachings, the Mishnah (Oral Torah) is also referred to as wisdom (*hikma*). The Mishnah is a collection of writings that contains examples and clarifications on the meaning of Torah. However it is pointed out that the Mishnah is not wisdom in and of itself but the means to arrive at wisdom. So perhaps both opinions are correct: *hikma* is both the "capability to understand" (the result) as well as the *sunnah* and *hadith* (the means) to achieve that understanding.

An analogy would be a math teacher who wants to teach the principles of math. First the rules are explained but they are beyond the understanding of the student, and then many examples are given. The student, by reviewing the examples, eventually arrives at a greater understanding of the principles. The examples are the means to arrive at a deeper understanding.

The same is true for a student of law, who reviews many case studies to arrive at the general principles. The case studies are not "the law", nor do they have authority. They are merely applications of the law, yet through them one can achieve understanding of "the law".

Yaqub: *Sunnah* and *hadiths* can't be different from Qur'an. And they aren't completing Qur'an. Qur'an is complete.

Ben: I still wish to point out that verse 2:151 says *"wayu allimukumu* (and teaches you) *l-kitāba wal-ik'mata"*. This *'ayah* puts *l-kitāba* (the Qur'an) one level above the *ik'mata,* yet both are connected by the same verb: They were taught. One cannot "teach" a capability.

A friend suggests that one can teach scripture and wisdom without the use of ahadith.

Ben: How does one teach wisdom? Through approved examples. Take the book of Proverbs, it opens by saying that it teaches wisdom and then is filled with hundreds of sayings and examples. Isn't this what we find in the *sunnah* and the *ahadith*?

Salman, our enthusiast for Qur'anic purity, insists: A messenger has the truth but it is hard to communicate it. Without the skills needed to intelligently communicate the message, he cannot do his job. This is exactly what is called *hikmah*/wisdom.

A human can not explain the word of God better than God himself. (25:33)

Ben starts a new thread on a related topic: *Sunan* Abu-Dawoud Book 25, Number 3644:[1] Narrated Jundub: The Prophet (pbuh) said: If anyone interprets the Book of Allah in the light of his opinion even if he is right, he has erred.

In my understanding the best way to interpret the Book of Allah is according to the *ahadith* (legends), *sunnah* (traditions), and the consensus of the *ulema* (scholars).

Gambo responds to an assertion that familiarity with Arabic is essential in understanding the Qur'an: What has the knowledge of Arabic to

---

1. Collection of *ahadith*. *Sunan* is another word that refers to *hadith*.

do with my faith? I don't bother myself to study Arabic. I am proud of my native language.

Ben: It is impossible to have a full understanding of the Qur'an without reading it in Arabic. There is a proper and correct interpretation of the Qur'an, and it is not hard to find. The proper interepration it is not based on our own wishes and desires but rather on the meaning that was intended when it was revealed.

I don't see that studying *ahadith* contradicts the use of one's own sense and intelligence. Ultimately we must use our own reason to decide what we will believe and what we will reject, but the basis for this decision must not be our own personal wants and desires, but rather based on the original intended meaning which Allah promises to safeguard. Every person colors what he or she knows based on how he or she views the world, only people who have nullified their own self-interests and dedicated themselves wholly to the service of Allah are fitting vessels for the reception and transmission of this original intended meaning. I believe this *hadith* above is saying that we need to understand scripture in the light of the vehicles that convey that meaning: *sunnah*, the *ahadith*, and the consensus of the *ulema* (scholars). Otherwise, even if one comes up with the right understanding, it may be for the wrong reasons.

Gambo: I can only trust the Qur'an and nothing else!

Salman: The idea that the word of God needs word of man to be explained is completely flawed and defies all common sense and logic.

Ben: Surely if God revealed His word, He also revealed the correct understanding of that word.

For example, in another thread on this Facebook® page, I discuss with a very popular Sheikh and a student of his concerning his interpretation of the Qur'an. He holds that the Torah that is mentioned in the Qur'an is a completely different book than the Torah that we have today. Why does he believe this? Because he figured it out using his own logic. He understands the Qur'an to be quoting the Torah word for word, and he cannot find these exact word-for-word quotes in the Torah. This is his "common sense". Almost without exception this is not the opinion of Islamic *tafsir*. The consensus is that the Torah has been corrupted in some way, but we are talking about the same book. It is my opinion that his interpretation works against the unity of believers and several clear teachings of the Qur'an.

It has been my experience that when people throw out the *hadith*, the *sunnah*, the *tafsir* as "the work of man" —even the original Arabic wording as "not necessary" —they end up disagreeing on interpretation and come up with incorrect meaning, which is exactly what I understand this *hadith* to say. This in turn can cause great conflict and difficulties.

Mike: The Qur'an does suggest that there is some corruption in the Bible, but in light of these verses that require belief in the Bible, applying common sense suggests that this corruption is in the meanings of certain words.

As far as the *hadith* literature is concerned, there appears to be some confirmation that the corruption in the Torah is *tahrif e mani* (scriptures have been incorrectly interpreted) not *lafzi* (corrupted). On the other hand, there is also some evidence in *hadith* that the Prophet (pbuh) had forbidden the *sahabah* (companions) from reading the Bible. However, the strongest arguments in favor of the Bible come directly from the Qur'an.

Salman: Rabbi, I think you are missing the point. You mentioned that the disagreement between people when they use their own common sense is a problem. Can you please explain how you see it as a problem? If my view differs from yours, how can it be a problem for you or anyone else?

Each individual is responsible for him/herself and all of us have the common sense to lead our own way.

I find that most scholars are always worried about what others believe and why they differ in their opinion or understanding from that of the scholars. This shows their insecurity.

You continue to talk about the importance of *hadith, sunnah,* and man made *tafsirs* yet you fail to realize that the divisions, hatred, violence, sects etc among most of those who call themselves "believers" is due to all these sources. Each group calls itself "righteous" and claims to have their exclusive *hadiths, sunnah,* and *tafsirs.* You also claim to belong to one of these groups and perhaps this why you feel that people should not think for themselves if they disagree with the consensus of the so called scholars.

Ben: You stated: "If my view differs from yours, how can it be a problem for you or for anyone else for that matter." Because it can lead to ideas that are against Islam, and in my case against the People of the Book. It seems to me to be that any group which has a "Qur'an only" view is bound to lead to error. It was for this reason that I brought the above *hadith.*

I was asked the question, "Do you think it's acceptable for Muslims to rule by Qur'an alone without external sources (such as *sunnah* or *hadith*)?" I answered no.

If the Qur'an is equally self-evident, then everyone should be free to interpret it as he or she sees fit, without giving any precedence to scholars or righteous believers who shed many tears to arrive at the full meaning of text.

Of course, as a Jew, my opinion regarding Islamic jurisprudence is of almost no importance. In the spirit of Rabbi Joseph Ber Soloveitchik I am stepping down from this discussion.[1]

---

1. See Rabbi Soloveitchik's discussion about interfaith dialogue in Chapter 2.

But still, according to the opinion of Rabbi Benamozegh, Jews should not oppose but rather encourage Muslims to be proper, stronger, devout Muslims just as Muslims should encourage Jews to be proper, stronger, and devout Jews.

18. Prophets of Ancient Times, Spiritual Leaders of Today:

Choosing a Path

Ben Abrahamson:

> **To every people** [was sent] **a Law Giver: when their Law Giver comes** [before them] **the matter will be judged between them with justice and they will not be wronged.** (Qur'an, *Al-Yunus* 10:47)

> **We sent not a messenger except** [to teach] **in the language of his** [own] **people, in order to make** [things] **clear to them. Now Allah leaves straying those whom He pleases and guides whom He pleases: and He is exalted in power, full of Wisdom.** (Qur'an, *Ibrahim* 14:4)

Alexander: A Prophet like Moses can be found in every generation according to the Torah.

> **A prophet will the LORD thy God raise up unto thee, from the midst of thee, of thy brethren, like unto me; unto him ye shall hearken** … (Deuteronomy 18:15)

> **And thou shall come unto the priests the Levites, and unto the judge that shall be in those days; and thou shalt**

inquire; and they shall declare unto thee the sentence of judgment. (Deuteronomy 17:9)

Nevertheless, the intent of the Creator of the world is not within the power of man to comprehend, for (to paraphrase Yeshayahu 55:8) **His ways are not our ways, nor are His thoughts our thoughts.** As Maimonides stated, the deeds of Jesus and Muhammed will pave the way for the improvement of the entire world, motivating the nations to serve God together, as it is written (Zephaniah 3:9), **"I will make the peoples pure of speech so that they will all call upon the Name of God and serve Him with one purpose."**

> How will this come about? The entire world has already
> become filled with talk of Messiah, as well as of the Torah
> and the *mitzvos.* Some of them (the Christians) say: "The
> 613 commandments used to be true, but are not all in force
> in the present age." Others (the Muslims) say: "Implied
> in the commandments are hidden concepts that cannot
> be understood simply; the Messiah has already come and
> revealed them."(Rambam, Laws of Kings 11:4)

Riaz on diversity:

> **And We have revealed to you,** [O Muhammed], **the Book
> in truth, confirming that which preceded it of the Scripture
> and as a criterion over it. So judge between them by what
> Allah has revealed and do not follow their inclinations
> away from what has come to you of the truth. To each of
> you We prescribed a law and a method. Had Allah willed,
> He would have made you one nation, but** [He intended]
> **to test you in what He has given you; so race to** [all that
> is] **good. To Allah is your return all together, and He will**

[then] **inform you concerning that over which you used to
differ.** (Qur'an, *Al-Maedah* 5:48)

Satnam Singh: Doesn't the Qur'an contradict itself on this point? Some
verses say that monotheistic traditions will be accepted while others
say none but Islam will be accepted!

Malik: Islam refers to the natural, innate religion of mankind. Everyone,
regardless of religious custom, who adheres to proper ethical monotheism, is a Muslim who practices Al-Islam. Proper Hinduism, proper Judaism, etc are all Islam.

Satnam Singh: Hinduism advocates the belief in reincarnation and kar-
ma. In Islam, these beliefs are only found among the extreme Shia
groups. Muhammed Dara Shikoh, the Sanskrit and Persian Scholar
from the early seventeenth century, in his book *Majma Ul Bahraain*
did a great job in trying to reconcile Hinduism and Islam, however
he purposefully ignored the position of reincarnation.

Malik: You misunderstand. Differences in theological praxis are not the
core issue. Whether or not reincarnation takes place is irrelevant.
The real issue is salvation. Those who believe in one God and do
good deeds are Muslims and their religion is *Al-Islam.*

Alexander: If the natural monotheist religion is called "Islam" by you, it's
called "Noahidism" by Jews, that is, the religion of Noah and his descendants. However, the term *Islam* in its usual sense requires belief
in Muhammed and Qur'an which is not required in Noahidism.

Malik: Noahidism also has its requirements; it demands submission to the
rabbis. The Rambam, the principle authority of Jewish law, states the
only option for gentiles is direct observance of the Noahide system
under the guidance of rabbis or conversion to Judaism.

Alexander: Noahidism demands acceptance of the revalation on Mt. Sinai. What you call "submission to rabbis" is actually a very wide spectrum of views. In the same way we can say that Islam both refers to general, ethical monotheism, or to submission to Muhammed and Qur'an.

Malik: As for the recognition of the vice-regency of the Prophet of Islam, things are a lot more complex than what you have presented. The word *"kafir"* means to "cover up" (the truth). As the Qur'an says, Allah guides whom he wills. Only someone who knows beyond the shadow of a doubt that the *shari'a* of the Prophet Muhammed is true should follow it. The Qur'an acknowledges that not everyone is guided towards the Islamic faith in terms of submission to Muhammed and Qur'an.

A friend: The Qur'an is not contradicting itself when it says all faiths are accepted and when it again says only Islam is accepted. You see, it comes down to what the Qur'an means by "Islam". The Qur'an makes it clear that whatever faith you claim to adhere, if you devote yourself to God only and strive to do good, then you have done "Islam", which correctly means "submission to God's will" and is not a name for a new kind of faith.

It is human beings who have a tendency to group themselves according to their differing beliefs and stamp a name (Jew, Christian, Muslim, Hindu, Buddhist, etc.) to their man-made religions. But God reminds mankind repeatedly of the true religion which is submission to his will; in Arabic it means "Islam".

And, not to let the followers of Hinduism feel excluded, a friend refers to reincarnation:

> **How can you reject faith in God? Do you not recall that
> you were once without life, and Allah gave you life; then**

**God will cause you to die, and will again bring you to life;
and finally to Allah will you return.** (Qur'an, *Al-Baqarah*
2:28)

**Set forth to them the similitude of the life of this world:
It is like the rain which we send down from the skies:
the earth's vegetation absorbs it, but soon it becomes
dry stubble, which the winds do scatter: It is Allah Who
prevails over all things.** (Qur'an, *Al-Kahf* 18:45)

Many mystics believe these verses hint at reincarnation. This is not
the orthodox view today, but the Qur'an has many layers of meaning,
some clearly expounded and some ambiguous.

Malik: Nahjul-Balagha notes that God made mankind out of different
sands and each person is thus tested according his *fitrah* (nature).
For some people the test comes through Islam. For other people God
uses other means to test them.

For some people the test is not even based on acceptance of religious code but other choices that God presents them in their life.

This is why in Islamic philosophy some atheists are given leeway.
Righteous atheists worship God by contributing to science, philosophy and the like.

Choosing a Path

A friend: Each must free oneself from past conditioning, and have one's
own experience of the revelation.

*A heated discussion follows on the heels of this advocacy for a
divinely inspired personal choice. What is the role of "modern day
prophets"? Where do the Chassidic Rabbis of today, revered by
their followers, or the Mormons' "latter day saints" fit into the
concept of following all of God's prophets?*

Daoud: Islam is the present Regent of the Dynasty of The Living Revelation, being the last inheritor. The different prophets are the faces of the same Man so to speak.

You have to free yourself from the conditioning you received from dominant forces in your life and have your own experience of the revelation.

His regency is on and nobody has replaced him yet, not even you gurus.

Farah: Your sincerity in your quest will make the revelation "reveal" itself.

Amal Omar: There is no contradiction between the verses:

> **Surely those who believe, and those who are Jews, and the Christians, and the Sabeans, whoever believes in Allah and the Last day and does good, they shall have their reward from their Lord, and there is no fear for them, nor shall they grieve.** (Qur'an, *Al-Baqarah* 2:62)

> **And whosoever seeks as religion other than Islam it will not be accepted from him, and he will be among the losers in the hereafter.** (Qur'an, *Al Imran* 3:85)

The first verse refers to those Sabeans, Jews, and Christians who sincerely followed the teachings of their respective prophets, without ever corrupting the true message, and believing in the prophecy of the advent of Muhammed made known by Musa, Isa, and other prophets (see sahih Baqarah: 40).[1] Allah knows best.

S Cohen: I'm kind of confused right now. What about these quotes?

---

1. Collection of *ahadith*

Muhammed is God's apostle. Those who follow him are ruthless to the unbelievers but merciful to one another. (Qur'an, *Al-Surah* 48:29)

O you who were given the Scripture, believe in what We have sent down [to Muhammed], **confirming that which is with you, before We obliterate faces and turn them toward their backs or curse them as We cursed the Sabbath-breakers. And ever is the decree of Allah accomplished.** (Qur'an, *An-Nisa* 4:47)

So here's a clearer question: the Qur'an seems to say I must believe in Muhammed and the divinity of the Qur'an to be "saved". If I don't, am I doomed?

Farah: It says "hard", which means tough, not ruthless. The general consensus is that the verse concerns spiritual quest and that the unbelievers in question are ego, Satan, anger, and vain pursuits.

Satnam Singh demands sources: General consensus? Which *tafsir* (commentator) are you referring to?

S Cohen: My question still hasn't been answered.

Farah: Only you can eventually answer it! As long as you resist the revelation, the revelation will resist you.

Satnam Singh is not giving up: Again, which *tafsir* are you referring to?

His question remains unanswered for now.

Alexander: I am led by a certain revelation, others by different ones, who is to say that one is more or less true?

Farah: *If* you accept it is a Dynasty of the One revelation from the One God, then you accept the final acting one, and that is loyal to the spirit of every one of them.

Alexander: Then according to your logic you should accept Mormonism. Their prophet appeared in the 1820s, long after Muhammed.

I, on the other hand do not accept that there is a prophet equal to Moses. I can respect that Muhammed is a prophet to you, however.

Moreover, I follow a dynasty of prophets within Judaism, from Rav Shneur Zalman of Liadi to Rav Menachem Mendel, the Lubavitcher Rebbe. They are all very recent, spanning the last 200 years to the present, and they rouse my soul into fiery flames of love and awe of God.

Mormons believe Rev. Joseph Smith Jr. was a true prophet of the One God.

Farah: You present scholars and rabbis as equal to prophets. I cannot agree with that.

Alexander: I presented quotes from the Torah above stating that there shall be prophets like Moses in every time period. Of course they are also sages and rabbis at the same time. Moses was also a rabbi. It simply means teacher or master.

The dynasty of prophets didn't end 2,000 years ago. It was just concealed during the time of exile.

Isma'eel AbdulKhaliq Alemao shares from his Facebook® page: Muhammed is predicted in the Torah, and Jews must accept him: If Muhammed was sent only to the gentiles, then one expects such a restriction to be stated in the Qur'an.

What we see in the Qur'an is to the contrary:

Whatever of good reaches you, is from Allah, but whatever of evil befalls you, is from yourself. And We have sent you

[Muhammed] **as a Messenger to Mankind, and Allah is Sufficient as a Witness.** (Qur'an, *An-Nisa* 4:79)

This should suffice in refuting the claim that a Jew can remain under the *shari'a* of Moses. If there is lingering doubt:

O Mankind! Verily, there has come to you the Messenger (Muhammed) with the truth from your Lord. So believe in him, it is better for you. But if you disbelieve, then certainly to Allah belongs all that is in the heavens and the earth. And Allah is Ever All-Knowing, All-Wise. (Qur'an, *An-Nisa* 4:170)

And We have sent you [Muhammed]: **not but as a Mercy for the *'alamin*** [mankind, *jinn* and all that exists]. (Qur'an, *Al-Anbiya* 21:107)

Say [Muhammed to mankind]: **"If you** [really] **Love Allah then follow me, Allah will Love you and forgive you your sins. And Allah is Oft-Forgiving, Most merciful."** (Qur'an, *Al-Imran* 3:31)

Narrated Abu Huraira:

Allah's Apostle said "How will you be when the son of Mary [ie, Jesus] **descends amongst you and he will judge people by the law of the Qur'an and not by the law of Gospel.** (Fateh-ul Bari page 304 and 305 Vol 7) (Book 55, Hadith 658) Sahih Al-Bukhari.

Had the Christian community been exempted from the *shari'a* of the Qur'an, why is the teacher of the law of the Gospels (Jesus) ruling according to the law of the Qur'an?

If Moses were alive amongst you, he would have had no option but to follow *me. (Musnad Ahmad 14104. Musnad Abu Ya'la Hadith 2081. Tafsir Ibn Kathir 2/68. Shaykh Hamztul Zain classified it as Hasan in his classification of Musnad Ahmad 11/500 pub. Dar al-Hadith Cairo, 1995)*

This is in conformity with this *ayah:*

And [remember] **when Allah took the covenant of the prophets, saying: "Take whatever I gave you from the Book and** *hikmah* [understanding of the Laws of Allah], **and afterwards there will come to you a messenger** [Muhammed] **confirming what is with you; you must, then, believe in him and help him." Allah said: "Do you agree** [to it] **and will you take up my covenant** [which I conclude with you]**?" They said: "We agree." He said: "Then bear witness; and I am with you among the witnesses** [for this]**."** (Qur'an, *Al-Imran* 3:81)

And when there came to them a Messenger from Allah [Muhammed] **Confirming what was with them, a party of those who were given the Scripture threw away the Book of Allah behind their backs as if they did not know!** (Qur'an, *Al-Baqarah* 2:101)

O you who have been given the Scripture [Jews and Christians]**! Believe in what We have revealed** [to Muhammed] **confirming what is already with you, before We efface faces** [by making them like the back of necks; without nose, mouth] **and turn them hind wards, or curse them as We cursed the Sabbath-breakers. And the Commandment of Allah is always executed.** (Qur'an, *An-Nisa* 4:47)

If the prophets said that when Muhammed comes they must follow him, what about the followers of those prophets, especially since Muhammed has been explicitly mentioned as being sent for the whole of the human race in the Qur'an?

I ask Allah to guide you and me to what He loves and pleases Him.

Isma'eel AbdulKhaliq Alemao continues: The obligation to become Muslim is written in the Torah and *Tanakh* (Bible).

> **I will raise them up a Prophet from among their brethren,**
> **like unto thee, and will put my words in his mouth; and**
> **he shall speak unto them all that I shall command him.**
> (Deuteronomy 18)

All the tribes of Israel were assembled at Horeb, were they not? If so, **"I will raise them up a Prophet from among their brethren."** The God of Israel was speaking about them as a collective. Ishmael is included in the brethren of the children of Israel:

> **And as for Ishmael, I have heard thee: Behold, I have**
> **blessed him, and will make him fruitful, and will multiply**
> **him exceedingly; twelve princes shall he beget, and I will**
> **make him a great nation.** (Genesis 17:20)

Moses consolidated the twelve tribes of Israel into one entity. Muhammed did the same with the tribes of Arabia.

Already we are seeing the likeness of Muhammed to Moses, peace be upon both of them, are we not?

Moses was a lawgiver, he by Allah ordained what was permissible for the Tribes of Israel. The same is true of Muhammed with the tribes of Arabia.

When thou art come into the land which the LORD thy God giveth thee, thou shalt not learn to do after the abominations of those nations.

There shall not be found among you any one that maketh his son or his daughter to pass through the fire, or that useth divination, or an observer of times, or an enchanter, or a witch … . For all that do these things are an abomination unto the LORD: and because of these abominations the LORD thy God doth drive them out from before thee … .For these nations, which thou shalt possess, hearkened unto observers of times, and unto diviners: but as for thee, the LORD thy God hath not suffered thee so to do. (Deuteronomy 18)

The Hebrews made *Jihad fi sabilillah*—struggle for the sake of Allah—under Joshua to take control of the Levant didn't they?

It is the same thing that occurred after the death of Muhammed, with the Muslim armies that marched into the Levant and Persia.

Muhammed is thus similar to Moses.

I will raise them up a Prophet from among their brethren, like unto thee. (Song of Solomon 5)

The Jews say of this chapter that the subject is King Solomon, peace be upon him. The Christians claim that Jesus, peace be upon him, is being described.

I adjure you, O daughters of Jerusalem, if ye find my beloved, what will ye tell him? That I am love-sick. (Song of Songs 5:8)

If the Tribes of Israel are being told to go out and look for the "beloved" can it be Jesus or Solomon?

King Solomon was the King over the Tribes of Israel, the tribes therefore have no need to go out and look for him, he is there plain to see.

Jesus is the Messiah, the anointed and successor of Kings David and Solomon. The Jews have no need to go out and look for him, the Messiah is coming to them.

His mouth is most sweet; yea, he is altogether lovely (Mahmadim—מַחֲמַדִּים) This is my beloved, and this is my friend, O daughters of Jerusalem. (Song of Solomon 5:16)

This is the name Muhammed explicitly mentioned.

The Tribes of Israel who were given the Song of Solomon had clear prophecy of the coming of Prophet Muhammed, and knew him by name.

Not only did the *Bani Israel*, Tribes of Israel, know they were under obligation to follow a non-Hebrew Prophet they were given his name in the Song of Solomon as noted above.

If there is dispute about the name of Muhammed being a name and not as is translated "altogether lovely", harken unto the following example of the name of David, peace be upon him, in the Hebrew language:

Then all Israel gathered themselves to David (דָּוִיד) unto Hebron, saying: 'Behold, we are thy bone and thy flesh." (1Chronicles 11)

And David (דָּוִד) was the youngest; and the three eldest followed Saul. (1 Samuel 17)

Note the different spellings of "David", one with the *yod* and one without. The addition of the *yod* connotes aggrandizement.

**Neither shall thy name any more be called Abram (אַבְרָם),
but thy name shall be Abraham (אַבְרָהָם) ; for the father of a
multitude of nations have I made thee.** (Genesis 17)

The addition of the letter *heh* connotes that he became a Prophet
of Allah. In Semitic languages, there are two plurals, the plural of
number and the plural of grandeur.

**… and the sign or the wonder come to pass, whereof he
spoke unto thee — saying: "Let us go after other gods,
which thou hast not known, and let us serve them."**
(Deuteronomy 13)

The word for gods is אֱלֹהִים – this refers to plural in number. Yet
in Genesis 1:

In the beginning God created the heaven and the earth.

The word for God is אֱלֹהִים — this refers to the plural in grandeur.
מַחֲמַדִּים is therefore the name Muhammed aggrandized, just as the
name Abram was transformed and given the grandiose status of
Abraham.

Alexander: AbdulKhaliq, you do realize that one can find whatever he desires
by spinning the verses. Chrisitians "prove" that God is really a trinity.

Arabic and Hebrew share the same roots and the word *Mahmadim*
is a Hebrew word that doesn't necessarily refer to Muhammed. In
comparison, the Christians "prove" that Jesus is the Messiah because
his name in Hebrew means Salvation. Same weak logic. Most Hebrew
names mean something like God is great or God is the savior, or God
is grace or slave of God.

I am religious because of what was shown to me, and it wasn't
just spiritual.

Different people receive the light in the way they are familiar with, using the prisms of their culture and knowledge.

Farah: See we return to the question of conditioning and the necessity to free oneself from it.

Alexander: I am a skeptic by nature and will believe nothing if I am not convinced beyond doubt. I am not saying that the Muslim or the Christian paths are false. They are true relative to the audience.

You speak of the need to divest oneself of prejudices and stigmas. The only way to do that is to critically examine everything, starting from ground zero.

You mentioned the ego as synonymous to evil ... We should all have a personal *jihad* with our own ego. Then we may actually progress together. Not just our personal ego ... But also our national and religious ego which is even more dangerous.

Farah: We should realize our humanity as our father Abraham wished for all of us.

Isma'eel AbdulKhaliq Alemao, undeterred, returns to sources and etymology: The *mem* prefix in Semitic languages serves as a pointer or directional. In Arabic we have *min* (from), *mahn* (who, that is) and *mu* (a direct object prefix).

What does the word *Mahmud* mean? *Mahn* (who) *h-m-d* (is praised).

We have a precedent in the Hebrew name Matityahu, gift of God. The same linguistic construction prevails; the *mem* prefix (the pointer) and then the phrase gift of God. We as well, like in the case of *Mahmadim* in the Song of Solomon, have a *patach* vowel marking on the *mem*, illustrating a parallel with the Arabic use of this prefix. Thus one can claim that *Mahmadim* in the Song of Solomon is a name.

Alexander: AbdulKhaliq, I am fluent in Hebrew. I am telling you. It's not a reference to Muhammed but just a word that the name Muhammed shares a root with.

Also, Moses didn't unite the twelve tribes. They were already united. And the parallel of conquering land is common to any warlord or leader. You claim that Jews knew that a prophet named Muhammed would come and that he was a true prophet. This is simply not true at all, even if you really would like it to be.

Isma'eel AbdulKhaliq Alemao keeps up the pace: Deuteronomy 18:18 — **"I will raise them up a Prophet from among their brethren, like unto thee."** Has this prophecy been fulfilled, if not, what are the criteria this prophet must fulfill in order to be a Prophet? What is being alleged by the Muslims is that in like manner as the Messiah has been prophesied, so too has Prophet Muhammed; the Jews have been given information about whom to follow in the future, in like manner as they are told to follow the Messiah.

Alexander: Even if you examine the context of the verses you quote:

> **Thou shalt be whole-hearted with the Lord thy God. For these nations, that thou art to dispossess, hearken unto soothsayers, and unto diviners; but as for thee, the Lord thy God hath not suffered thee so to do.** (Deuteronomy 18:14)

> **A prophet will the Lord thy God raise up unto thee, from the midst of thee, of thy brethren, like unto me; unto him ye shall hearken;** (Deuteronomy 18:15)

It speaks of a Prophet like Moses that Jews should listen to and not to those who invoke ghosts and spirits, etc. Not that some super special Prophet is coming, but in all times that is where guidance shall be drawn from. The Torah is followed by Holy Scriptures that follow exactly that pattern of prophets in each generation. During exile prophecy is hidden and the whole nation of Israel "disappears", scattered among the nations, but the prophecy continues in a concealed form.

I think Muhammed was sincere in his beliefs. But Jews never considered him a prophet for them or awaited a prophet specifically by that name. I think Jesus was also sincere. Not every spiritual leader or a teacher for certain people is necessarily a prophet, but I have nothing against others considering them prophets.

Isma'eel Abdulkhaliq Alemao:

> **A prophet will the Lord thy God raise up unto thee, from the midst of thee, of thy brethren, like unto me; unto him ye shall hearken**. (Deuteronomy 18:15)

Two points must be made here: There is reference to only one prophet to come, not a multiplicity. And, "Of thy brethren" cannot mean from among the tribes of Israel because the tribes are being addressed as a collective. When the term "brethren" is used with a collective, how can it refer to within the group when there is a better phrase, namely "from among yourselves" or Genesis 13:15: "thy seed"?

Alexander: AbdulKhaliq, actually it doesn't say just from thy brethren, but literally from among your brothers, which means from the children of Israel.

The children of Israel are one nation and the children of Ishmael another. You suggest that there are better ways to refer to "brothers", but it is not convincing to think that "among your brothers" means from another nation.

All the back and forth seems to exhaust the participants, ending with this final comment. You can almost hear him sigh.

Alexander: The real question I think we should all ask ourselves is what are the teachings that are worthy to stand on their own, without feeling forced to accept dogmas. There are certainly many good teachings in Islam, in Buddhism, in Judaism ... I wish we could just share those without the "who is closer to God" contest.

This goes naturally into the next thread.

Ben: Jews and Muslims have the same religion. The differences between them are only a little more different than the difference between Sunni Islam and Shi'ah Islam. All the basic religious beliefs are the same. The only difference between Judaism and Islam as it is practiced today is that Judaism believes that *shari'a* of Torah is still valid and that each nation has its own *shari'a,* whereas Islam today believes the *shari'a* of the Quran binding on all nations.

A friend concurs: Exactly ...

Imad: Another big difference is that Jews do not accept Jesus and Muhammed as Allah's prophets and messengers.

By the way, what is the origin of the term "Judaism"?

Ben: The Jews do not call themselves "Jews" in religious law, rather "Israel" or "Children of Israel". The name "Israel" was given by Allah in Torah and the Qur'an.

The name "Judaism" does not appear in the Torah; rather we call our faith "those who follow the Law of Moses".

The question of prophethood is secondary to that of covenant, because if we define the term "prophet" by means of the Torah and then that Torah is invalidated, that would be faulty logic.

Imad: But there were two kingdoms, Israel and Judah.

Ben: The kingdoms of Israel and Judah were political kingdoms which ended 2,000 years ago. The definition of the Jewish people—Children of
Israel—is the community of people who are obligated to keep the
shari'a of *Musa* (Moses). The Torah says:

> **And he said, The LORD came from Sinai, and rose up from**
> **Seir unto them; He shined forth from mount Paran, and**
> **He came with ten thousands of saints** [prophets]: **from His**
> **right hand went a fiery law for them** [*shari'a*/covenant]."
> (Deuteronomy 33:2)

The idea that each of the seventy descendants of Noah became
a nation, with a land, language, and religion is discussed in the Talmud, tractate *Bava Kama* 38a. This is developed in detail by Rabbi
Benamozegh in his book, *Israel and Humanity*. [1]

Christianity however is different; it proposes that the Torah has
been invalidated. When I asked where does Islam prove that the Torah is no longer valid? Two Islamic scholars told me "the New Testament proves it".

A friend asks: Didn't the Jewish scriptures mention the coming of prophet
Muhammed? So why don't Jews believe in him now?

Ben responds, different prophets for different *ummas*: The Torah teaches
that prophecy is not limited to the Jewish people. There were many
prophets who were not Jewish; some were from Arabia, as noted in
the above quote.

---

1. Published posthumously in 1914 by his student Aime Palliere, whom Rabbi
Benamozegh guided in following the Noahide covenant.

Thus we are taught that prophets were sent and covenants were made with the seventy nations of the world. (Since the Great Sanhedrin was disbanded in the fourth century CE, we cannot formally rule that anyone was a prophet.) Allah could have made us one *umma* with one *shari'a*, but He chose not to. Instead we are to compete as if in a race for virtue.

The Torah says it is eternal and will never be changed. It also says that a prophet cannot change the Torah. This means that any Muslim or Christian who claims that his prophet invalidated the Torah, essentially invalidates the claim to prophethood, from the point of view of Torah. As I said above, the question of prophethood is secondary to the question of the validity of the covenant of Torah.

Asif: You said, "When I asked where Islam proves that the Torah is no longer valid? Two Islamic scholars told me 'the New Testament proves it'.". But I disagree. The Qur'an says that Jesus did not bring any new laws.

> And [I have come] **confirming what was before me of the Torah and to make lawful for you some of what was forbidden to you. And I have come to you with a sign from your Lord, so fear Allah and obey me.**

Ben: This is a matter of great debate, and the lack of agreement is the only reason why we are not all sitting together as brothers. May the *Al-Mahdi* (Messiah) come quickly and answer all our questions, and explain where we are different.

Asif: Early Christianity did believe in following the Torah, it was Pauline Christianity that diverged.

A friend: There are verses in the Qur'an that say that Allah will seek out our differences on the Day of Judgment. That means we need to accept that we differ. There are verses too that show us where to find common ground, especially in that we worship none but Allah.

Ben: On the eternity of Torah,

> **Thou shalt keep therefore His statutes, and His commandments, which I command thee this day, that it may go well with thee, and with thy children after thee, and that thou mayest prolong [thy] days upon the earth, which the LORD thy God giveth thee, for ever.**
> (Deuteronomy 4:40)

It also says that a prophet cannot change the Torah. (Deuteronomy 18:13-22)

Sada: Muhammed never changed the original message of Torah; he confirmed it and corrected some things that had changed.

Faried: The Qur'an does not say that everything was changed; it says certain words were changed from their places; it instructs its messenger to tell Christians and Jews to judge according to their own scripture. Interference with the word of God happened in Islamic history as well. Here the interference came about with attributing false *ahadith* (legends) to the messenger and misrepresenting the meaning of the Qur'an.

Ben: Rabbinic Jews today also believe that there were Jewish scriptures that were tampered with: the Septuagint and the Samaritan Bible. Perhaps Muhammed was referring to these when speaking of words that were changed from their places.

Faried: Muslims are reminded right at the beginning of the Qur'an to believe in what was sent to the Messenger of the Qur'an and what was revealed before it.

A friend: The ultimate truth is beside Allah, the All-Knower. If we want the truth, then sincerely ask Allah for his guidance. We are indeed rewarded or punished on individual account. May Allah guide us to His blessed truth. Amin.

Ben: There is *deen* (basic religion) and *shari'a* (covenant). Islam refers to both a *deen* and a *shari'a*. Judaism is only the name of the *shari'a* of Torah.

Islam as a *deen* is equivalent to what we call Noahide Law. It is obligatory on everyone. In that sense it is the foundation of all proper religion, even Judaism.

Islam as the *shari'a* of the Qur'an is for the *umma* (people) of Muhammed (pbuh). From a rabbinic point of view, there have been at least seventy covenants, one for each of the seventy nations of the world. It is certainly possible for the whole world to join one covenant, especially the one that is closest to the simple faith *(millat)* of Abraham (pbuh).

However, from the point of view of *tikkun olam* (rectifying the world) one would expect the natural diversity of mankind to cause individuals to continue to be attracted to the covenants that have been assigned to their nation, albeit in their corrected form. The Rambam says that Islam has a role in assisting this rectification.

A short note on government:

A friend asks*:* Do you think democracy is the best system to choose the leader in country?

Ben: I don't know if this applies to every country, but in the Torah it is shown that the country must be run through agreement by two people: a king and a prophet. The former represents the wants and desires of the people, and the latter represents the rights and obligations to God. In modern terms a king would be replaced by a democratically elected parliament. The prophet would be represented by the best and most worthy scholars of the nation. Together this upper and lower house, when they agree, would be in my opinion the best system to run a country.

A friend: Salam, every *masjid* (mosque) will have its *imam* (religious leader) who knows the Holy Qur'an and studies each situation best in preparation of his weekly *kuthbah* (sermon).

Ben responds: *Wa alikum salaam.* The concepts of *ijma', al-sawad al-a'zam, jumhur, al-tarjih bi-al-kathra* and legal teachings *al-qawa'id al-fiqhiyya* are related to the principle of majority rule. This relates to popular sovereignty, equality, popular consultation, and the adoption of majority decisions by all the participants in political processes.

This concept is expressed in the *hadith*, "My *umma* will not agree on an error, and when you see a disagreement you have to follow the majority *(fa-idha ra'aytum ikhtilafan 'alaykum bi-al-sawiid al-a'zam)."* It has been argued that *al-sawad al-a'zam* means the majority group *(al-jama'a al-kath'ra)* because their agreement is closest to the *ijma* (consensus).

In my own opinion, I would favor the adoption of the majority principle within the framework of other principles validated by *shari'a* or *halachah* in an Islamic or halachic state.

Many fear that a state run by *shari'a* would lead to endless religious coercion; this misconception comes from a misplaced idea of what divine law is. Common law is essential to the functioning of society and is enforceable. Divine law reflects the ideal state that all people must strive for, but it is not enforceable on earth. Both Islam and Judaism agree on this.

In the Roman (Western) view of law, for every law there must be a punishment. If a law has no punishment, it is effectively thought of as nullified. Laws are thus limited to what is enforceable. If not enforceable, the legislature would not have made the law in the first place. If something is not forbidden because it is not enforceable, then it is permitted.

In the Torah/Islamic concept of law, God is the sovereign. While technically this is a theocracy, the word theocracy has been given a bad name because it is confused with Western style enforcement. There are visions of minions of religious police monitoring compliance with "God's law". However this is mistaken, since neither the Torah nor the Qur'an spend anything more than a few words discussing enforcement of law. The Islamic concept of law is guidance. Ideally, it is a rich reservoir of information from which to draw on to decide how to act appropriately in any given situation. Enforcement is done by God who sees all and knows men's hearts. However, in a real world, there are unbelievers, hypocrites and criminals who would take advantage of this situation. So the earthly sovereign is empowered to enforce a small subset of these laws, being limited to those laws which allow the proper functioning of society.

Take for example the Torah punishment for picking up sticks on the Sabbath. The Sabbath is one of the distinguishing characteristics of the Children of Israel. Carrying in public places and lighting fires on the Sabbath is prohibited. However, the Torah only records one person who was stoned for picking up sticks for a fire, even though the violation of the Sabbath probably happened countless times. In this specific case, the person was warned beforehand and did his actions publicly in direct defiance to the commandment of Moses (pbuh). In this limited case, where rebellion would begin to degrade social order, did Moses (pbuh) require that the rebel be physically punished with capital punishment instead waiting for some spiritual accounting at a later time.

The same is true with the punishment for adultery. It is absolutely true that sin of adultery is extremely severe, detracts from the family unit, and causes imeasurable spiritual damage to the individual and society. It is also absolutely true that God is just, and will punish sins. However, it is never suggested in the Torah or the Qur'an to set up informants to seek out adultery. Instead the temporal sovereign is empowered to enforce a physical version of the spiritual capital punishment, when it becomes a threat to civil society. In the Talmud, adultery guidelines are set forth that it should be punished physically with capital punishment when the person was warned beforehand, understood what they were doing, and performed the act publicly with witnesses.

Unlike Western law, this does not mean any unpunished act is permitted. It will surely be punished but not necessarily by the temporal court. And even if not convicted, there may be enough evidence to be grounds for immediate divorce, affecting alimony, child support, and visitation rights depending on what is needed for civil society.

A friend: May Allah make you firm and useful to the rising of Islam.

Ben: *Insha'Allah.* May we all be proper and complete in our faith.

A disillusioned friend: Today, worldwide (no conspiracy theory needed), only the corrupt, or only those who are willing to corrupt, are promoted to leadership positions, whether in the military, the government, and even in religious councils.

Another: The system mentioned above is currently implemented in a form in Iran. However, one distinction is that the religious leaders first vet the elected officials if they are theologically eligible to run. Also, the religious leaders have supreme veto power which is definitely needed as people without deeper theological convictions are susceptible to make rash, short-sighted decisions.

A second friend: Democracy could work fine with minor changes in the way it operates. People should be involved in running the government rather than just making the government.

And a third: Islam teaches us to follow the Prophet and leaders who are righteous and learned. In matters religious, even the Prophet has to follow the edicts from Allah that are the form of revelations. He cannot change them or follow other teachings. In matters temporal, he should consult the experts and those who are close to him. This teaching should apply to all leaders. Democracy or elections are no guarantee that the voters will choose the right leaders. There is also no guarantee that those who impose themselves on the people in revolutions and overthrowing of governments can be the right leaders. Only those who fear Allah are able to lead the people aright.

19. The Amman Message

Friends discuss The Amman message, which condemned terror and promoted a more peaceful Islam.

Ben Abrahamson summarized the main points: Based on the *fatwas* provided by the following great scholars (who included the Shaykh Al-Azhar; Ayatollah Sistani and Sheikh Qaradawi), in July 2005 CE, King Abdullah II of Jordan convened an international Islamic conference of 200 of the world's leading Islamic scholars or *'Ulema* from fifty countries in Amman. The scholars unanimously issued a ruling on three fundamental issues (which became known as the 'Three Points of the Amman Message'):

1. They specifically recognized the validity of all eight *madhabs* (legal schools) of Sunni, Shi'a and Ibadhi Islam; of traditional Islamic Theology (Ash'arism); of Islamic Mysticism (Sufism), and of true Salafi thought, and came to a precise definition of who is a Muslim.

2. Based upon this definition they forbade *takfir* (declarations of apostasy) between Muslims.

3. Based upon the *madhabs* they set forth the subjective and objective preconditions for the issuing of *fatwas* (rulings), thereby exposing ignorant and illegitimate edicts in the name of Islam.

These Three Points were then unanimously adopted by the Islamic world's political and temporal leaderships at the Organization of the Islamic Conference summit at Mecca in December 2005. And over a period of one year from July 2005 to July 2006, the Three Points were also unanimously adopted by six other international Islamic scholarly assemblies, culminating with the International Islamic *Fiqh* Academy of Jeddah (the Islamic World's leading juridical body) in July 2006. In total, over 500 leading Muslim scholars worldwide as can be seen online (at www.ammanmessage.com) unanimously endorsed the Amman Message and its Three Points.

Here are some direct quotes:

The primordial religion of Islam is founded upon equanimity, balance, moderation, and facilitation: …. (2:143) The Prophet Muhammed—peace and blessings upon him—said: **"Facilitate and do not make difficult, bear good tidings and do not deter."**

No day has passed but that this religion has been at war against extremism, radicalism and fanaticism. They are not from the true character of the tolerant, accepting Muslim.

Islam calls for treating others as one desires to be treated. It urges the tolerance and forgiveness that express the nobility of the human being: **"The recompense for an evil is an evil equal thereto, but who forgives and reconciles, his recompense is from God"** (42:40). **"Good and evil are not equal. Repel with what is most virtuous. Then he between whom and you there is enmity will be as if he were an intimate friend"** (41:34).

Islam recognizes the noble station of [human] life, so
there is to be no fighting against non-combatants, and no
assault upon civilians and their properties, children at their
mothers' bosom, students in their schools, nor upon elderly
men and women. ... On religious and moral grounds, we
denounce the contemporary concept of terrorism that is
associated with wrongful practices, whatever their source
and form may be.

... And the last of our supplications is that praise be to God,
Lord of the worlds.

Amman
Ramadan 1425 Hijri
The Hashemite Kingdom of Jordan
November 2004 A.D.

A friend: Sadly, these messages fell on deaf ears. It was conveyed in 2004,
and look at all those terrible wars which happened afterwards.

Ben: Why do you think that happened? Was the approach wrong?

Our friend's response: The approach was not wrong, what is written and
declared is correct, the intention is good, but sadly, nobody paid attention. I believe Muslim leaders must work extra hard, double hard,
even triple hard to propagate the ideas to their people. But what can
we do? The Amman declaration was not even mentioned in school
books in my country, post 2005. If they are not propagated properly,
how will the young generation benefit from it?

Ben: So you are saying that the propagation of correct ideas is limited by
the leadership support for those ideas? I would ask, why can't people pick up on truth on their own?

Our friend's response: I can't speak for other countries, so I use my own country as an example. We have Internet access for the general public since the mid-to-late 1990s. But I can gather ten random Muslim from the streets in my city (the Capital) and ask them: "Do you have access to the Internet?" and I am very sure at least eight will say, "Yes I have". Then take those eight people and ask them, "Do you know about the Amman Message?", and maybe only one will say "Yes I do". (I just randomly asked nine Muslims in my office, and surprisingly none of them knows about the Amman Message). So you see, even with open internet access, the Amman message does not reach my country's Muslim population. How could they pick up on the truth of the Message if they don't even know that the Message exists?

Ben: This sound more like people don't find it interesting, not worth passing on.

Our friend responds: That is because the messages spread by radical groups are far more prevalent. This is a Muslim-majority country, and the government tolerates the radicals. They are allowed to publish everything they like, and sadly, our young generation found their messages more often than the peace messages as embodied within the Amman Message.

Ben: But everyone theoretically has access to the same material on the internet, why isn't the Amman Message talked about more by moderate people?

Friend: Moderates have far less Internet presence in Indonesian-language websites. I know of only two—www.nu.or.id and www.islamlib.com. Besides, our Muslim moderates, like moderates everywhere, are not very passionate about campaigning for their cause. Unlike the radicals, who are better organized and better funded.

Some see problems in the Amman Message itself, which explains
why it was not a popular as hoped.

Mustafa Kamil Ata believes that the participants overstepped their authority, that the Qur'an should be the guide, not self-appointed leaders: : Let me explain why "The three points of failures" are not interesting.

1. "They specifically recognized the validity of all eight *madhabs* (communities) ... and came to a precise definition of who is a Muslim."

    Since they did not show an *ayah* (verse) or *hadith* (commentary) mentioning any *madhab* as valid/invalid, they are inventing things:

    And do not say, about what your own tongues put forth falsely. "This is lawful, and this is forbidden," so that you invent a lie against Allah. Indeed, those who invent a lie against Allah will not prosper. (Qur'an, *An Nahl* 16:116)

    Who are they to define "who is a Muslim", while Allah clearly defines:

    Say [O Muslims]: **"We believe in Allah and that which has been sent down to us, and that which was sent down to Abraham, and Ishmael, and Isaac, and Jacob, and the tribes, and that which was given to Moses and Jesus, and that which was given to the prophets from their Lord. We make no distinction between any of them, and to Him we have submitted."** (Qur'an, *Al-Baqarah* 2:136)

    So if they believe in the same that which you believe, then they are (rightly) guided. And if they turn away, then

they are only in schism. So Allah will be sufficient for you against them. And He is the All Hearer, the All Knower. (Qur'an, *Al-Baqarah* 2:137)

So you see, Allah defines no *madhab;* indeed Allah accepts the people of the scripture as rightly guided if they believe as defined in the following verses:

Say [O Muhammed]:"O People of the Scripture, come to a word [of agreement] equitable between us and you, that we shall not worship except Allah, nor shall we associate with Him anything, nor shall one of us take others for lords besides Allah." So if they turn away, then say: "Bear witness that we are those who have submitted [to Allah]." (Qur'an, *Al-Imran* 3:64)

Certainly, those who believe [in the Qur'an], and those who are Jews, and Christians, and Sabeans, whoever believed in Allah and the Last Day and did righteous deeds, shall then have their reward with their Lord, and there shall be no fear upon them, nor shall they grieve. (Qur'an, *Al-Baqarah* 2:62)

Say: "O People of the Book, you are not on anything [as to guidance] until you observe the Torah and the Gospel and that which has been sent down [the Qur'an] to you from your Lord." And that which has been revealed to you from your Lord will surely increase many of them in rebellion and disbelief. So grieve not for the disbelieving people. (Qur'an, *Al-Maida* 5:68)

And so many other verses to be recounted defining "who is Muslim".

2. "Based upon this definition they forbade *takfir* between Muslims." They are once again overstepping their boundaries. Allah is the only authority to allow or forbid anything.

3. "Based upon the *madhabs* they set forth the preconditions for the issuing of *fatwas*, thereby exposing ignorant and illegitimate edicts in the name of Islam." So they are exposing their own ignorant and illegitimate edicts in the name of Islam.

As if these *madhabs* are not enough, now they are inventing new categories as moderate, non-moderate, extremist, etc. As I see it there are no midways, no categories. A person is either a Muslim or not, depending on whether he or she matches the criteria defined clearly in the above verses. The time for those self appointed prophets and gods has come to an end, *insha'Allah*.

When asked for more clarification of his position, Mr. Ata replied: While I feel I am challenging mistaken leaders, that's not because I have a great deal of self confidence. The strength I feel stems from the following verses, and some other verses not included below:

> **And say: "Truth has come and falsehood has vanished away. Indeed, falsehood is ever bound to vanish."** (Qur'an, *Bani Isra'il*, 17:81)

> **There shall be no compulsion in the religion. The right path has indeed become distinct from the wrong. So whoever disbelieves in false deities, and believes in Allah, then certainly he has grasped the most trustworthy handhold that will never break. And Allah is All Hearer, All Knower.** (Qur'an, *Al-Baqarah* 2:256)

And do not become weak, nor grieve, and you shall gain the upper hand if you are [true] **believers.** (Qur'an, *Al-Imran* 3:139)

While I feel that I am a true believer, I try not to forget the fact that what actually matters is what Allah says for His servants. As servants, it is none of our business to judge anyone as more or less worthy — this doesn't mean we cannot have opinions; it means we cannot assume that Allah also thinks the way we think.

It is the result of this belief that I strongly disagree with whoever tries to categorize and brand people generally, and worse yet, officially. Such attempts are always dangerous that may easily divide people into many hate camps.

The above discussion should indicate to readers truly interested in interfaith dialogue that such dialogue must be done with extreme sensitivity to each party. The Amman Message sounds nice to the uninitiated, but it apparently did not make the Qur'an the final word on what is Islam, who is a Muslim, etc. This overstepping of boundaries was enough to disqualify the Amman Message in the eyes of many Muslims, even if it was well meant, and even if one agreed with the intentions and the message itself. Note that Mr. Ata quotes the Qur'an more frequently than the leaders involved in the Amman Message.

*Remember — Sunan Abu-Dawud Book 25, Number 3644: Narrated Jundub: The Prophet (pbuh) said: **If anyone interprets the Book of Allah in the light of his opinion even if he is right, he has erred.***

Dialogue with serious Muslims must include an awareness of their great reverence for text and tradition. To those used to Western relativism, this is an adjustment indeed. And a needed one.

Note the Hajj *to Mecca—rich and poor, Arab and Chinese, Black and White, are wearing two simple white garments showing our innate equality.* Kitab *(scripture) is equalizing as well. Mr. Ata, unimpressed by titles, stood up to hundreds of leaders just by brandishing scripture. He was empowered, whatever his status, by his knowledge of* kitab. *He will not be imposed upon by influences other than those grounded in scripture. Any efforts to do otherwise will be met with resistance.*

This brings us naturally to the next topic—Cultural Diplomacy, also known as Track III Diplomacy.

20. Cultural Diplomacy

Track III Diplomacy

The Road Map to a Culture of Peace in the Middle East

Ben Abrahamson: Track III diplomacy involves dialogue along cultural
and religious lines to foster understanding between various peoples
in areas of conflict. I have been involved in some of the meetings that
have brought leaders of different faiths together in Istanbul, Ankara,

Paris, Jerusalem, Jordan, Oxford and Yale Universities, the House of Parliament and the United Nations, as well as in areas of conflict such as Hebron, in the Holy Land.

Dr. Emil Constantinescu, president of the Institute for Cultural Diplomacy, Berlin, defines cultural diplomacy as "a course of actions, which are based on and utilize the exchange of ideas, values, traditions and other aspects of culture or identity, whether to strengthen relationships, enhance socio-cultural cooperation or promote national interests; cultural diplomacy can be practiced by either the public sector, private sector or civil society."

He maintains that such diplomacy has existed as a practice for centuries. See more at: http://www.culturaldiplomacy.org

Religious Affairs Chairman for Foreign Relations of Turkey, Mehmet Gormez, has stated "… the impact of religion in international relations is becoming increasingly more valuable, and we will see it peak in the future."

As Dr. Mordechai Kedar, lecturer in Arabic at Bar-Ilan University, noted, "… traditional Islamic people find it easier to talk to traditional Jews who share the same cultural world, and perhaps it is time that the (Israel) Foreign Ministry also understand this… . It is important for Israel to be represented in a way that will make it easier for our traditional neighbors to accept us, and that the state of Israel is not entirely secular and liberal."

Former Israeli Ambassador Alan Baker noted: "It requires ongoing spiritual and practical dialogue between religious leaders, clergy, and lay leaders in order to establish common interests and principals."

Understanding the Erastian Roots of Western Institutions

From The Permanent Forum for Global Ethics and The Culture Of Peace—Track III Cultural Diplomacy; United Nations. Conf. Room 1. Main Bldg., June 24, 2013; "Implementation of The Levant Initiative: The Academic Dimension"

Ben Abrahamson: What is the role of religion in peacemaking? What is the role of religion in contemporary political theory?

In the UN declaration "Declaration and Programme of Action on a Culture of Peace" *(A/53/L.79)* 53/243 there is a definition of what is a culture of peace.

Article 1

A culture of peace is a set of values, attitudes, traditions, and modes of behaviour and ways of life based on: (*a*) Respect for life ... (*b*) respect for sovereignty ... (*c*) respect for human rights and fundamental freedoms; (*d*) commitment to peaceful settlement of conflicts (*e*) meet the developmental and environmental needs ... (*f*) respect right to development ... (*g*) respect for equal rights and opportunities for women and men; (*h*) Respect freedom of expression ... (*i*) principles of freedom, justice, democracy, tolerance, solidarity, cooperation, pluralism, cultural diversity, dialogue, and understanding

In this declaration, religion is not explicitly mentioned. It is only mentioned once, with regard to discrimination against the individual:

Recognizing the need to eliminate all forms of discrimination and intolerance, including those based on race, colour, sex, language, religion, political or other opinion, national, ethnic or social origin, property, disability, birth or other status,

What is not explicitly stated is the "respect for the religious community", ie the rights of religious people when they combine with each other, and respect for the hierarchy of indigenous religious leadership.

***

In the UN declaration, "Elimination of all forms of religious intolerance" *(A/59/503/Add.2)* 59/199, it recalls that

... all States have pledged themselves, under the Charter of the United Nations, to promote and encourage universal respect for and observance of human rights and fundamental freedoms for all without distinction as to race, sex, language or religion, ...

Also in this declaration, religion is only recognized as the right of the individual and not the community.

***

In the UN Declaration, "International Decade for a Culture of Peace and Non-Violence for the Children of the World (2001–2010)" 53/25 *(A/53/L.25)*, the governments of member states:

> ... are invited *to take the necessary steps* to ensure that the practice of peace and nonviolence is taught at all levels in their respective societies, including in educational institutions;

Here the governments of member states are invited to take the role of moral guides.

***

This is even more explicit in the UN Declaration on "Elimination of all forms of religious intolerance" *(A/59/503/Add.2)* 59/199.

> ... restrictions on the freedom to manifest religion is permitted if necessary to protect public safety, order, health or morals or the fundamental rights and freedoms of others.

Here we have the government restricting religion on moral grounds. What moral grounds are there if not based in some kind of religious thought?

***

Eric Nelson is a Professor of Government at Harvard University. His research focuses on the history of political thought in early-modern Europe and America, and on the implications of that history for debates in contemporary political theory.

In his essay, "The Religious Origins Of Religious Tolerance—

Analysis", he notes the popular way of thinking about the Western intellectual history:

> The West moved from an indefensibly theological frame
> of mind to a confusedly metaphysical one, and then
> finally to a respectably rational one. In the sixteenth and
> seventeenth centuries in Europe, we are told, that a titanic
> shift occurred in the way that European Christians thought
> about moral and political philosophy. In this period, under
> the influence of a specific set of circumstances and events—
> the rise of the new science, philosophical skepticism, and
> the carnage of the religious wars—Western theorists turned
> away from religion, regarding its claims as lacking in
> authority, and also as being fundamentally dangerous and
> inimical to peace.

The result of all of this was the "Great Separation", a decision made by Western theorists to sequester religion from moral and political theory and to allow those disciplines to get on according to their own rational criteria without any recourse to religious claims. This is an old and established view.

However, Professor Nelson asserts that many, if not most, of our most fundamental freedoms, commitments to human rights, and political institutions emerged instead out of a deeply theologized context and were explicitly justified in the first instance on the basis of religious claims. Committed early modern Christians found themselves arguing in favor of fundamental freedoms, rights and institutions, and doing so on religious grounds. Such leaders included Abraham Lincoln, the founding fathers of the United States of America, 16th–17th century political theorists such as Henry Ainsworth, Erastus, Gomerus, Armenius, Hugo Grotius, John Lightfoot, Thomas Coleman, John Seldon, and in recent history, Martin Luther King Jr.

The UN should be no exception, as in its founding charter, also emblazoned on the statue outside, quotes the verse in Isaiah, "men shall beat their swords into plowshares ..."

16th-18th century Christian Hebraists explored rabbinic texts in search of creating the ideal commonwealth. The Talmud, Midrash and medieval codes of Jewish law were consulted. As Henry Ainswoth said (1611):

> One must consult "Hebrew doctors of the ancienter sort, and some later of best esteeme for learning" if one wishes "to give light to the ordinances of Moses touching the externall practice of them in the commonwealth of Israel, which the Rabbines did record, and without whose helpe, many of those legall rites (especially in Exodus and Leviticus) will not easily be understood."

Ainsworth and other Hebraists proceeded under the fervent belief that the proper form of government was a theocracy, in which all would be guided by scripture in an effort to approximate the ideal heavenly standard on earth—however, at the same time, God himself restricted the enforcement of religious law to those laws of civic consequence as determined by the civil magistrate. Although there was no separation of religion and state, the only laws that were enforceable were those that if broken would threaten civic order. Thus, what sorts of religious practice and observance have important civic consequences? Not many. These Hebraists concurred with the rabbinic view that there are virtually no "thought crimes", ie, thoughts are not punishable by earthly courts.

Thomas Lüber (Erastus) (1568) passionately supported theocracy based on the ancient Hebrew commonwealth. Note here how such a theocracy gives ample room for religious tolerance: "Although the Israelites could, of course, punish those who had committed civil offences, there was no spiritual sanction for errors in doctrine or belief." and "While 'externall Religion' falls within the purview of the magistrate (because it can affect civil peace and order), internal religion does not. For "who judgeth the heart but God?"

Concerning tolerance for the minority, Grotius stated: "Within the Hebrew republic itself, there always lived some strangers [not bound by Mosaic religious law], known as hasidei ummot, or Righteous among the Gentiles.

"These people were not bound by the Mosaic law, yet were allowed to live amongst the Israelites unmolested, provided that they observed a minimal standard of general morality." This he argued, was the basis of civil, i.e. natural law. Grotius did advocate for regulation of blasphemy if the blasphemy would interfere with civil order, ie, questioning God's omnipotence. Later English Hebraists disagreed with Grotius on this point, and relegated such "thought crimes" to the peculiar needs of the Hebrew commonwealth and not applicable to English society. Here we have an opening for understanding that given the variety of human culture, some countries will tend towards reinforcement of beliefs and some will not.

John Selden, John Lightfoot, James Harrington, and Thomas Coleman were seventeenth century English political theorists, heavily influenced by Erastus and the model of the Hebrew commonwealth. Seldon's "De jure naturali et gentium iuxta disciplinam Ebraeorum" (1640) was published three years before the convening of the Westminster Assembly, and contained Selden's derivation of a universal morality from the "Praecepta Noachidarum", the Noachide laws.

While the civil magistrate was limited to enforcing infractions of laws regarded as criminal, employed to disturb the peace, or against universal morality as expressed in the Noachide laws, the Parliament was free to legislate on the full range of civil and religious law.

Selden owes all of this to rabbinic literature—specifically, to the canonical account in Talmudic tractate *Sanhedrin* 56a-b, and its elaboration in Maimonides' *Mishneh Torah*.

God's Embrace of Toleration

While the national religion was to be the main focus of Parliament, minority religions were guaranteed religious freedom based on the *praecepta Noachidarum*.

The existence of the category of sojourners *(proselyti domicilii)* who were allowed to live within the Hebrew republic even though they did not acknowledge or abide by the full Mosaic law, and were not subject to punishment for refusing to participate in public worship—proves, for Selden, that Israelite theocracy practiced toleration.

In the Qur'an this message is reinforced:

To each among you have we prescribed a Shar'ia [law] **and Minhaj** [custom]. **If Allah had so willed, He could have made you a single Ummah** [faith community], **but** [His plan is] **to test you in what He hath given you: so strive as in a race in all virtues. The goal of you all is to Allah; it is He that will show you the truth about the matters in which you are different.** (Qur'an, *Al Maeda* 5.48)

To each is a goal to which Allah turns him; then strive together [as in a race] **towards all that is good. Wheresoever ye are, Allah will bring you together. For Allah hath power over all things.** (Qur'an, *Al Baqara* 2.148)

To every people [was sent] **an Apostle/Law Giver** *(rasûl)*: **when their Apostle/Law Giver** *(rasûl)* **comes** [before them] **the matter will be judged between them with justice and they will not be wronged.** (Qur'an, *Al-Yunus* 10.47)

The word *Islam* is used in two ways, as a *deen* (Law) and as a *shari'a*. One will find that everywhere the word *deen* is used it refers to the universal nature of religion and where the word *shari'a* is used it refers to the particular nature of religion as it applies to one faith community.

***

We see that early European religious thinkers found themselves arguing in favor of religious toleration, and doing so on religious grounds. When it comes to the founding fathers of the United States of America, Thomas Jefferson's advocacy of separation of religion and state was in order to protect the churches from interference from the government, but not to place the government in a position of being able to trump religion. He stated in a letter to the minority Baptist congregation in Connecticut:

> Believing with you that religion is a matter which lies
> solely between man and his god, that he owes account to
> none other for his faith or his worship, that the legitimate
> powers of government reach actions only, and not opinions,
> I contemplate with sovereign reverence that act of the whole
> American people which declared that their "legislature"
> should "make no law respecting an establishment of
> religion, or prohibiting the free exercise thereof," thus
> building a wall of separation between church and State.
> Adhering to this expression of the supreme will of the nation
> in behalf of the rights of conscience, I shall see with sincere
> satisfaction the progress of those sentiments which tend to
> restore to man all his natural rights, convinced he has no
> natural right in opposition to his social duties."

His intent was to assure a minority denomination of its right to practice its form of religion, not, as has been used since, to put the government in a position of power over religion. Indeed, like the 16th-18th century Hebraists, he encourages the development of faith.

A series of court cases beginning in the 1940s sought to use Jefferson's above noted declaration to defund auxiliary needs of religious bodies, such as transportation to religious schools. The unintended effects of these court cases led to the lack of meaningful religious contribution to political dialogue during the passage of legislation and the increasing role of the Supreme Court to provide moral direction in legislation, albeit in an adhoc and unchecked fashion.

The French model of separation of religion and state, "laicite" has been criticized as anti-religious, for example, in its banning of religious apparel in public institutions, thus actually preventing adherence to religious precepts. We thus see in the French and American model a movement towards the marginalizing of religion and discrimmination against religion rather than mere separation of powers.

***

Summary: So now we can answer the questions we asked at the beginning. Why wasn't religion explicitly mentioned in Article 1 of the "Declaration and Programme of Action on a Culture of Peace". And when it is mentioned once, it is only with regard to discrimination against the individual. There is no explicit recognition of the religious community: the rights of religious people when they combine with each other, as they have for thousands of years. Instead the governments of member states are invited to take the role of moral guides. And they may even restrict religious expression on moral grounds. What moral grounds are there if not based in some kind of religious thought?

Understanding the Erastian roots of Western institutions, it is possible to understand this in the sense we have described above. The civil magistrate, or executive branch of government, can legislate and even limit religious expression to promote civil order—but this was originally intended to be based on religious motives, under the guidance of spiritual leaders, and in an attempt to approximate what God would have us do.

Although the effect is the same, the recent idea that guidance of the civil magistrate should come from purely secular, that is humanistic norms, is a relatively recent innovation—and does not fit very well in the Levant.

***

It is true that the religion of humanism seems to be favored by UN declarations, such as the UN Declaration, "Global Agenda for Dialogue among Civilizations" *(A/56/L.3 and Add.1)* 56/6, where it says:

> *Recognizing* that human rights and fundamental freedoms derive from the dignity and worth inherent in the human person and are thus universal, indivisible, interdependent and interrelated, and that the human person is the central subject of human rights and fundamental freedoms and, consequently, should be the principal beneficiary and should participate actively in the realization of these rights and freedoms, ...

It is important to note that humanism in these declarations plays the role that religion plays, and in that sense functions as a religion. One cannot assume that because one is a humanist, that he or she is appealing to the common fundamental principles accepted by all mankind. Humanism is a world view with its own biases, bigotry, and prejudices. Often parliamentarians and political scientists gravitate to like minded intellectual elite, and shun religious intellectuals, not recognizing that the majority of fundamental freedoms, commitments to human rights, and political institutions were set in place by deeply religious intellectuals of the sixteenth through eighteenth centuries.

The role of the civil magistrate in Western tradition until very recently has been to arbitrate and administer religion for the good of civil order. It was not intended to be an opening for humanism to trump religion but for the civil magistrate to act as a representative of indigenous moral values.

When detecting prejudice and bias within our institutions, we can look at the numbers of any given community which are represented. If an institution contains almost exclusively white Europeans, or almost exclusively male gender, we can say that bias is at work. If the number of religiously trained parliamentarians is a miniscule presence, while the majority of citizens, especially in the Levant, are deeply religious, then we may again be facing bias within the institution.

The fact that parliamentarians may not even be aware of the bias against traditional religious values and towards humanism, can be seen in the offhand comment by one parliamentarian—who when asked about the number of religious intellectuals participating in the peace process—responded by saying that such people are very rare and almost don't exist.

***

Variety is thus not a new phenomenon; rather, it is inherently Abrahamic. We need not strategize social revolutions, thus threatening indigenous peoples who already have their own scripturally based mechanism for peacemaking. Indeed, to strategize influences into other cultures is to create a sense of antagonism towards them, which these peoples do indeed sense. Those involved in such efforts at social change end up creating another form of bigotry in a secular liberal guise and having the opposite effect from their original intent. Working with the positive, indigenous scriptural values of the peoples of the Levant will bring a lasting peace.

Peace efforts in the Middle East have been ongoing for the past few decades. Despite the peace treaties signed between Israel and Egypt, and Israel and Jordan, the region remains a powder-keg for hostilities at large in particular between the Palestinians and Israel. The Arab Spring, which brought new developments in Arab countries, made efforts to reach an encompassing solution to the Mideast conflict so far without success.

The UN must have a team of religiously trained leaders, approved of by indigenous religious authorities, who can act as advisors to the UN and liaisons between the UN and the peoples of the Levant. The people will feel represented and lasting peaceful change can finally take place.

Cultural diplomacy can succeed where other efforts have failed because it brings leaders together in an environment of familiarity, credibility, and trust.

Fadzilah: *Masha'Allah*, Rabbi.

Habib: Very good work ... keep going.

Rachel: UN initiatives state their intention to change societies via the arts, media, and educational systems. These efforts are likely to be seen as colonialism in disguise, certainly if they are not in line with *al kitab* and approved of by our religious leaders.

The Qur'an is replete with a framework for theocracy-cum-tolerance: in *Surat An-Nisa 4, ayat* 162-163:

> **But those among them who are well-grounded in knowledge, and the believers, believe in what hath been revealed to thee and what was revealed before thee: And [especially] those who establish regular prayer and practice regular charity and believe in Allah (*Subhanahu wa-ta'ala*) and in the Last Day: To them shall We soon give a great reward. We have sent thee inspiration, as We sent it to Noah and the Messengers after him: we sent inspiration to Abraham, Isma'il, Isaac, Jacob and the Tribes, to Jesus, Job, Jonah, Aaron, and Solomon, and to David We gave the Psalms.**

Make allowances for people, command what is right, and turn away from the ignorant. (Qur'an , *Al-Araf* 7:199)

Tolerance of different races and peoples:

O Mankind! We created you from a male and female, and made you into peoples and tribes so that you might come to know each other. The noblest among you in God's sight is that one of you who best performs his duty. God is All-Knowing, All-Aware. (Qur'an, *Al Hujurat* 49:13).

Freedom of thought:

There is no compulsion in religion. (Qur'an *Al Baqarah* 2:256)

So remind them! You are only a reminder. You are not in control of them. (Qur'an, Al Gashiyah 88:21-22)

If your Lord had willed, all the people on earth would have believed. Do you think you can force people to be believers? (Qur'an, Yunus 10:99)

There is no separation of religion and state in Islam or Judaism. A state indeed must have laws, enforcement, and punishment for crimes that upset the fabric of society. However, in both Islam and Judaism, law enforcement must occur through a justice system, courts and witnesses, not via the media and majority opinion. Connecting the West with its Erastian roots will return us to both a God-fearing and tolerant framework. Muslims need not view the West as a foreign threat but as an entity in need of revival. What is needed is for Muslims to both cleave to Qur'anic teachings, and educate themselves about Western political science, especially about Erastus and his followers. Muslims can take an active part in reconnecting the West with its own theocratic roots as well as expressing the authentic beauty of Islam.

Jeffrey identifies himself as a Reform Jew and asks Ben: Where does all this interfaith dialogue leave him? Are the religious Muslims and Jews going to band together against people like him?

Ben answers: All that is required is that you point to your covenant and identify it as the one under which you are bound. No one is checking up on your level of observance.

Jeff: I don't really trust religious people. I hope what you say is true; if it is then that is okay.

A Rope of Three Cords

An enthusiastic friend encourages Ben: Teach brother!

Ben responds: It's time for religious leaders to stand up and say what is right, even if it doesn't agree with politics or the media. It's time for believers to stand together.

> **And hold fast, all together, by the rope which Allah**
> [stretches out for you], **and be not divided among**
> **yourselves; and remember with gratitude Allah's favour**
> **on you; for ye were enemies and He joined your hearts**
> **in love, so that by His Grace, ye became brethren; and ye**
> **were on the brink of the pit of Fire, and He saved you from**
> **it. Thus doth Allah make His Signs clear to you: That ye**
> **may be guided.** (Qur'an, *Al-Imran* 3:103)

In Judaism we are taught that the strongest rope is made of three cords. This reminds me of the three Abrahamic faiths, Islam, Christianity, and Judaism. If the proper believers of these faiths would bind together there would be no stronger rope.

> **Two are better than one ... and a strand of three cords is not easily broken.** (Ecclesiastes 4:9-12)

Another friend: Right on brother, make it plain.

But another: Muslims, Jews, and Christians cannot bind in one rope because those three faiths can't let them bind, unless we say there is no religion.

Ben: Why not? Musavi Muslims, Isavi Muslims and Muhamadi Muslims have much in common.

Faried De Bruyns: I agree with the rabbi on his rope interpretation.

> **And those who believe in the oneness of Allah and do righteous good deeds, they are dwellers of paradise, they will dwell therein forever.** [And like I said some people love opposition and want to be divided.] **Wake up to yourselves and evil and obey All come to common terms as Allah commanded.** (Qur'an, *Al Baqarah* 2:81)

Ibrahim: Truly, there is no deity but He!

Tim: God bless you.

Marcus: Gracias.

***

Stan Tenen shares an excerpt from his essays, "An Organic Model of Civilization: The Tree of Abraham" and "The Three Pillars of Love":

Stan: There is an historical flow from the perennial tradition to Abraham, and then to Judaism, Christianity, and Islam. When we look back in time through Islam, we see Christianity, and when we look back in time through Christianity, we see Judaism, and before that, perennial and unbounded history. This is the flow of civilization and time, moving from a metaphoric Jewish seed, through a metaphoric Christian tree, to a metaphoric Islamic fruit.

We also have all three traditions as three phases of life, together at the same time in our time. The conceptual phase is identified with Judaism, the gestational phase with Christianity, and the letting-go (birthing) phase with Islam. Of course, each of these phases of faith must include the other two, because this is all happening all at once, right now, just as it is also happening eternally, cyclically, and throughout history.

Life grows both ways. Life grows sequentially in time, and it grows spread out in different organs within an organism at any given time.

Each of the three phases of the Abrahamic traditions necessarily includes the highest qualities of the other two, while at the same time, each is the primary representative of only one. So, I associate the conceptual stage with Judaism, and I identify it embryologically with the seed, and functionally with reason and law (Torah), the priestly tradition, and integrity. The Christian tradition is associated primarily with passion, compassion, "good works," and what the Eastern traditions call "Dharma". Embryologically, it is identified with the tree that manifests the seed's life-force in the world (the tree as the cross is the symbol of Christianity). Moslems must submit to Allah, and let go of their ego and worldly attachments. This is the function of the fruit, which must let go of the tree to provide the fertile ground for the next cycle of life. The Moslem covenant specializes in community and hospitality.

Put simply, Judaism is known for its Torah of integrity, Christianity is known for its Gospel of love, and Islam is known for its Quran of submission.

Of course, all three phases also include the other two.

Stan adds: When you see peacemaking among the children of Abraham as based not only upon scripture and history, but upon science and mathematics, then our proposals can be no more controversial that the law of gravity.

In geometric metaphor, the three cords are also the three edges, and/or the three ribbons, of the tetrahelical column. There's also extensive description of "wave-work" in the Letter of Aristeas, which outlines the gifts Ptolemy gave to encourage the Septuagint translation

For more information about the work of Stan and Levana Tenen in merging the scientific with the sacred, see www.meru.org.

21. Speech in the Abrahamic Faiths
Slander and War

*What follows is an example of such a cord. It is part of Ben's efforts
in Cultural Diplomacy. He spoke on April 15, 2012 at the Queen
Elizabeth II Conference Center, London*

Ben Abrahamson: I have been asked to speak about promoting social justice. But that is a very big topic. Sometimes in order to tackle a big topic, it is worthwhile to start with a small topic. I propose to begin by understanding "What is gossip?"

Gossip is idle talk or rumors about the personal or private affairs of others. It is one of the oldest and most common means of sharing information and views, but it also has a reputation for passing on errors and variations into the information transmitted, sometimes accidentally, sometimes intentionally. With the advent of the internet, gossip can be spread from one place in the world to another. Information that used to take a long time to transmit is now available in an instant.

Gossip is Roundly Condemned by Judaism, Christianity and Islam.

In Judaism

Judaism considers speaking about someone without a constructive purpose (known in Hebrew as an evil speech, *lashon hara*) as a sin. Speaking negatively about people, even if retelling true facts, counts as sinful, as it demeans the dignity of man—both the speaker and the subject of the gossip. According to Proverbs 18:8: "The words of a gossip are like choice morsels: They go down to a man's innermost parts."

Psalm 34:12-16 says,

12 **Come, ye children, hearken unto me; I will teach you the fear of HaShem.**

13 **Who is the man that desireth life, and loveth days, that he may see good therein?**

14 **Keep thy tongue from evil, and thy lips from speaking guile.**

15 **Depart from evil, and do good; seek peace, and pursue it.**

16 **The eyes of HaShem are toward the righteous, and His ears are open unto their cry.**

Leviticus 19:16 says,

Thou shalt not go up and down as a talebearer among thy people; neither shalt thou stand idly by the blood of thy neighbour: I am the Lord.

In addition, the words "ye shall not wrong one another" in Leviticus 25:17 according to tradition refer to wronging a person with one's speech.

In Islam

Islam considers backbiting the equivalent of consuming the flesh of one's dead brother. According to Islamic commentators, backbiting harms its victims without offering them any chance of defense, just as dead people cannot defend themselves from abuse. Muslims are expected to treat each other like brothers, deriving from Islam's concept of brotherhood amongst its believers.

It is written:

> **O ye who believe! Shun much suspicion; for lo! some suspicion is a crime. And spy not, neither backbite one another. Would one of you love to eat the flesh of his dead brother? Ye abhor that** [so abhor the other]**! And keep your duty** [to Allah]**. Lo! Allah is Relenting, Merciful.** (Qur'an, *Al-Hujurat* 49:12)

> **You who believe! If a deviator brings you a report, scrutinize it carefully in case you attack people in ignorance and so come to greatly regret what you have done.** (Qur'an, *Al-Hujurat* 49:6)

> **O You who believe! Show integrity for the sake of God, bearing witness with justice. Do not let hatred for a people incite you into not being just. Be just. That is closer to faith. Heed God alone. God is aware of what you do.** (Qur'an, *Al-Maedah* 5:8)

In Christianity

Romans 1:28-32 associates gossips ("backbiters") with a list of sins including sexual immorality and with murder:

> 28 **And even as they did not like to retain God in their knowledge, God gave them over to a reprobate mind, to do those things which are not convenient;**

> 29 **Being filled with all unrighteousness, fornication, wickedness, covetousness, maliciousness; full of envy, murder, debate, deceit, malignity; whisperers,**

> 30 **Backbiters, haters of God, despiteful, proud, boasters,**

inventors of evil things, disobedient to parents,

31 Without understanding, covenant breakers, without natural affection, implacable, unmerciful:

32 Who knowing the judgment of God, that they which commit such things are worthy of death, not only do the same, but have pleasure in them that do them.

We see here that they are covenant breakers, included with sins that are ranked among the Ten Commandments.

James 3 says,

1 My brethren, be not many masters, knowing that we shall receive the greater condemnation.

2 For in many things we offend all. If any man offend not in word, the same is a perfect man, and able also to bridle the whole body.

3 Behold, we put bits in the horses' mouths, that they may obey us; and we turn about their whole body.

4 Behold also the ships, which though they be so great, and are driven of fierce winds, yet are they turned about with a very small helm, whithersoever the governor listeth.

5 Even so the tongue is a little member, and boasteth great things. Behold, how great a matter a little fire kindleth!

6 And the tongue is a fire, a world of iniquity: so is the tongue among our members, that it defileth the whole body, and setteth on fire the course of nature; and it is set on fire of hell.

7   For every kind of beasts, and of birds, and of serpents,
    and of things in the sea, is tamed, and hath been tamed
    of mankind:

8   But the tongue can no man tame; it is an unruly evil,
    full of deadly poison.

...

13 Who is a wise man and endued with knowledge among
    you? let him shew out of a good conversation his works
    with meekness of wisdom.

14 But if ye have bitter envying and strife in your hearts,
    glory not, and lie not against the truth.

15 This wisdom descendeth not from above, but is earthly,
    sensual, devilish.

16 For where envying and strife is, there is confusion and
    every evil work.

17 But the wisdom that is from above is first pure, then
    peaceable, gentle, and easy to be intreated, full of
    mercy and good fruits, without partiality, and without
    hypocrisy.

18 And the fruit of righteousness is sown in peace of them
    that make peace.

Where Does Gossip Fall in the Ten Commandments?

It seems to clearly fall in under the ninth commandment, "You shall not bear false witness against your neighbor." The Ten Commandments are part of the Mosaic covenant, but the Bible speaks about previous covenants made with Adam and Noah.

A covenant is based on a contract between man and God, bound up in his following God's commandments. The very first time in the

Bible that the verb *tsavah* (צִוָּה, "to command") appears is in the verse Genesis 2:16, "And the Lord God commanded the man saying, of every tree of the garden you may freely eat." Rabbinic tradition understands this first commandment to Adam to include seven of the Ten Commandments.

1) **And** [He] **commanded**—refers to legal system, and thus it is written: **For I know him, that he will command his children and his household after him, and they shall keep the way of the L-rd, to do justice and judgment.**

2) **The L-rd**—is [a prohibition against] blasphemy, and thus it is written: **and he that blasphemeth the name of the Lord, he shall surely be put to death.**

3) **God**—is [an injunction against] idolatry, and thus it is written: **Thou shalt have no other gods before Me.**

4) **The man**—refers to homicide, and thus it is written: **whoso sheddeth man's blood, by man shall his blood be shed.**

5) **Saying**—refers to sexual immorality, and thus it is written: **They say, If a man put away his wife, and she go from him, and became another man's.**

6) **Of every tree of the garden**—but not of the tree of life, this refers to theft.

7) **Thou mayest freely eat**— but not limb of a living creature.

We see that the seven commandments given to Adam and renewed with Noah correspond:

1) I am the Lord your God.

2) You shall have no other gods before me, You shall not make for yourself an idol (1st Noahide).

3) You shall not make wrongful use of the name of your God (2nd Noahide).

4) Remember the Sabbath and keep it holy.

5) Honor your father and mother.

6) You shall not murder (3rd Noahide).

7) You shall not commit adultery (4th Noahide).

8) You shall not steal (5th Noahide).

9) You shall not bear false witness against your neighbor (7th Noahide).

10) You shall not covet your neighbor's wife, You shall not covet anything that belongs to your neighbor (6th Noahide).

Basically the Seven Commandments of Noah are the same as the Ten Commandments minus three commandments. The commandment to keep the Sabbath was specifically given to the Children of Israel. Perhaps the other two are, "I am the Lord your God" which includes the unique four letter name of God which was revealed to the Children of Israel and "Honor your father and mother" which was given "so that you should live long in the land I am giving you" again referring to the Children of Israel.

The Qur'an puts it this way:

But those among them who are well-grounded in knowledge, and the believers, believe in what hath been

revealed to thee and what was revealed before thee: And
[especially] **those who establish regular prayer and practice
regular charity and believe in Allah** [*Subhanahu wa-ta'ala*]
**and in the Last Day: To them shall We soon give a great
reward. We have sent thee inspiration,** *as We sent it to
Noah* **and the Messengers after him: we sent inspiration
to Abraham, Isma'il, Isaac, Jacob and the Tribes, to Jesus,
Job, Jonah, Aaron, and Solomon, and to David We gave the
Psalms.** (Qur'an, *An-Nisa* 4:162-163)

So we see that those who gossip are covenant breakers as it says
in Romans 1:31. Which covenant? The covenant of Noah.

According to Christianity the covenant made with Noah was an
incomplete covenant. According to Islam, the covenant made with
Noah was not the last covenant. But it is a covenant nonetheless.
Those who keep the Seven Commandments, what we call the Noahide Law, which were given to all humanity, are keeping what may
be called biblical Common Law. These commandments are a fundamental necessity for any God-fearing nation, a fundamental *deen*
which is obligated upon all humanity.

But Let's Look at This Further.

Gossip appears to be prohibited under the general prohibition of
"You shall not bear false witness against your neighbor". This in turn
corresponds to the Noahide Law of "Setting up Courts of Justice".

James 3:18, after discussion the tremendous damage Gossip and
Evil Speech can do, says:

**And the fruit of righteousness is sown in peace of them
that make peace.**

In Hebrew the word for righteous is *tzedek*. This is also the word
for justice. So one could understand James to be telling us that the

prohibition of gossip is related to "not bearing false witness", which in turn is related to courts of justice.

Let us review this verse again:

You who believe! If a deviator brings you a report, scrutinize it carefully in case you attack people in ignorance and so come to greatly regret what you have done. (Qur'an, *Al-Hujurat* 49:6)

One must collect evidence and scrutinize it carefully. These are the actions of a court.

A hundred years ago we used to think that the industrial revolution would solve all the world's problems. We saw with World War I and World War II and its destruction of humanity as well as environmental pollution and the destruction of the world we live in that this was not so. Now we have turned to secular humanism to provide us direction, to provide moral guidance where there is none. But the biblical system of God-fearing judges is too cumbersome for modern policy makers. Instead, the courtroom has been replaced with the evening news.

For Two Generations We Have Suffered Wartime Propaganda.

For two generations we have suffered wartime propaganda. Each side in the Middle East, and other countries throughout the world, tries to demonize the other, making them less than human. This is being done by the secular non-religious and sometimes anti-religious media. They benefit when believers fight against each other. We need religious judges, who fear God more than politics or the media, to call witnesses, examine facts, and come to a true conclusion. We cannot rely on the TV to bring us a balanced view of the truth.

How do you know what is a "fact" without a proper trial and God-fearing justices? How many religious courts have ruled on this? How many *fatwas*[1] have been issued? Where are the verdicts of religious, God-fearing courts who have called witnesses, examine facts, and come to a true conclusion?   They have been sidelined by the thirty-second media, with people who want their three minutes of fame.

A proper Muslim, and a proper Jew, is forbidden by religious law to go to a non-religious court. How much more so, to decide something based on what amounts to—by religious law—gossip. Verdicts of guilty or innocent must be issued by judges, not journalists.

One might say, "Journalists report the truth—the camera doesn't lie." But one should try reading the reports of propaganda efforts by the British and the Germans during WWII, or during the Cold War between the Russians and Americans.   Photos often do not hold up in a court of law.

One might say "one doesn't need a judge or a trial jury to know the truth, especially when you're a witness." Have you ever been at a trial? Do you know how widely testimony can differ when you experience a bombing, terrorist attack, or even car accident?

It is forbidden by scripture to come to a guilty or innocent verdict on the basis of the report of a journalist.

As religious Jews, Christians and Muslim, we are obligated to go back to the legal system, and not make conclusions until a trial has been held. We are forbidden to judge people as guilty or innocent on the basis of news reports.

The minute one judges a person based on a news report, or journalistic article, and does not bring it to a proper trial, where there are divinely mandated strict rules on the quality of evidence and testimony, one has allowed himself to be manipulated, biased, and swayed. One who does this strays from their faith.

Common Law

Christianity has allowed common law to fall into the hands of the secularists, in the guise of "rendering up to Caesar what is Caesar's",

---

1. Order by Muslim cleric

which has worked to provide a minimum of law that is equally applied towards all citizens, a standard praised by scripture "that there should be one law for citizen and stranger". But by letting both the authorized judicial system, as well as what might be termed "trial by the media", abandon the scripturally mandated requirements of justice, one deviates from the commandment of God for Justice and Righteousness.

In Judaism, common law and religious law are merged into a single system; this is true with Islam as well. In Christianity, common law has been relegated to the temporal authorities, but it is meant to be shaped, molded and guided by Christian morality and ethics. Without a compass, mighty sailors can travel with all their might but never arrive at their destination. Scripture is our compass—a standard worthy of emulation, and the only method to achieve justice.

The elements are all there for peace, just the order has been mixed up.

We have become accustomed to letting the television be our courtroom, and public opinion our judge. We let secular, anti-religious media tell us what the "truth" is, even though we know they want to increase conflict. We need true religious, sincere judges, who fear God, to collect evidence, hear testimony, and come to a righteous conclusion.

In most trial systems, one must go to great lengths to convict someone of murder. Yet a single news report can cause riots where hundreds of people are killed. It is forbidden for a religious Jew, Christian, or Muslim to act on this kind of information. And if the people were not guilty of the crimes that they were accused of, every person who passed the "news report" along by email or Facebook® posting, shares the guilt of their murder and will need to answer for this before God.

Some Final Thoughts

We must search for opportunities for peace:

But if they incline to peace, you incline to it, and trust in God. Verily, He is the All-Hearer, the All-Knower. (Qur'an, *Al-Anfal* 8:61)

We must seek judicial solutions to disputes, not violent solutions.

Dispute not with the People of the Book save in the fairer manner, except for those of them that go wrong; and say: "We believe in what has been sent down to us, and what has been sent down to you; our God and your God are One, and to Him we have surrendered." (Qur'an, *An-Ankabut* 29:46)

We must forgive:

God did aforetime take a covenant with the Children of Israel; and We raised up from among them twelve chieftains. And God said, 'I am with you. Surely, if you perform the prayer, and pay the alms, and believe in My Messengers, honour and assist them, and loan to God a beautiful loan, verily I will wipe out from you your evils, and admit you to gardens with rivers flowing beneath; but if any of you, after this, resisteth faith, he hath truly wandered from the path of rectitude. But because of their breach of their covenant, We cursed them, and made their hearts grow hard; they change the words from their places and forget a good part of the message that was sent them, nor wilt thou cease to find them ever bent on new deceits, except a few of them. Yet pardon them, and forgive; surely God loves those who do good. (Qur'an, *Al-Maedah* 5:12-16)

But above all, we must submit to God. Psalm 34:14 says, **"Seek peace and pursue it,"** yet most people forget the first part of the verse, **"Turn from evil and do good."**

Establishing a mutually agreed upon system of justice is the first step. The rabbinical commentaries, echoing a tradition that has been passed down since Mount Sinai, teach that setting up God-fearing judges comes first, before setting up a king, government or even the Temple.

In other words, we need a government, justice system, and media which adheres to universally accepted moral standards before we can "seek peace".

A friend: Thanks Rabbi Ben Abrahamson, may Allah bless you ... shalom and peace!

Ben: Muslims shouldn't gossip. Allah said:

> **Successful are the believers, who are humble in their prayers, and who turn away from pointless talk.** (Qur'an, *Al-Mumamim* 23:1-3)

> **Those who do not bear witness to what is false, but when they pass by pointless talk, pass by with dignity.** (Qur'an, *At-Furqan* 25:72)

> **When they hear pointless talk, they turn away from it.** (Qur'an, *Al Qasas* 28:55)

Salman: Great message. Thank you.

Muhammed : May Allah bless us *Insh'Allah*.

O You who believe! Show integrity for the sake of Allah, bearing witness with justice. Do not let prejudice for a people incite you into not being truthful. Be truthful! That is closer to faith. Heed Allah [alone]. Allah is aware of what you do. (Qur'an, *Al-Maedah* 5:8)

Zair: It is refreshing to know that such persons exist who acknowledge the spirituality and truth of another religion. Brother Ben, in you we have a kindred soul and it is a privilege knowing you.

What thrills me the most is that in one of his writings he unearthed evidence to show that Islam is actually older than Christianity. I am going to study a bit of Judaism now. In all my hunger for knowledge, I never considered looking at Judaism because of Israeli conduct. Thanks to brother Ben, I even understand Islam better. *Allahu Akbar.*

You who believe! If a deviator [the media: newspapers, television, the internet] **brings you a report, scrutinize it carefully in case you attack people in ignorance and so come to greatly regret what you have done.** (Qur'an, *Al-Hujurat* 49:6)

Ahmed: Mr. Abrahamson this message is very nice, thanks.

Ben: We have become accustomed to letting the television be our courtroom and public opinion our judge. We let anti-religious media dictate to us, even though we know their aim is to increase conflict. We need true religious, sincere judges who fear Allah to collect evidence, hear testimony, and come to a righteous conclusion. May Allah speedily reveal the *Mahdi* in our days.

Conclusion

Ben: The Muslim who truly understands the teachings of his religion is
gentle, friendly, and likeable. Honesty and earning trust is one of the
most important duties of a Muslim

> **"Shall I not tell you who among you is most beloved to
> me and will be closest to me on the Day of Resurrection?"
> He repeated it two or three times ... He said, "Those of you
> who are the best in manners and character."** [1]

There is a basic faith called *deen* or the Noahide covenant, which is
common to all mankind. Beyond that our laws and traditions differ.

Jews believe that God made a covenant with the Children of Israel.
God made covenants with each of the nations of the world. Each of
us is bound to his respective covenant, and will be judged by the law
revealed to his or her nation.

We must "compete" with each other in good deeds "as if in a race".
We respect the true covenant that God has revealed to each nation,
but we must operate in an entirely orthodox, fundamental, and "true
to the sources" fashion concerning what God has revealed to us.

There will come a day when "God will be One and His Name
One" (Zechariah 14:9). When all our questions will be answered, and
all the seventy paths of righteousness will be shown to be leading to
the same place. But each nation has a different divine mission, and
diversity is necessary. We need each other. We need each other to
function faithfully.

Our own actions will help bring about world peace:

> **The believer gets along with people and they feel
> comfortable with him. There is no goodness in the one**

---

1. The Musnad Ahmad ibn Hanbal *ahadith* collection. This *hadith* is considered *sahih*
(reliable).

who does not get along with people and with whom they do not feel comfortable. (Ahmad and al-Bazar; *sahih*)

The way of God is indeed the way of peace.

Appendices

The Seven Laws of Noah
The Torah View of Religion Among the Nations

*Much of this material is covered elsewhere in the book
and is condensed here.*

Ben Abrahamson: In *Baba Kama* 38a , we see that each nation was assigned a land and language. Noahide Laws are a measure of a proper religion. A faith is divine and its followers guaranteed a portion in the hereafter if it fulfills the minimum requirement of Noahism.

We can thus say that proper Islam is a divine religion, not because we have studied its teachings, or claim to understand it, but because the Torah says so.

'Avodah Zarah 26a. A Gentile studies Torah for the purpose of observing the laws of Noah. R. Meïr says he is as good as a high priest, and quotes: Ye shall therefore keep my statutes, and my judgments, which if a man do, he shall live in them. The text does not specify an Israelite or a Levite or a priest, but simply "a man"—including a Gentile.

The Seven Laws are:

1. **Justice:** Commandments to set up courts of law and pursue social justice

2. **Respect and praise G-d**: prohibitions against blasphemy.

3. **Belief in God:** prohibitions against worshipping any being except God.

4. **Respect the family:** sexual morality.

5. **Respect human life:** prohibitions against murder.

6. **Respect for others' property:** prohibitions against theft.

7. **Respect all creatures:** prohibitions against eating the limb of a living animal.

And he said: **HaShem came from Sinai, and rose up from Seir unto them; He shined forth from mount Paran, and He came from the myriads holy ones** [prophets]**, at His right hand was a fiery law unto them. Yea, He loves the peoples, all His holy ones—they are in Thy hand; and they sit down at Thy feet, receiving of Thy words.** (Deuteronomy 33:2-4)

Seir, in the land of Edom, is a fitting symbol of Rome, which has always been identified with Edom, and Paran was the original home of lshmael, father of the Arab peoples. (*Baba Batra* 25a; Sffirei, *Piska* 343; Midrash *Tannaim* 209)

Scripture links Seir and Paran with Sinai; the commentaries say that this is because these two names stand for all of mankind, for they represent the two great powers which at that time contended for domination of Judea: the Arabs and the Romans, the East and the West. God thus renewed His covenants with the Gentiles at Sinai. (*Avodah Zarah* 2b).

--

The Lord spoke those words—those and no more to your whole congregation at the mountain, with a mighty voice. (Deuteronomy 5:19)

R. Yochanan asserts that this refers to a multiplicity of voices; the sound of the holy voice divided into seventy voices so that all the nations might hear it. (Midrash *Shmot Rabbah* 28.6)

The Lord giveth the word: They that publish the tidings are a great host. (Psalms 68:12)

The School of R. Ishmael taught:: every single word that went forth from the Holy One, blessed be He, split up into seventy languages. (Sabbath 88b)

Hear, for I will speak princely things. (Proverbs 8:6)

R. Hananel b. Papa said, why are the words of the Torah compared to a prince? Just as a prince has power of life and death, so have the words of Torah power of life and death. Thus Raba said; to those who go to the right hand thereof it is a medicine of life; to those who go to the left hand thereof it is a deadly poison. Another interpretation: "princely" denotes that on every word which went forth from the mouth of the Holy One, blessed be He, two crowns were set. (Sabbath 88b)

Although the nations rejected the Torah that was accepted by the Children of Israel, "two crowns" means that there must have been another covenant based on Noahism that was offered them.

Know for sure that I will then enable the nations to give me acceptable praise. All of them will invoke Hashem's name when they pray, and will worship him in unison. (Zephaniah 3:9)

R. Joshua b. Levi said: Had the heathen nations of the world known how excellent a thing the Tent of Meeting was for them, they would have encompassed it with encampments and fortifications. One finds that before the Tent of Meeting was erected, the heathen nations of the world, on hearing the voice of divine speech, rushed in fright out of their camps. (Vayikra Rabba 1:9-12)

God cometh from Teman, and the Holy One from mount Paran, selah. His glory covereth the heavens, and the earth is full of His praise... He stood, and measured the earth: he beheld, and drove asunder the nations; and the everlasting mountains were scattered, the perpetual hills did bow: His ways are everlasting. (Habakuk 3:3,6)

The word "measured" in Hebrew is the same word as "character-ized", and "drove asunder" is related to "excesses", so this verse is understood to teach: "He stood, and characterized [the nations of] the earth: He saw the excesses of the nations; and the everlasting mountains were scattered, the perpetual hills did bow [they were given a path to overcome their bad traits]: His ways are everlasting [His scripture will never change].

Rabbinic commentary says that Jethro (Shu-ayb) was a "Bnei Noah" (righteous non-Jew). The "Children of Jethro" were "God fear-ers" also called "Kenites". Targum Onkelos translates "Kenites" as Salamai or Muslamai.

Prophecy is not limited to the Jewish people

From His right hand went a fiery law for them (Deut 33:2)

The "fiery law" was the supernal Torah translated into seventy languages.

Sifre to Numbers 12:2. "[And suddenly the Lord said to Moses and to Aaron and Miriam,] **Come out, you three, to the tent of meeting.** [And the three of them came out...]:" This teaches that the three of them were called in a single act of speech, which an ordinary mouth cannot accomplish and an ordinary ear cannot hear. And so Scripture says,

And God spoke all these words, saying. (Exodus 20:1) **One thing did God say, but two did I hear** (Psalms 62:12). **Is not**

**my word like fire, says the Lord, and like a hammer that
breaks the rock** (Jeremiah 23:29).

Sifre connects Numbers 12:2 to Exodus 20:1, Psalms 62:12 and
Jeremiah 23:29. The common theme is that the "Voice of God" is a
metaphor, which has qualities unlike a normal voice.

The connection with fire is significant. Just as fire appears differently to different people looking at different angles, sounds different,
and feels different, so too does the Lord have the ability to speak at
one time to many people. This multifaceted Voice of God is described
with the imagery of "fire".

At Mount Sinai there was a noise, thunder and fire. In rabbinic
tradition the "fire" is related to the fact that the Torah was spoken
simultaneously in seventy languages at the same time (Talmud *Shab-
bos* 88a; *Exodus Raba* 5). The supernal Torah was written in seventy
languages in order that the nations should not be able to plead ignorance as their excuse for rejecting it (Tosefta, *Sotah* 8).

Perhaps this can explain Deuteronomy 18:

**When thou art come into the land which the LORD thy
God giveth thee, thou shalt not learn to do after the
abominations of those nations. There shall not be found
among you any one that maketh his son or his daughter to
pass through the flame** [Molech worship], **one that useth
divination, a soothsayer, or an enchanter, or a sorcerer,
or a charmer, or one that consulteth a ghost or a familiar
spirit, or a necromancer. For whosoever doeth these things
is an abomination unto the LORD; and because of these
abominations the LORD thy God is driving them out from
before thee.** (Deuteronomy 18:9-12)

**A prophet will the LORD thy God raise up unto thee, from
the midst of thee, of thy brethren, like unto me; unto him**

**ye shall hearken; according to all that thou didst desire
of the LORD thy God in Horeb in the day of the assembly,
saying: "Let me not hear again the voice of the LORD my
God, neither let me see this great fire any more, that I die
not." And the LORD said unto me: "They have well said
that which they have spoken."** (Deuteronomy 18:15-17)

**I will raise them up a prophet from among their brethren,
like unto thee; and I will put My words in his mouth, and
he shall speak unto them all that I shall command him.
And it shall come to pass, that whosoever will not hearken
unto My words which he shall speak in My name, I will
require it of him.** (Deuteronomy 18:18-19)

There is a repetition between Deuteronomy 18:15 and Deuteronomy 18:18. Both say that the Lord will raise up a Prophet like Moses
(pbuh), but the former is in the second person (of your brethren) and
the latter is in the third person (from their brethren). In between is the
verse: **"Let me not hear again the voice of the LORD my God, neither
let me see this great fire any more, that I die not."** This verse means
that originally the entire Children of Israel were to accept the Torah
(the voice of the LORD) and the supernal Torah (this great fire), but
they could not bear this, and would have died. Instead God would
raise up Prophets. The Prophets would be for you (children of Israel)
and for them (seventy nations of the world). This is supported by
the use "whosoever" (*ish*) which is a general word for mankind, not
limited to the Children of Israel.

The Pesikta invokes:

**All the kings of the earth shall praise You, O LORD, for
they have heard the words You spoke. They shall sing of
the ways of the Lord, Great is the majesty of the LORD!**
(Psalm 138:4,5)

Know too that in every generation, [Gentile] witnesses appear to confirm the giving of the Torah. These are Eliphaz the Temanite, Bildad the Shuhite, Zophar of Naama [The friends of Job]; Job of the land of Uz; and last of all, Balaam son of Beor.

The term Muslim

It is a fact of Jewish Law that Muslims are perfect monotheists.

Rabbinic literature teaches that there is common faith, a fundamental "religion" which all are born into. Jews have called this *yireh shomaym, ger toshav* or *bnei noah* in Hebrew, *theosebeia* in Greek.

In the Torah, "Kenite" is translated to Aramaic as *salamai* or *muslamai*. This refers to the great numbers of non-Jewish believers who came to sacrifice the *korban shlamim* in Jerusalem: Salamai, Musalamai, Muslims. This could be a clear indication in our literature that Islam is an ancient religion, dating back to second temple times, at least. And if Islam's roots are the same as what we call *bnei noah*, then it is much older, it is the religion of Noah and Adam himself.

The closeness of Islam and Judaism was always understood by biblical scholars up until recent years. The close relationship between Jews, the ten lost tribes, the Arabs and Rachabites was all assumed. With the advent of German revisionists such as Wellhausen and Büchler, this all changed. They introduced ideas that Islam started with moon or rock worship. Devout Jews know that this is not true.

In the following verses we have three circles: the Children of Aaron (the priesthood), the Children of Israel and the God-fearers / Muslamai :

O Israel, trust thou in the Lord: He is their help and their shield. O house of Aaron, trust in the Lord: He is their help and their shield. You that fear the Lord, trust in the Lord: He is their help and their shield. (Psalm 115:9-12)

Let the Children of Israel say: "His love endures forever."
Let the Children of Aaron say: "His love endures forever."
Let the God Fearers say: "His love endures forever." (Psalm 118:2-4)

Attempts to water down Judaism make it difficult for Muslims to relate to the nation of Israel. The nation of Israel's loyalty to the Torah will make Jews more accessible to Muslims and make Muslims more accessible to Jews.

We need our divine diversity.

The nation of Israel and the nations of the world are to work in harmony to bring completion to humanity and peace to the world.

Babylonian Exilarchs

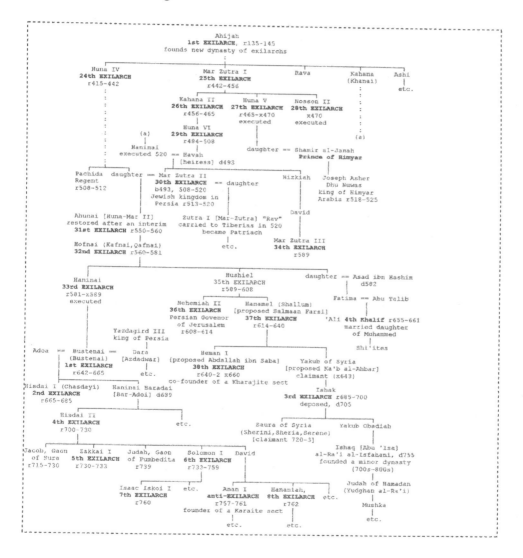

Ahijah
1st EXILARCH, r135-145
founds new dynasty of exilarchs

Huna IV
24th EXILARCH
r415-442

Mar Zutra I
25th EXILARCH
r442-456

Rava

Kahana
(Khanai)

Ashi
etc.

Kahana II
26th EXILARCH
r456-465

Huna V
27th EXILARCH
r465-x470
executed

Nosson II
28th EXILARCH
x470
executed

Huna VI
29th EXILARCH
r484-508

(a)

Haninai
executed 520 == Havah
[heiress] d493

daughter == Shamir al-Janah
Prince of Himyar

(a)

Pachida
Regent
r508-512

daughter == Mar Zutra II
30th EXILARCH == daughter
b493, 508-520
Jewish kingdom in
Persia r513-520

Hizkiah

Joseph Asher
Dhu Nuwas
king of Himyar
Arabia r518-525

Ahunai [Huna-Mar II]
restored after an interim
31st EXILARCH r550-560

Zutra I [Mar-Zutra] "Rav"
carried to Tiberias in 520
became Patriarch

David

Hofnai (Kafnai,Qafnai)
32nd EXILARCH r560-581

etc.

Mar Zutra III
34th EXILARCH
r589

Haninai
33rd EXILARCH
r581-x589
executed

Hushiel
35th EXILARCH
r589-608

daughter == Asad ibn Hashim
d582

Fatima == Abu Talib

Nehemiah II
36th EXILARCH
Persian Govenor
of Jerusalem
r608-614

Hanamel (Shallum)
[proposed Salmaan Farsi]
37th EXILARCH
r614-640

'Ali **4th Khalif** r655-661
married daughter
of Muhammed

Shi'ites

Yazdagird III
king of Persia

Adoa == Bustenai ==
(Bustenai)
1st EXILARCH
r642-665

Dara
[Azdadwar]

etc.

Heman I
[proposed Abdallah ibn Saba]
38th EXILARCH
r640-2 x660
co-founder of a Kharajite sect

Yakub of Syria
[proposed Ka'b al-Ahbar]
claimant (x643)

Hisdai I (Chasdayi)
2nd EXILARCH
r665-685

Haninai Baradai
[Bar-Adoi] d639

Ishak
3rd EXILARCH r685-700
deposed, d705

Hisdai II
4th EXILARCH
r700-730

etc.

Saura of Syria
(Sherini,Sheria,Serene)
[claimant 720-3]

Yakub Obadiah

Ishaq [Abu 'Isa]
al-Ra'i al-Isfahani, d755
founded a minor dynasty
(700s-800s)

Jacob, Gaon
of Sura
r715-730

Zakkai I
5th EXILARCH
r730-733

Judah, Gaon
of Pumbedita
r739

Solomon I
6th EXILARCH
r732-759

David

Judah of Hamadan
(Yudghan al-Ra'i)

Isaac Iskoi I
7th EXILARCH
r760

etc.

Anan I
anti-EXILARCH
r757-761
founder of a Karaite sect

Hananiah,
8th EXILARCH
r762

etc.

Mushka
etc.

etc.

etc.

Definition of Terms

In some cases the following are parallels rather than strict definitions:

Arabic	Hebrew	English
Allah	*Elohim/ HaShem*	God
Qur'an	*Qur'an*	Revelation to the Prophet Muhammed (phuh)
Tawrat	*Torah*	Five Books of Moses or Written Torah: revelation to Prophet Moses (pbuh). More generally used as meaning the entire written and oral Torah
Deen	*Din*	Law: Basic unversal faith binding on all humankind. Known in Jewish tradition as the Noahide Laws and in Islamic tradition as Islam or submission. The one *Deen* has many *shari'a*s
Shari'a	*Brith*	Covenant/law: A subset of *Deen* and the expression of serving God. *Shari'a* differs among the peoples of the world. *Shari'a* is sppecific to each prophet and binding on each people. Each *shari'a* has many *madhabs* (communities).
Fiqh	*Halachah*	Jurisprudence: Practical application of divine law in daily life. Binding on each *umma* (people)
Minhaj	*Minhag*	Custom: Way. Enhances the keeping of religion but has no punishment if broken

Arabic	Hebrew	English
Hadith (ahadith–plural)	Midrash (Also can parallel Mishnah or Baraisa)	Tradition/ legend: In Islam known as the hidden revelation, these are teachings that were transmitted from Muhammed (pbuh) to his companions (sahaba), later written down. Its parallel in Judaism is midrash— teachings that were transmitted from Moses (pbuh) and later written down.
Sunnah Clear and well-trodden pathway	Halachah "The way to go"— law in daily life	Sometimes used interchangeably with the term hadith, sunnah has a more legal connotation
Misani	Mishnah	To review one's study: Jewish oral tradition
Isnad	Mesorah	Chain of transmission of ahadith from Muhammed (pbuh); tradition
Tafsir	Perush	Commentary: Traditional teachings, this contrasts with Ijtihad / Pilpul
Ijtihad	Pilpul	Independent legal reasoning based on scripture; not necessarily accepted by entire community
Bidah	Chadash / Chidush	Religious innovation: In Islam this is heretical. In Jewish thought, not necessarily accepted by entire community; positive when enriches understanding of Torah, negative if seen as heretical

Arabic	Hebrew	English
Ayah (Ayat–plural)	Pasuk	Scripture verse
Surah	Perek	Chapter; surat means "the sura of"
Umma	'Am	A people bound by a shari'a/brith/covenant
Madhab/Maslak	Edah	Legal community. Subset of umma, a group that follows a certain set of customs
Ulema	Sanhedrin	Group of scholars; National religious council
Mu'min	Ma'amin	Believer, trustworthy person
Kafir	Kofer	Apostate. In Islam is someone who rejects the truth after knowing it to be true.
Iman	Emunah	Faith
Aqeeda	Dath	Religious theology
Rasul	–	Lawgiving prophet
Nabi	Navi	Prophet

Names of Prophets and Leaders

Arabic	Hebrew	English
Nuh	Noach	Noah
Ibrahim	Avraham	Abraham
Musa	Moshe	Moses
Shu-ayb	Yisro	Jethro
Dawood	David	David
Ismail	Ishma'el	Ishmael
Isa	Yeshua'	Jesus
Muhammed	Machmud	Muhammed
Mahdi	Melech HaMoshiach	King Messiah: righteous leader at end of days

Different groups mentioned in the Qu'ran

Arabic	Hebrew	English
Bani Yisrael	Bnei Yisrael	Children of Israel

The Children of Israel, as written about in the Torah. In the Qur'an, this term generally has positive connotations.

Ummatun Qaimatun	Bnei Yisrael	Rabbinic Jews

Descendants of Pharisees. The term Pharisee comes from the Hebrew word *perush*, which connotes interpreting scripture on many levels, in line with tradition; they believed in the Oral Tradition later preserved in the Mishnah and Talmud. In the years before Islam, there were only a few rabbinic immigrants from Persia to Arabia. In the Qur'an, they are barely mentioned.

'Al Saduqiyyh	Tzadukim	Sadducees

A Jewish community named after Tzadok, a Jewish scholar in the second century BCE who taught that one should serve God without expecting a reward. His followers adopted Hellenism. They embraced rationalism, literal interpretation of the Torah, and rejected the authorized interpretation of Torah (Oral Torah). A large community of Jews derived from the Sadducees dwelled in Arabia at the time of the Prophet Muhammed. This group no longer exists as a Jewish community.

Al Yahudi	Yehudim	[Edomite] Jews

In the Qur'an, this term refers to the descendants of Priests and their Edomite, Moabite, Amonite and Nabatean followers who had converted to Sadducean Judaism five centuries before Islam. In the Qur'an it generally has negative connotations. Another name is the 'Al Saduqiyyh.

Al Nasaara	Notsrim	[Gnostic] Christians

A portion of the Al Yahudi adopted gnosticism and they were referred to as the Al Nasaara. Their gnostic teachings were based in monasticism, living in caves, self deprivation and seeking revelations from Angels. They continued to observe Jewish customs such as Yom Kippur (*Ashura*) but also believed in Jesus as the literal son of God, the Trinity and virgin birth.

Sabi / Hanifa	Tsabim	Sabeans

The descendants of Southern Arabians that had adopted monotheism and pilgrimage, without taking on the obligations of Judaism, in the centuries before Islam. They are associated with King David (pbuh) and adopted the Psalms as their scriptures.

Muslamai	Kenim	God-Fearers

Any believer who had adopted the true religion (*Deen*) of God, known in the Torah as God-fearers. The first God-fearer mentioned in the Five books of Moses is Jethro (pbuh), the father in Law of Moses (pbuh). His children and followers were called the Kenites. In the translation of the Torah to Aramaic, first century CE, they were called *Salamai* and *Muslamai*.

Shamiri	Shomrim / Shamronim	Samaritans

A name for the community of non-Jews which took on Judaism during the first exile, sixth century BCE. The Qur'an attributes the sin of the Golden Calf to a **Shomri**; the Talmud attributes it to a member of the *erev rav*, also a community of non-Jews which outwardly took on Judaism. In a general sense, this term also refers to the remnants of the Northern tribes of Israel who had embraced Hellenism and later Sadducean Judaism. Its five books of Moses and book of Joshua differ from the Masoretic text used by rabbinic Jews.

Different scriptures mentioned in the Qu'ran, and related works:

Arabic	Hebrew	English
Tawrat	Torah	Five Books of Moses

The scriptures given to Moses (pbuh) at Mount Sinai for the Children of Israel. In rabbinic Judaism this term also means the Torah, Prophets and Writings, called the "written Torah" as well as the Talmud and related writings that are called the "oral Torah". In Islam the word Tawrat is also inclusive, referring to both the written and oral Torah.

Ingel	—	Gospel

The texts associated with the four Gospels and, from the point of view of the Qur'an, may or may not include the letters of Paul the apostle. Since the Qur'an teaches, **"We send not a Law Giver except (to teach)**

in the language of his (own) people…" (Qur'an, *Ibrahim* 14:4), the original language of the Ingel is assumed to be Greek.

Zibur	*Tehilim*	Psalms

The psalms written by King David (pbuh). They were the central scripture for the Sabeans.

Tahrif-bil-Ma'ani	—	Misinterpretation

Refers to the concept in Islam that ancient scriptures have been incorrectly interpreted. Scholars Imam Razi and Imam Tabari held this opinion.

Tahrif-bil-Lafz	—	Textual corruption

Refers to the concept in Islam that ancient scriptures have been corrupted. Scholars Ibn Hazm and Al-Biruni held this opinion.

Tarjum	*Targum Onkelos*	Aramaic translation of Torah

The translation of the Five Books of Moses to Aramaic by Onkelos, first century CE. He refers to righteous gentiles as *Salamai* or *Muslamai*, ie, those who bring the Temple sacrifice known as the *shelamim* sacrifice

—	*Targum Hashiv'im*	Septuagint

The translation of the Torah into Greek in the second-century BCE. It differs from the Masoretic text used by rabbinic Jews as it switches the order of words, leaving some words out, and repeating phrases so that the text reads more logically and rationally. Additional books were added, known as the Apocrypha. This was the main text used by the Sadducees and early Christians.

Other concepts

Arabic	Hebrew	English
Musavi Muslim	*Bnei Israel*	Jew who properly keeps the covenant of the Torah
'Isawi Muslim	*Bnei Noah*	Christian who properly keeps the covenant of the Gospel
Muhammadi Muslim	*Bnei Noah*	Muslim who properly keeps the covenant of the Qur'an
Dhimmi	*Ger Toshav*	Foreign resident: In the Torah, the largest group of non-Jews who had adopted either partial or full Judaism were the Edomites. It is proposed the name *Dhimmi* is derived from *Edomi*.

Calendar/festivals

Arabic	Hebrew	English
Hijri	—	Muslim calendar
Hijra	—	Journey that Muhammed took from Mecca to Medina in the year 622 CE; this marked the first year of the Islamic calendar

Months

In pre-Islamic times the Hebrew and Arabic calendars coincided. The following is a table of correspondence of months and holidays as it was during the early years of the Prophet (pbuh).

Arabic	Hebrew	Holidays
Muharram	*Tishrei*	*Ras as Sana, Ashura;* *Rosh Hashana, Yom Yippur, Sukkot*
Safar	*Heshvan*	
Rabi I	*Kislev*	*Milaad-Un-Nabi;* *Hanuka*
Rabi II	*Tevet*	
Jumada I	*Shevat*	

Jumaaa II	Adar I	
Rajab	Adar II	Milaad-Imam Ali, Lailat al-Ma'raj; Purim
Shabaan	Nisan	Lailat al Baraat; Pesach (Passover)
Ramadan	Iyyar	Month Long Fast; Sefirah Mourning
Shawal	Sivan	Eid al Fitr; Shavuot (Pentacost)
Dhu al Qa'dah	Tamuz	
Dhu al Hijjah	Av+Elul	Roz e Arafat, Eid al Hajj, Eid al Adha; Fast of Av

Conversational terms

Arabic	Hebrew	English
Insha'Allah	Be'ezrat Hashem	God Willing
Hamd'Allah	Baruch HaShem	Praise God, Blessed be the Name
Mash'Allah	Hodu L'Hashem	God knows best. Praise God. Used when speaking of something in the present or past, not the future.
Jazak'Allah	Kol HaKavod	May God reward you
Salaam Aleykum	Shalom Aleichem	Peace unto you
SWT/Subhanahu Wa Ta'ala	HaKadosh Baruch Hu	Glorified and Exalted be He (Written after the word Allah as a show of reverence)
Subhan'Allah	Halleluyah	Glory be to God
Swall Allahu alaihi wasallam (saw)	alav haShalom (as)	May he rest in peace; literally: peace be upon him/her (pbuh)
Hazrat		The honorable

Bibliography

See **www.alsadiqin.org**

Index

48624461R00188

Made in the USA
Lexington, KY
07 January 2016